PRAISE FOR *OWN YOUR LIFE STORY*

Dr. Lidia Lae brings a global and deeply human perspective to the question of who we are and who we can become. *Own Your Life Story* invites readers to move beyond inherited narratives and step into lives shaped by choice, courage, and joy. It's a compelling guide for anyone seeking a life of meaning and impact.

Marci Shimoff
New York Times Bestselling Author of *Happy for No Reason* and *Chicken Soup for the Woman's Soul*

Own Your Life Story is a thoughtful and encouraging companion for anyone trying to make sense of who they are and where they're going. Dr. Lidia Lae writes with real warmth and insight about how our families, cultures, and experiences shape us—but also reminds us that we still have a say in the story moving forward. This is a book that will speak to many women, especially in times of change, and help them feel less alone as they find their voice, their strength, and their direction.

Dr. Kirsty Sword Gusmão AO
Former First Lady of Timor-Leste, Activist, and Author of *A Woman of Independence*

With insight and compassion, Dr. Lidia Lae shows how the stories we live shape our relationships, our work, and our sense of what is possible. This book offers a thoughtful, practical framework for becoming the author of your own life and creating success that feels both prosperous and deeply aligned. A meaningful and empowering read for anyone ready to redefine success from the inside out.

Ellen Rogin
New York Times Bestselling Author of *Picture Your Prosperity*

Dr. Lidia Lae is sharing the privilege of travelling part of the journey of life with you as the reader in an incredibly deep and meaningful way, and you will be truly enriched. The enjoyment of that journey depends on your traveling companions. The book takes us on a journey of self discovery and an exploration of cultural identity. This book gives us a brilliant insight into how to live a life well lived!

Dame Sylvia Morris DBE
Former Headteacher, National Leader of Education, and Education Consultant

PRAISE FOR *OWN YOUR LIFE STORY*

I believe this book will be invaluable to women of any age and culture. The book will be a wonderful guide for women to understand and appreciate themselves, whilst being encouraged to follow their desires through their own story. I loved the personalized format and structure, which gives the book credence, whilst supporting the reader to develop their own story. An amazing book!

Dr. Leonie Clyne OAM DJSJ
Founding Managing Director, Angus Clyne Australia, Former Deputy Chancellor, Flinders University, and Independent Director and Chair of the Academic Board, Barton Business School

Own Your Life Story struck a chord with me. Lidia Lae has an extraordinary ability to hold both tenderness and rigour as she explores how culture, identity, and lived experience shape the stories we carry. Through her own story and the voices of women from around the world, she invites us to slow down, reflect, and gently reclaim authorship of our lives. This is a book for anyone ready to move from surviving inherited narratives to living with intention, meaning, and heart.

Jane Phipps
Visionary Leader and Author of *The Heart-Centered Leader*

This book offers a thoughtful, compassionate framework for understanding your life as a story, one shaped by desire, opposition, guidance, and choice. By inviting readers to step out of inherited cultural scripts and into authorship of their own lives, it reframes personal growth as both an inner reckoning and a creative act. With clarity and heart, the chapters guide readers from reflection to alignment, helping them identify what truly matters and how they want to live next. It's a meaningful roadmap for anyone ready to move beyond survival mode and toward a life of purpose, joy, and legacy.

Kerry Kriseman
Memoir Mentor and Author of *Accidental First Lady*

With warmth and clarity, Dr. Lidia Lae shows how small shifts in self-understanding can create meaningful change in everyday life. Her approach invites readers to release what holds them back and step into a life shaped by purpose and joy. A thoughtful and uplifting read for those committed to living happier, more intentional lives.

Reen Rose
Bestselling Author of *Your Happiness Connection*

PRAISE FOR *OWN YOUR LIFE STORY*

In *Own Your Life Story*, Lidia skillfully weaves in the life stories of courageous women to demonstrate the power of the StoriCompass and CulturAlign tools in helping women embrace their unique makeup and frame their lives from hereon. The depths of wisdom and insight presented in this book, so beautifully conveyed through poignant life stories, including her own, can bring the transformation you seek if you would take the courage to pick it up and engage with it.

Professor Marie Yap OAM
Professor of Psychology and Psychologist, Monash University

Own Your Life Story invites readers to see their lives not as fixed narratives, but as evolving journeys shaped by awareness and intentional choice. Dr. Lidia Lae offers a thoughtful roadmap for letting go of limiting patterns and embracing a future shaped by purpose and meaning. A beautifully written invitation for anyone seeking to live with greater clarity and authenticity.

Dr. Julie Donley
Author of *Leading at the Speed of People* and *The Journey Called You*

Own Your Life Story beautifully reveals how the stories we tell ourselves shape our capacity to heal and grow and how we learn to rewire our brains. Dr. Lidia Lae blends psychological insight with compassionate storytelling to guide readers toward rewiring limiting beliefs and creating lives of clarity and purpose. This is a powerful companion for anyone seeking lasting emotional and mental well-being.

Patt Lind-Kyle
Author of *Heal Your Mind, Rewire Your Brain: The New Neuroscience for Mental Health, Anxiety, Depression, Cognitive Decline and Creativity*

Own Your Life Story felt highly relevant to my experience as both a woman and an airline captain. Lidia's StoriCompass framework offers a thoughtful and compassionate lens for understanding self-doubt and opposition, helping women make sense of their culture, lived experiences, and reconnect with their values in demanding environments. Many psychology books I've read tend to focus on a single aspect of us such as values, attachment, or personality, but this is the first I've read that truly captures the whole picture of a human being.

Rebecca Bryan
Airline Captain, Jetstar

PRAISE FOR *OWN YOUR LIFE STORY*

Lidia's text is a blueprint to find our personal journey in a world context that is disrupted, facing an escalating sense of the era of chance, and appearing to lean toward uncertainty, nihilism, and idiocracy. Lidia's content is based on academic rigor, lived experience, and a wonderful sense of empathy. Her content addresses, with responsibility, the need for education as spelled out in the UNESCO Sustainable Development Goals (SDG 4) in their entirety. The depth of ethical understanding of humankind makes this book mandatory study, significant for us all.

Dr. Berise Heasly PhD
Educator, Researcher, and Author of *Beyond the Boundaries*

Any book that encourages people to 'own their life story' gets a huge thumbs up from me. Helping people to see the value in their lived experience and become the author of their next chapter is a true gift. I highly encourage you to embrace the steps this book offers!

Verity Price
2021 World Champion of Public Speaking and Author of *Present with Power*

Own Your Life Story is a compassionate guide to understanding how our stories shape not only who we are, but how we heal, grow, and live with purpose. Dr. Lidia Lae cleverly invites readers to see their lives not as fixed narratives, but as evolving journeys of intentional choice. She offers readers a compelling roadmap for letting go of limiting patterns and understanding the role that one's background and culture play in one's life. It's a beautifully written and inspiring read for anyone seeking to live with greater clarity and authenticity.

Rosalind Ferry
Author of *One Journey*

In *Own Your Life Story*, psychologist Lidia Lae PhD, recognizes your cultural identity and with her practical tools, helps you navigate life on your terms. She cites real life stories from multicultural women, including her own, to show how to use these tools to live the life you want to live. This book could change your life.

Linda Lau Anusasananan
Author of *The Hakka Cookbook, Chinese Soul Food from around the World*

There's power in owning your story, something deep inside that takes root and propels you forward in a meaningful way. Lidia Lae gives us a road map about how our pieces fit not just for our own self discovery but for our legacy. She also speaks of story loops that keep us stuck.

PRAISE FOR *OWN YOUR LIFE STORY*

I am living one right now that Lidia's book showed me how to close.

Rhoda Bangerter
Split Location Specialist, Podcast Host, and Author of *Holding the Fort Abroad*

This book offers a valuable insight to a person in all stages of their lives. Whether you are the one currently feeling stuck and desperate for change, or the one who has recently achieved something great, or the one on the brink of a massive life change. It offers food for thought and reflection, a chance to look at your own life, background, personality, and relationships through both analytical and compassionate lenses. Additionally, it offers a great practical tool for said analysis, and for making the changes you need.

Emma Pihlajamaa
Security Specialist and Former Higher Education Expert, University of Oulu

I found *Own Your Life Story* immensely readable. I enjoyed it predominantly because it felt like a shared story rather than an instructional work; that's not to say it isn't instructional. Reading this work both challenged and reassured me in equal, comforting measure. Sometimes it even moved me to tears. At the conclusion of this book, I felt like I knew the author as a friend; a caring, supportive, inspirational friend.

Louise Faulkner
Tourism & Partnerships Manager and Photographic Artist

Own Your Life Story by Dr. Lidia Lae is an empowering guide to embracing cultural identity and navigating life on your own terms, a perspective I deeply relate to as a migrant woman. Through practical tools, it invites readers to move beyond inherited narratives and redefine success with intention, meaning, and heart.

Fabiola Campbell
Founder and CEO, Professional Migrant Women and Author of *Own It: A Call to Migrant Women Who D.A.R.E. to Be Seen*

We live in a moment when the noise around us drowns out the voice within—and the stories we inherit replace the ones we're meant to tell. *Own Your Life Story* meets that tension with psychological rigor and real compassion. Dr. Lidia Lae shows that identity isn't something you discover. It's something you claim. This book is for anyone ready to stop performing their life and start authoring it.

Camille Preston PhD
Business Psychologist and Author of *Living Real*

OWN YOUR LIFE STORY

Embracing Cultural Identity & Creating a Life of Joy, Meaning, & Legacy

Lidia Lae PhD

First published in Australia in 2026 by InkLume Media
www.inklumemedia.com

Copyright © Lidia Lae 2026

All rights reserved. StoriCompass™ and CulturAlign™ are trademarks of their respective owners. All other trademarks, service marks, and logos are the property of their respective owners. No part of this publication, including the StoriCompass™ and CulturAlign™ frameworks, may be reproduced, stored in a retrieval system, or transmitted in any form or by any means, electronic, mechanical, photocopying, recording, or otherwise, without the prior written permission of the publisher/author, except as permitted by law.

Excerpt from *The Hakka Cookbook* by Linda Lau Anusasananan reprinted by permission of the author.
Excerpt from the writings of Julia Cameron reprinted by permission of the author.

Edited for US Publication by Cortni L. Merritt
Cover art by Ashish Joshi
Layout by Sophie White
Author photo by Daniel Mu

This book is intended for educational and inspirational purposes only. It is not a substitute for professional legal, psychological, or medical advice. The author and publisher make no representations regarding the accuracy, completeness, or outcomes of applying the content presented herein. We expressly disclaim any liability for any loss, harm, or consequence arising directly or indirectly from the use or application of the information, stories, or insights shared in this book.

 A catalogue record for this book is available from the National Library of Australia

Lae, Lidia
Own Your Life Story: Embracing Cultural Identity & Creating a Life of Joy, Meaning, & Legacy.

ISBN 978-1-7641326-0-2 (paperback)
ISBN 978-1-7641326-1-9 (hardcover)
ISBN 978-1-7641326-2-6 (epub)

INKLUME MEDIA

For my family,

the women who have shaped my story,

and women everywhere who are writing their own.

Table of Contents

Foreword by Dr. Wendy Cahill	1
Introduction	5

Part 1 Mapping Your Story Landscape — 15

1	Stories We Didn't Choose to Live	17
2	Who Are You in Your Life Story? (The Agent)	35
3	What Do You Really Want? (The Desire)	55
4	Who or What Guides You? (The Guide)	73
5	Who or What Benefits from Your Success? (The Beneficiary)	93
6	Who or What's Assisting You Forward? (The Supporter)	110
7	Who or What's Standing in Your Way? (The Opposition)	125
8	What Does Your Life Look Like? (Your Story Frame)	141

Part 2 Moving Beyond the Cultural Script — 165

9	Breaking the Patterns That No Longer Serve You	167
10	Becoming the Author, Not Just a Character or Victim	189
11	Living Aligned	207

Part 3 Creating a Life of Joy, Meaning, and Legacy — 227

12	Framing Your Future: Your Next Chapter Starts Now	230
13	Reframing Success: What Joy Really Looks Like	252
14	Living Your Meaning and Legacy	273

Helping Children Build Healthy Life Stories	290
Acknowledgements	291
Bibliography	293
Beyond These Pages	300
About the Author	301

Foreword

Dr. Lidia Lae raises the bar with *Own Your Life Story*! It would be a mistake to dismiss this work as 'just another set of life stories'. Every woman has a story worth telling—a story that is uniquely hers, shaped throughout her life journey by culture, identity, challenges, and triumphs. In *Own Your Life Story*, Lidia invites you to step into the driver's seat of your narrative, offering a roadmap to navigate the twists and turns of life with clarity, courage, and a touch of humor.

Nor is this your typical self-help book. It's a vibrant, deeply human exploration of what it means to live with intention and authenticity. With her signature blend of academic rigor, lived experience, and heartfelt empathy, Lidia has crafted a guide that is as practical as it is profound. Whether you're a high-achieving professional, a woman balancing family and career, or someone simply seeking to understand yourself better, this book will resonate with you.

Through the innovative *StoriCompass* framework, Lidia reframes life's challenges—not as obstacles to overcome, but as opportunities to understand ourselves more deeply. She empowers readers to break free from inherited narratives, close the story loops that keep us stuck, and embrace the power of choice. Her approach is refreshingly honest, encouraging reflection without judgment and growth without pressure.

This book *is* a gem! What makes this book truly special is its ability to speak to women from all walks of life, across cultures. From airline captains navigating male-dominated industries to mothers reflecting on their cultural identities, *Own Your Life Story* is a universal call to reclaim your voice, your values, and your vision for the future. It's a celebration of the stories we carry from the different cultures we inhabit and the legacies we create.

Lidia's writing is both tender—compassionate at times—and sometimes punchy, weaving humor and wisdom into every page. You'll laugh, you'll cry, and most importantly, you'll think about who you are, where you've been, and where you want to go. This book is not just a guide; it's a companion for the journey, a spark for *transformation*, (*change that is significant, substantial and sustained*) and most importantly, a reminder that your story matters!

So, dear reader, take a deep breath and dive in. Let *Own Your Life Story* be the compass that helps you navigate the terrain of your life with purpose, joy, and a renewed sense of self. Your story is waiting to be written—by you.

Wendy Cahill AM DSG PhD
Chair, Academic Board, Texila College Australia
Board Director, Barton Business School
Former Director of Academic Leadership, University of Melbourne

Disclaimer

The stories shared in this book come from lived experience—my own, and those generously offered by women from around the world. Out of respect for privacy and ethical integrity, certain names, identifying details, and specific circumstances have been thoughtfully changed. While the emotional truths, challenges, and insights remain intact, any perceived resemblance to actual individuals, communities, or organizations is purely coincidental unless clearly indicated.

This book is intended for educational and inspirational purposes only. It is not a substitute for professional legal, psychological, or medical advice. The author and publisher make no representations regarding the accuracy, completeness, or outcomes of applying the content presented herein. We expressly disclaim any liability for any loss, harm, or consequence arising directly or indirectly from the use or application of the information, stories, or insights shared in this book.

If you are facing emotional or mental health difficulties, please seek support from a qualified professional. Help is available, and you do not have to navigate life alone.

The stories and reflections within these pages span cultures, languages, and worldviews. While every effort has been made to honor the richness and complexity of each voice, cultural interpretations and individual experiences may vary. This work is offered in a spirit of respect, connection, and shared humanity.

Introduction

The bravest thing a woman can do is to look her own history in the face and accept it as her own.

— Attributed to Margaret Oliphant

I became a refugee as a toddler. Born the year before Operation Lotus, the invasion of East Timor (now Timor-Leste) by Indonesia, I must've soaked up the restlessness of a country on the brink of war. After the Indonesian occupation, life became unbearable, so plans were put in motion for my family to escape.

My parents and brothers—Ba, Ma, Sien, Kian—and I became separated from our large extended family when we sought asylum and flew to Portugal. In this new Western culture with my family, housed in commission flats, we found the Portuguese welcoming.

The year I turned six, my little hands clutched the armrests of the plane, knuckles white, as the rhythmic beat of my pounding heart took over my senses, embodying both my fear of the unknown and my thrilling anticipation. I was going to see my grandparents, Poh Poh and Goong Goong, again. They had escaped to Australia with many of my extended family. My eyes stared through the oval window to fix onto the serene, endless expanse of clouds, finding a brief, beautiful calm as we descended.

I ran into the arms of my grandmother, Poh Poh, at our heartfelt reunion at Tullamarine Airport in Melbourne. My face buried into her soft tummy, she smelt of sweet perfume. Joyful tears covered our faces; we were all together again. I couldn't wait to start school in this land of great opportunities, but life is bittersweet.

As refugees in the '80s, we were outcasts in White Australia. I had never felt shame like I did when I was repeatedly told by the school bully to go home with my ching-chong eyes. *Where was home, after all, when you are a Third Culture Kid?*

Though my emotional wounds have healed, the scars remain. Ma and Ba drummed it into us that education was our way of redemption. They knew because neither of them had the chance to complete high school in East Timor.

So I poured myself into books. Many nights, I read the dictionary so I could grasp the English language, translating for Ma and Ba, who worked at the factories only to come home to their second job as textile machinists to support our family.

At the end of my first school year, my teacher gifted me a box of books. It was priceless. Through her presence and her present, I fell in love with language and somehow understood it was the key to my success. In words, I found solace, tenderness, and a world of possibilities.

Stories from fiction and nonfiction books have been woven into every aspect of my life. Immediately before my sixteenth birthday, I discovered psychology when I read Chaim Potok's *The Chosen*, which planted a seed in me to become a psychologist. Helping people seemed a noble way to live. I also dared to dream I could reach the pinnacle of educational achievement: obtaining a PhD!

***

Years later, the dream of that PhD was finally within reach. I was sitting in my study, stuck in my own story, wondering how I was going to complete my thesis and cross that finish line; tears welled in my eyes. My mind vacillated between hope and doubt. *Was I PhD material? Who was I to believe I could achieve this childhood dream? Did I have it in me?* Imposter syndrome set in.

Wiping away the wet streams on my cheeks with my palms, I swallowed the taste of failure and the fear of it. No, I was not ready to give up. Faith had taught me that anything is possible for those who believe.

As with all great feats in life, I was learning that when we yearn for something and aspire to become more, to obtain our heart's desire, obstacles arise.

And I had a lot working against me. I was already in my early thirties, a newlywed, and we wondered if the PhD would derail our plans to start a family. The clock was ticking.

When my Poh Poh found out, she exclaimed, "Ayor, why do you want to study more? You could have babies!" She questioned whether my previous qualifications were really valuable when family is what makes a person. She spent her life giving birth to twelve children and nurturing the eleven who survived. I'm sure she thought I was nuts to pursue a PhD when I could be holding something more precious.

Fate would have it that after I got accepted into the PhD program, I found myself pregnant.

I was already a therapist running my own consultancy, a wife, a student, and now becoming a mother. Life was full, hectic. To add to the equation, three years after my first baby, I had another. In those early days, I felt like a zombie, surviving on minimal sleep. Life happened so fast, I felt like a character in my own story.

Motherhood stretched me to the limits of coping, those sleepless nights, dripping tops because the breast milk leaked all over. The cries that wouldn't cease. The minute I would put the baby down, the screaming was so loud and persistent I had to pick the baby up again. Even taking a shower became a luxury. I had no idea how I was going to find the time to do research for graduate school.

With the two new young ones, we outgrew our apartment. I question my life choices now, but while in the middle of working toward my PhD, my husband and I started building our house, on top of all my other roles. I felt so overwhelmed.

Owning up to my life story, admitting these decisions, and being vulnerable are not easy for me. Especially as a psychologist. We are seen as having it all together. But we are human, imperfect, and flawed like any other person. We are highly trained, but we juggle life with all its different roles and demands like everyone else. We have our own struggles and times when we feel like giving up on our life dreams.

My lingering thoughts of self-doubt never truly left. But Susan David's *Emotional Agility* got me to face my overwhelm and self-doubt. I remember listening to her on Audible while I was picking up my youngest from a party. As I turned at a suburban Melbourne intersection, her words drilled into my mind, "Just show up!"

I couldn't give up. Ma and Ba had sacrificed so much, looking after my two young daughters so I could work and study. The rest of the family all had made sacrifices. *What would those two precious girls think? That Mom pursued her dreams but never got to realize them? What message would I be sending them if I gave up?* That was what sealed my grit! My family is the *why* behind everything I do.

Come Monday morning, instead of making an excuse not to attend my supervisory meeting and throw in the towel, I showed up. I confessed to my supervisor that I was in a mess of struggles. The pressures of my different roles and identities had taken their toll. However, I found out later these were only the external obstacles hindering my progress. (I'll explain later.)

My honesty released me. My supervisor promised he was going to help me get over the line. He kept his word.

We were discussing my research applying Greimas's Actantial Model (GAM)—which literary scientist Algirdas Greimas claimed as a framework for analyzing the universal deep structures underlying all narratives—to people's life stories. Then he asked, "Why don't you use the model on yourself?"

What? The same tool on myself?

"It'll help you work out what's going on in your own life," he added.

I took my supervisor's advice and applied this model—which I have now adapted to clinical practice and called it the *StoriCompass*—to explore why I was stuck and the story I was telling myself.

Doing this helped me gain insight into the obstacles that were underlying my work toward my goals. What I learned empowered me to persevere, and it transformed my life.

Why I Wrote This Book

Over a decade after starting my PhD, I walked with the other academics, all draped in black regalia highlighted with the colors of our faculty. Like emperor penguins in procession, we walked solemnly down the aisles past seats filled with other graduates gathered at the Royal Exhibition Building, where this University of Melbourne graduation was held.

As higher-degree graduates, we stepped onto the stage to be seated. As my name was called, I heard applause and walked to the designated position to hear my citation read. I felt the unspoken pride and beaming smiles of my parents, witnessing their daughter, a little refugee girl, become a psychologist dedicating her life to helping people, and now, awarded her childhood dream.

I've spent most of my adult years unraveling people's problems to improve their lives and investigating culture, memory, self-narratives, and how we make meaning of life. I explored how culture shapes the way individuals interpret and narrate their life experiences. My studies on the cross-cultural differences of the personal stories of Westerners and Easterners showed different, unique ways we build our identities and how those are shaped by culture.

As a psychologist, I am honored and privileged to be allowed into the inner chambers of peoples' lives, working with individuals, couples, and families who invite me into their secret worlds. The worlds no one else, not even family members or closest friends, know. I get to hear the inner voices we all have, the ones trapped in adult bodies but still children within: the forty-year-old housewife struggling in her marriage, her nervous system highly reactive due to childhood abuse. Or the successful general manager crippled with anxiety and intimidated by a subordinate because the person reminds him of a high school bully. Countless times I've seen these old stories and past experiences still operating powerfully in my clients' present lives.

Their stories humble me. In my work, I've heard many stories of abuse, suffering, and depravity. But I have also glimpsed tremendous resilience, hope, courage, and strength despite challenging experiences.

I used to be puzzled, as a teenager and young adult, when complete strangers approached me on trains or buses, in shops or parks, to share their life stories with me. I had always been drawn to autobiographies and had a fascination with people's lives. And people were drawn to that fascination like a magnet and felt comfortable sharing their stories with me.

It was no wonder then that I pursued psychology, and the PhD opened up to me. It's been no coincidence also that my love of cultures and the diversity of people led to investigating the puzzle pieces of how life stories differ cross-culturally and how we all make sense of life.

People are worlds to explore, oceans we can dive deep into to discover the treasures within.

The treasures unearthed from investigating life stories in both research and clinical practice are what I want to share with you. This is a story of my own life and of others who have allowed me in. As an East Timorese–Chinese Portuguese Australian woman, I have embraced who I am and the complexities of my cultural background. I have spent my career helping others explore their own complex stories and learn to navigate the world through the lens of their cultural identities.

My life intersects with many others, including yours and the women you will be introduced to in these pages. I interviewed these women specifically for this book and they volunteered their life stories, which I recorded verbatim. They did so because they believed in the book's vision of owning and sharing personal narratives to help each other grow. They are not my clients but come from all parts of the globe—teachers, students, homemakers, corporate professionals, executives, writers, health practitioners, and more—young to mature, ordinary but extraordinary women who have allowed you in so that in sharing, you will know you are not alone.

Scattered in the book are also stories of famous women whose lives touched mine. We all have dreams and struggles. Together, all our lives form the cultures—the meaning system of values, beliefs, customs, practices, behaviors—we inhabit and embody.

How This Book Can Help You

This book is about exploring and understanding your cultural identities. Your cultural identity is simply *who you are*. We are not created in a vacuum. Like fish that swim in the ocean and need the medium of water to survive, we are immersed in culture from the time we are soaked in amniotic fluid in our mother's wombs. We are born into the fluid cultures of our family, community, country, and society. The medium of culture is the invisible substance that directs the flow of our lives, the force that shapes us.

Understanding how your life story is influenced and shaped by the cultures with which you identify gives you the power to understand what powerful cultural scripts direct your life: your decisions, your struggles, your relationships, your path.

Through this exploration, you can discover the cultural stories that help you succeed and the ones that no longer serve you. And if there are stories no longer serving you, this method helps you break free from them, change so you can live life on your own terms.

Through understanding your individual story, you will be empowered to honor the cultural scripts sacred to you, enabling you to create a life you desire and deserve, one that is fully aligned with your values and who you choose to be. You can develop and own a meaningful life that brings you joy and that makes a positive impact.

Ultimately, we are all vessels of greatness. The art we make of our lives is rooted in the stories we live while in this world. Like all of us, one day you and I will leave this world, and it's up to us to make sure the story we leave behind is one we truly owned because when we are gone, we are only remembered by the story we lived. This is our legacy.

Too often though, people live trapped inside a story they didn't choose, repeating roles they didn't question, chasing goals never truly their own. I have seen too often in the clinic room how these stories come to manifest as anxiety, depression, and other mental health and relationship issues. Many people fall short of their potential when they become trapped in narratives not of their own choosing. With false selves and life stories punctuated with a sense of failure, of not having achieved dreams, of disappointment, and of stagnation.

If you're in a time of transition, perhaps you've lost your job and aren't sure where to go from here. You may have recently become a parent and feel like you're struggling. Or someone dear has left, and you don't know how to navigate life without them. This book can help you make sense of it all.

Maybe you simply feel lost in the story of your own life, and you think, "There must be more! This can't be it." If you're unsure what your life is about, if you're questioning decisions you've made, if you're determined to move forward and build a strong, positive, meaningful life: in these pages, you will find you are not alone. This book is written for you. The women who vulnerably share their lives in this book, including me, open our hearts to you, to welcome you into a culture of belonging. This time of transition in your life is an opportunity to grow and learn. In this book, I present tools and maps for you to learn about your unique self and path.

This book was born from the many women who came to me asking questions like, "Who am I? Where do I belong? How do I accomplish my goals and dreams? How do I live a life worth living?"

If these are your questions, too, this book gives you a step-by-step guide to building your life. I've read hundreds of self-help books, and many have helped, but as a culturally diverse woman, the "Self" explained in those books did not fully capture the powerful cultural influences that shape each of our lives. This is my attempt to highlight the cultural dimensions of our lives and bring together real-life stories, psychology, neuroscience, philosophy, sociology, semiotics, and more to help you explore and reflect on your life story.

In the following pages, you will find in part 1 that when you map your story landscape using the StoriCompass, you will gain language, structure, clarity, and vision. You can become the *author*, not a character or victim, in your own life. There are prompts after each chapter for you to go deeper to map out where you are, where you want to be, and what is required for you to get there. Part 2 will show you culture's influence on your life and how you can pick up your story at any turning point. Or how you make your own turning point that will change the plot of your life story. No matter how your story began, you have the power to determine the next chapter and how it ends.

You will realize the creative power you have in authoring a life of meaning and purpose in part 3, where you'll find answers to the question, "How do I achieve my wildest dreams, goals, and desires?" You will learn how *Life Framing* can help you.

The story you start owning and sharing is the very thing culture is made of. Culture is transmitted through the medium of narratives. Our life stories shape the cultures we swim in, can become the template that others aspire to, and craft the legacy for which we will be remembered when our story ends.

Let's begin now with the end in mind. Live the story you want to own and embrace the person you are becoming.

PART 1

Mapping Your Story Landscape

To narrate is to put meaning into order.

— Attributed to Algirdas Julien Greimas

The StoriCompass™

The StoriCompass is a tool I developed to help people make sense of who they are and the life they're living by seeing it as a story. It was inspired by Greimas's Actantial Model, a structural framework I used in my PhD research to explore cross-cultural differences in *what* people share in their stories and *how* they tell them. Over time, I reimagined it into a practical, human-centered process that helps us reflect, realign, and reconnect with what matters most.

In the following chapters, you will gain insight and tools to understand who you are and that the life you are living can be seen as a story you can create. The StoriCompass has three *pathways* with six important *elements*, which will be explained in the next eight chapters. These pathways with their elements are: 1) The *Pathway of Pursuit*, explains the *Agent-Desire* relationship; 2) The *Pathway of Impact*, illustrates the *Guide-Beneficiary* that operate in any pursuit; and 3) The *Pathway of Forces*, highlights the *Supporter-Opposition*, which act on the Agent in their pursuit of the Desire. This part 1 of mapping your story landscape using the StoriCompass offers you not only direction but clarity, as well as a process that you can apply in your everyday life.

It's about seeing our stories more clearly. And when we do, we can reclaim authorship of those stories. Whether you're navigating a life change, leading a team, raising children, or simply trying to reconnect with yourself, the StoriCompass offers a structure to help you realign with what matters most. You simply need a place to start, situate yourself in your own story. This is that beginning—a map to walk alongside you as you make sense of where you've been and who you are, then choose what comes next.

1

Stories We Didn't Choose to Live

Through others we become ourselves.

— Attributed to Lev Vygotsky

What goes on in the minds of a few can move a whole culture.

— Attributed to Margaret Mead

Tessa's day was not going well. Hundreds of Lego pieces littered across the lounge room, which her young kids had not cleaned up. She was late for their dental appointment. And now she couldn't find her keys. The disorder around her home felt like it mirrored the mess she felt within.

Growing up, Tessa struggled with being mixed race. Her mom was Chinese, but her dad was Anglo Australian. At school, she had never felt like she truly belonged with the studious Asian kids; she struggled academically. Neither did she feel comfortable with the Anglo Aussie group who were often playing sports. She wasn't great at sports either. She had never really known where she fit.

Where life growing up had been dominated by her Chinese mother, now as an adult, it felt controlled by her Greek Australian husband. These two strong figures in her life sometimes conflicted, and she felt caught between, unable to take sides. She dared not disappoint her mother, but if she took her mother's side about anything, her husband would get angry. Their home was a place of frequent arguments. The kids learned to hide in their rooms when they heard things start to get tense.

She worried about her kids, with their complicated background. She was biracial, and her husband was too. *What culture would they identify with? Mine or his?* she thought. *What kind of a role model am I?* She felt a wave of self-loathing. Unheard by those she loved.

"Where is my voice in all this?" Tessa whispered to herself, collapsing onto her sofa, wondering, *Who am I?*

Tessa, a thirty-three-year-old homemaker, is one of the women I interviewed. As a friend, she kept many struggles private, but she agreed to share about her life, hoping it would help other women. The story above was a typical scenario in her life, but we never truly know what people go through unless they share their stories. Tessa tried to make sense of her past and present, wondering what was in store for her future. She told me, "I feel like I've actually never known who I am, even since I was little."

Tessa is not alone. Many women struggle with identity issues. They may ask themselves questions like:

* "What is my place in this world?"

* "Who am I? (If only I knew!)"

* "How do I find myself?"

* "How do I even love myself if I don't know who I am?"

I often hear these voices in clinical practice. Struggles with identity, self-worth, and self-love often sit disturbingly at the root of many emotional and relational challenges. If you can relate to any of these struggles, this book was written for you to let you know there is a path forward.

What Does It Take to Love Ourselves?

Ancient Greek philosopher Plato admonished people to "know thyself." He learned from Socrates that "the unexamined life is not worth living." Both believed that self-knowledge is the foundation of wisdom and ethical living. Socrates taught Plato about the fundamental importance of self-knowledge. Plato, in turn, developed his thesis that virtuous self-love is a direct result and consequence of genuine self-knowledge.

During the COVID-19 pandemic, cosmetics retailer The Body Shop and research company Ipsos surveyed twenty-two thousand people across twenty-one countries, measuring the Global Self-Love Index, including factors such as self-worth, well-being, and happiness. The study revealed how age, gender, country, and living standards impact people's feelings about themselves. Results identified a self-love crisis for women around the world, with one in two women feeling more self-doubt than self-love, and 60 percent of female respondents wishing they had more respect for themselves.

Self-love may mean many things, but it has to start internally, by choosing to know and love who you are. Then you treat yourself like someone worth caring for.

But how do you get from not knowing who you are to loving yourself *and* believing that you are enough and worth caring for the way you are?

To answer this question, we explore how we got to where we are today, how culture influences our lives, and how our identity developed.

Understanding the root causes of issues in our lives helps us work through the underlying problems.

Once we understand the underlying issues, we use that information to achieve better emotional well-being, make better decisions, have more loving relationships, gain self-confidence, and experience greater overall life satisfaction. Owning our life's stories is our path to self-love.

The Importance of Identity

In 1951, psychoanalyst Erik Erikson pointed at identity as an organizing principle that humans use to work out who we are and who we want to be. You may be familiar with Erikson's work on human developmental stages. He studied how people form an identity in childhood, how that identity changes throughout life, and the factors that can affect identity. Our identity shapes our stories and beliefs about who we are and what we want; my research connects to the idea that we form identities through experiences.

Identity today can be fraught with confusion. Rapid technological, societal, and cultural changes impact each of us, and the changes seem to come faster and faster.

In 1951, it was considered science fiction to video call someone, or to have the entire knowledge of the world on a device that fits in our pockets. Besides technology, there are now more blended multicultural families, gender in Western cultures is no longer considered static or permanent, and the world is experiencing more mass migration than ever, to name a few changes. The concept of *identity* is vital for us to understand as we negotiate virtual worlds in addition to physical worlds; the ongoing task of crystalizing one's identity has become more complex.

With psychology expanding beyond the Western framework and incorporating diverse cultural perspectives, it's more important than ever to understand ourselves and our cultural identity. Unless we do, we will find it difficult to develop ourselves to our highest potential. How can you move forward to build a successful, joyful life and future if you do not know yourself or what you stand for? Here is the invitation to know who you are in your own story.

How Did We Get Like This?

Each of us is born in a time and place, within a family. We may be from rich or poor families, from a certain class in our society, a particular ethnicity, and may be born into a specific religion. These all impact how we see ourselves and influence our *self-concepts* (the thoughts we have about ourselves) and *self-esteem* (how we feel about ourselves).

Around the two-year-old mark, our autobiographical memory—the memory system that stores personal experiences—develops. Language use starts to expand and helps structure life experiences.

Tessa's mixed heritage was grounds for cultural tension; she sometimes felt torn between contrasting Western and Eastern values. In our conversation, Tessa mentioned that her dad, Jeff, was laid-back, uninvolved with parenting. He left most of the childrearing to her Chinese mom, Lin. She reflected, "Mom was the boss."

The Child Learns Who She Is

Researchers have found that parents—through conversations and reminiscing about things the child has done before she had memory—help the child build an understanding of herself. For example, parents might say things like, "You learned to walk quickly. You were always fast." "Remember the time of your first birthday? You had a big smile. You were always happy." These conversations help the child develop an understanding of herself. Reminiscing begins laying a foundation for the child's identity. Researchers call this *parent-child scaffolding*.

Tessa was the oldest of four children. Her sister was born soon after her second birthday, around the time her autobiographical memory was developing. At the time, she felt she lost the exclusive attention of her parents, which she enjoyed as the first child, a kind of dethroning that firstborn children can feel. That loss of attention meant she missed some of her parents' attention to help her make sense of her early experiences. The scaffolding became insufficient once her parents also focused on her sister.

These conversations and reminiscences start building the skills and meaning-making systems that give the child the know-how to make sense of life's experiences. Meaning-making is how we interpret ourselves, others, and the world, a process shaped by what we inherit from parents or caregivers. This process frames a child's interpretation of life and builds a foundation of coping skills for survival. When we learn our place in the world, our story, we are better able to adapt to what life throws at us.

One of the most important challenges in life is making sense of life experiences; giving meaning to what we've gone through. Do our hurdles and disappointments break us because we believe they are proof we are worthless? Or do we allow those experiences to strengthen us and nurture confidence as we overcome struggles?

Renowned psychiatrist and neurologist Viktor Frankl, and other researchers, have found that a proportion of adults may develop mental illness because they never fully developed meaning-making skills. They flounder because they aren't sure who they are or what they're supposed to be doing, which leads to problems such as depression, anxiety, and addictions. That is why evidence-based psychological treatments like cognitive-behavioral therapy (CBT), narrative therapy, and others help with some mental illnesses; they build the skills of making meaning out of what happens to us and understanding our role in the world.

For Tessa, the moment her parents brought her sister home from the hospital and began to spend less time with her, her childish confusion and sadness created the story that they loved her less.

Her parents continued to add to the family, and each sibling pushed her away from her parents to the edge of the family group. Her parents tried to make sure she still felt loved, but she never forgot the moment when she was no longer the center of their world. Now, as an adult, she has a tendency to collapse into a heap at any challenging or painful experience, believing her own story that she is not lovable, that she is incapable of coping with challenges. Her experiences of being on the outside, both in her family and in school, taught her that she didn't belong, and she believes it. *Who am I?* She keeps asking herself. She ponders her childhood marked by learning difficulties and social struggles; she uses those experiences to explain the struggles she continues with in adulthood.

During childhood, more and more experiences are stored in autobiographical memory. Research by psychologists Katherine Nelson, Robyn Fivush, and Michael Tomasello demonstrates that during childhood, language and social understanding develop rapidly as the child leaves home to start school and starts navigating different social worlds. As the child develops, they learn to express themselves and their needs, and they learn about the requirements of their social world. As they grow, a child's cultural understanding (and their absorption of cultural scripts) continues to develop their meaning-making framework of life.

The Child Learns Where She Fits

In adolescence, a child's brain goes through exponential growth, particularly in the prefrontal lobe—the seat of impulse control, where executive functioning skills are located. The child develops cognitive tools and psychosocial understanding, working out what is expected of them, and how they fit, from their culture. Adolescents start forming their identity, who they are and where they belong, by learning from the cultures around them; their family, peers, school, and neighborhood. As they develop, they begin to emulate different role models to build their identities through peer and interest groups. They may look at celebrities, influencers, sports stars, and others, like parents or teachers, to help develop their identities.

Creating Identity in Adulthood

In adulthood, using different work, home, and social settings, we continue to construct a coherent self-identity from life experiences. We identify within national and political groups as a citizen and engage with local communities. By this time, we have developed our cultural identity, which pulls together a story of who we are, what we value, and what we stand for. We often make important decisions in our lives—what career we pursue, where we live, who we choose to be in a relationship with, what hobbies we take up—based on these identities.

As events happen in our lives—loss, accidents, tragedies, or turning points, like getting married and having children—our lives change significantly, and how we make sense of these experiences impacts our self. As culture is in constant flux, so is identity.

Culture and Self

Our world feels like it's constantly spinning faster than we want. None of us can anticipate what's going to happen or how events will change our lives. Before COVID-19 hit, I hardly used the Zoom app to talk to people; I called them, or we would meet face to face. But now, years after the worst of the pandemic, online calls—with clients, international work colleagues, and friends—are a stable part of my week. The way I live, work, interact, and perceive the world has changed, and the same is true for most of us who lived through that time. The massive cultural change that happened during and after the pandemic was felt globally.

This feeling of everything in motion, never staying the same, is an example of how culture is in constant flux, whether it's work culture, family culture, community culture, or peer group culture. It's like a river that's always flowing. But with the rapid changes swirling around us, there are powerful, core ways groups of people tend to see themselves and each other, which don't change easily. Think of ethnic, religious, or political groups. Even if minor ways of expressing these cultures changes, the deeper identity stays consistent. These are deep currents that shape our very sense of who we are.

Web versus Island

These deep currents are where Tessa found herself caught. She had been brought up predominantly by an urban Chinese mother, Lin, who exerted more of her Chinese culture in the family home despite her Anglo Australian father, Jeff, in the background. In this Chinese culture, like other East Asian cultures researched, people often see themselves as connected to others, part of a big *web* or network. They focus on their family, friends, and groups, and their highest priority is everyone getting along. Tessa felt it was normal to lean on Lin. However, her husband John had grown up in Australia, where, as in so many other Western countries, people often see themselves as separate, unique individuals, much like an *island*. They focus on what makes them special, their own feelings, and on being independent from those around them.

Back in 1980, Dutch psychologist Geert Hofstede explored these cultural dimensions in a groundbreaking study. He surveyed thousands of employees at IBM, a global company, across many different countries. He revealed how their cultural backgrounds profoundly shaped their workplace values and behaviors. From his vast research, he discovered that cultures tend to lean in one of two directions on a spectrum: either promoting *individualism* (the *island* approach), where employees are encouraged to focus on their personal goals and stand out as their own unique people, or fostering *collectivism* (the *web* approach), where the emphasis is on fitting in, maintaining harmony, and prioritizing the well-being of the team and company.

It was Hofstede's research, particularly his cultural dimensions theory, which sparked the interest among researchers in cross-cultural psychology.

Until then, much of mainstream psychology operated under the assumption that core psychological processes in human brains, like the way we think and feel and what drives us, worked pretty much the same way no matter what culture a person came from. Similar to how a computer running a program will act like another computer running the same program. But in 1991, Hazel Rose Markus and Shinobu Kitayama showed that the cultures that influence us give us a different "operating system" for how we see ourselves and the world, for whether we see ourselves as an *island* or as a part of a *web*.

Cultural influence also affects our emotions and whether we feel prouder of our own achievements or of our group's achievements.

Lastly, cultural influence also impacts what drives us, our *motivation*: whether we are motivated to be better than someone else, or whether we focus on making sure everyone in our group is doing well. These cross-cultural differences impact each of us in profound ways.

In my research and work with clients, I've found this to be true; I've found that our cultural identity is the interaction of *culture* and *self*, and that both mutually constitute each other as proposed by the eminent psychologist Jerome Bruner. They dynamically influence each other so neither is building itself separately, but both develop together. Like DNA's intertwined strands, culture and self spiral together—each influencing how the other expresses itself.

* * *

Growing up, Tessa desired to belong, but she was torn between two groups of friendships, two contrasting cultures. On the one hand were her Asian friends who loved to read and were quite academic, but on the other hand were her Anglo Australian friends who loved sports: netball, cricket, football. They all congregated on the oval.

In truth, Tessa never felt like she belonged to either group, and so, her loneliness grew. She was torn, at times throughout high school spending time with one group more than another, then shifting alliances. Because she drifted between groups and hadn't built deep connections with either one, after school ended, her friends moved on in their lives and she drifted from them, feeling rejected that nobody from those groups tried to remain in touch with her. But then, she hadn't either. That experience of perceived rejection had a real impact on her life, and she carried it as a script into other experiences. When she didn't get into a course she wanted, she felt rejected by the university and ended up in technical college, where she met John. They fell in love, married, and started their family.

Establishing the Family Culture

When people gather, they bring a way of speaking, of making meaning, expressing values, behaving, building customs, and so on. When two people establish a home together, they establish a culture in their home.

As children come, the family develops their family culture. Usually, the family members don't always acknowledge or explore these invisible forces. Unfortunately, these hidden influences, if not addressed, can result in hard-to-resolve conflicts. For example, Tessa had no idea she was experiencing a conflict between her mother's understanding of the world as a web and John's individualistic vision, seeing himself and others as islands. He could not understand the cultural influences at play in Tessa's life because he only saw from the lens of his own cultural upbringing.

John couldn't understand why Tessa called her mom for advice on any problem or situation. When their children had fevers or when the family needed something, Tessa relied on her mom. John felt Lin had more power than he did in the home. So one night, in a fit of anger, he forbade Tessa to call her mom for help anymore. "We can handle our own problems," he told her.

Tessa couldn't help it; her mom was the anchor of her life, and she felt extremely lonely when no longer allowed to talk to her. She felt increasingly isolated from John because of his domineering behavior and couldn't relate to his individualism. Tessa had grown up with a sense that everything was connected, that one made decisions based on a complex understanding of social standing, not only to fulfil one's own needs. Their home culture felt toxic. They fought in front of the children, who absorbed it all. Home life was tense and emotionally unsafe. She told me, "I feel like I have ideas of what I like, but I guess I don't know how to actually get to that point of knowing who I am. I want to stop, I guess, worrying what people think, and I want to be able to know who I am…to stand up for myself."

If, like Tessa, you're tired, sick, or exhausted, it's time to understand yourself within the cultures where you grew up, within your current cultural contexts. Without that comprehension of our selves and the cultural influences that are deeply ingrained and currently operating, we fail to break free from invisible forces, to change ourselves and the cultures of our family, work, or society.

CulturAlign, the Cultural Identity Blueprint, helps us understand ourselves by showing what we value; our past, present, and future selves; and various cultural dimensions that impact us. We'll explore this further in chapter 2. But first, we need to understand our self and identity.

From research, clinical practice, and lived experiences, I found that how we see our life stories varies across cultures. As a therapist,

I found it paramount to understand how my clients' cultures impact their view of self, the world, and their roles in it.

Each person's frames of interpretation are deeply shaped by culture.

You can understand that for people like Tessa and myself, it becomes confusing when we've grown up between two cultures or within multiple cultures. We have both been Westernized, so we have integrated individual agency into how we view our lives. For Tessa though, she feels torn between the person she wants to become and the person sandwiched between her mother and husband.

More on Tessa later.

Who Was I in My Story?

Deep in the Baillieu Library of the University of Melbourne, a glass-covered building with a spiral staircase, I hunted down William James's 1890 book, *Principles of Psychology*. I wanted to read for myself what James wrote in his chapter on "The Consciousness of Self."

James argued that the Self consisted of two aspects of consciousness, "*I*"—the knower, which is the Self as subject of experience—and "*Me*" the empirical self, the Self as object of experience. The *I* was thought of as the "thinking self," referred to as the "pure ego," while the *Me*, which was the empirical self, was the Self as known. That is, all the aspects of myself, like my body, how others see me, my inner thoughts, and feelings; all the things I know about myself and what makes me, *Me*. For instance, you're reading this book. You are reading, but do you notice you also have an awareness that you are reading? Hence, in James's language, "the Self is both the knower and the known."

Reading those words, it hit me: I had made peace with Me. I am creating Me. The "story of my life" is the Me. I knew what I wanted to believe and feel in my life. I was conscious that I could make decisions about my life, have a sense of agency, and choose which direction to go. I have experiences that get stored in my memory, which contribute to a growing sense of who I am.

During my adolescent years, I, as many adolescents do, experienced some self-loathing. Not only had I been bullied as a child, but being Asian, I stopped physically growing at twelve years of age, while peers kept gaining height. Of course, when you're a teenager, image can be everything. The guys in early high school called me "a quarter." The name-calling stung, but I laughed it off. It dented my self-image; I didn't like Me because I was short and a bookworm in a tough, working-class school.

Later, as a graduate student, a psychologist, wife, mom, daughter, and friend, I finally became conscious of the Me that I was creating. We are complex selves, with different dimensions and roles. Being conscious of the I and Me relationship and how we relate to our "selves" is vital for our well-being. It is one of the keys to self-love.

Like Tessa, I needed to ask myself who I was in my own life story. The graduate student trying to complete her research? The exhausted mom who felt helpless about potty training her toddler and getting both kids to bed on time? The devoted daughter wanting to make her parents proud? The wife unsure how to carve out date nights with her busy husband? The friend who wanted to be there for her girlfriends but didn't know how when there weren't enough hours in the day? Was I in control of my own story?

It is a question we all must answer in order to build our lives well.

Our Life Story Is Our Identity

The answer to my questions came when I read eminent psychologist Dan McAdams's theory of identity as "the internalized and evolving story that integrates a reconstructed past, perceived present, and anticipated future." In simple words, McAdams saw the *life story* as *identity*.

McAdams explains that the psychological Self includes identities as *Actor*, *Agent*, and *Author*. We are social actors presenting ourselves to the world, performing social roles, and expressing our personality traits, like whether we are extroverted or introverted. We are also motivated agents: striving for, planning, and pursuing what we want in life. Lastly, we are autobiographical authors, constructing our life story. Identity helps us make sense of our past, present, and imagined future, providing our lives with a sense of unity, meaning, and purpose.

Though I was immediately drawn to his work, I wanted to know more about Self and identity and how cultural influences impacted them. Over the years, through hours in the library and hundreds of miles traveled, presenting my research at international conferences, and interviewing and listening to culturally diverse people, I've heard many life stories that reflect how influential cultures are on identity.

We're always in an ongoing dance where our identity and our culture shape each other.

So, to move with grace, the key to understanding who we are lies in how we actively construct our life stories and define our place in this world. In the next chapter, we'll explore more deeply who you are within your life story.

The StoriCompass

We all carry stories shaped by our upbringing, culture, struggles, and choices. But we're often so busy living them that we forget to stop and look at these scripts influencing our lives.

Working with many people in clinical practice, I developed the StoriCompass to help them unpack how they were constructing their lives from experiences and memory, as well as make sense of the stories they were living.

The StoriCompass gives us a way to pause and understand. It maps our life stories across three key pathways: our *pursuit* (what we aim for), the *forces* around us (what helps or holds us back), and the *impact* of others on our lives, as well as ours on theirs.

The StoriCompass also invites us to reflect on six core elements: the person we're becoming (*Agent*), what we truly long for (*Desire*), the guides that shape us (*Guide*), who benefits when we grow (*Beneficiary*), who/what supports us (*Supporter*), and who/what gets in the way (*Opposition*). In the following chapters, we will explore each of these important elements. Then in chapter 8, you can map your own life story with the StoriCompass.

The StoriCompass helps us clarify our life story and look at how we make sense of our lives. When we do not know ourselves, how are we supposed to teach a younger generation to develop their own voice? Their own opinions? If we do not gain self-awareness, we are at risk of never being able to author our own lives and use our voices. We will be on autopilot, dictated by the voices of domineering figures in our life, whether that be parents, bosses or spouses, or even our children. We are stuck in the stories we didn't choose to live.

Understanding yourself means you can choose control. You can know what steps you need to take to craft your own life. From your current self to your ideal self in the future.

The very selves we live in are a compilation of thoughts and feelings experienced in scenes: moments of our lives that form sentences and paragraphs to form a story. We create stories from what we've experienced, and this becomes our reality.

Stories repeated often form an identity. Remember, Erikson said that identity is greatly impacted by culture. It is through the interaction of culture and self that we come to know who we are. In the next chapter, take the important first step toward regaining self and controlling the next chapter of your life.

Key Takeaways

* Each of us is born into a family, community, country, etc., with different cultures that shape our self and identity.

* Our identity is our life story, weaving together the past, present, and anticipated future to give our lives a sense of unity, meaning, and purpose.

* From childhood to adulthood, we create stories and absorb cultural scripts to develop frames we use to make sense of life.

* StoriCompass is a framework that helps us explore our life stories using three pathways (pursuit, impact, forces) and six core elements (Agent, Desire, Guide, Beneficiary, Supporter, and Opposition).

Deeper Actions

Take a moment to ask yourself: Where am I in the unfolding story of my life?

The questions below will help you think deeply on this chapter of your life and what it is about:

1. Think about your story so far. If you could write your story in a book, what would each chapter be called?
2. What different cultures are you part of (or are a part of you)? Think about your country, cultural heritage/ethnicity, gender, sexual preference, religion/spirituality, interests or hobbies, and political views.
3. What kinds of conflicts have you felt between your cultures in your life? How have they affected your life?

If you like, start a journal to reflect on your life. You can write your answers to these questions. Wherever you are in your story, your willingness to pause and reflect is already an act of reclaiming. You are taking a step into the next part of who you are becoming.

2

Who Are You in Your Life Story? (*The Agent*)

> *I am no bird; and no net ensnares me:*
> *I am a free human being with an independent will.*
>
> —Charlotte Brontë

> *Become who you already are.*
> *There is no longer any other.*
>
> —Adapted from Meister Eckhart

Every life is a story—rich and layered, filled with desire, conflict, triumph, loss, and purpose. And every story is born of struggles within a cultural story. Mine certainly is.

Think about your own life. What have been your struggles? What has defined you? These can be difficult questions to answer. I understand, as I have asked these often in the clinic room, and many women need time to comprehend and process their internal issues to realize what defines them and how their story is part of a larger story.

With the StoriCompass, we can explore our stories the way a movie or book reviewer reviews a plotline. You will find your struggles embedded into this universal narrative structure: tension, suspense, hardship, and antagonism. These move a story and grip our attention; they are also how we can understand our own story and what it tells us about our values, dreams, and goals.

Our lives seem more interesting when there are problems, where obstacles abound but are somehow overcome. That's the winning Hollywood script! With our hardships and victories, we can generate rich stories of our internal and external experiences. The StoriCompass can capture the inner and overarching stories we tell ourselves and others.

In this chapter, as you understand your narrative and absorb the stories of other women who open up their lives to you, you begin to step into the role of Agent. As an Agent, you choose, act, and shape what comes next in your story by building a foundation for your life. This is done through reflecting on your past, present, and anticipated future; your values, and the cultural dimensions that shape you. By understanding your cultural identity blueprint, you gain clarity about who you are and what you stand for. This helps you become the Agent in mapping your story landscape, so you can move forward with direction rather than feeling lost or stuck.

Understanding Your Own Narratives

Tessa's story in chapter 1 is not unique. I also spoke to another friend, Tina, a thirty-five-year-old East Timorese–Chinese Australian woman working part-time in an IT/administrative role, who also felt the cultural tension of her parents' background, coming to Australia as refugees, like my own, as well as raising her children in a Western country.

Tina was struggling with health issues and controlling her weight. She wanted a life worth living, to be positive, energetic, and at peace within herself, but her overarching goal and true desire was to set a good example for her two children. However, she felt like her husband was negative and had no drive. She couldn't find role models for her children, as her parents' own marriage was full of tension.

In one of our conversations, Tina realized her issues were passed down from her ancestors. As we discussed her family history, she thought her grandmother was a bit narcissistic. Growing up, there was no warmth or affection from her maternal grandmother; she only recalls being scolded and told off. "Don't sit on the sofa." "Don't play outside." And so on. It was not a child-friendly place when she visited or stayed over. Then, as a young adult, when she was asked to take this grandmother to a party because her parents were away, she had come from the other side of town and unfortunately was running late. Instead of gratitude or understanding, Tina was put through a guilt trip and told off because this grandmother had to wait. Now they were late, she told Tina she'd rather not go anymore. Tina felt deflated.

The lightbulb moment came when she saw her mother on the phone with her grandmother, and she witnessed her mother rolling her eyes. No wonder, she thought: *Grandma and Mom had the same kind of relationship I have with Mom*. She realized her grandmother had pushed her own daughter away as she had pushed Tina away. Likewise, Tina's own mother lacked the nurturing and affection Tina had always craved. This helped her understand her own mother and why she hadn't been able to relate emotionally to Tina when she was little. Her parents could only give what they knew. Because of their own traumas, they weren't able to give little Tina the attention and life skills she needed to be a full Agent of her own life.

As we talked, Tina acknowledged that, despite their hardships, she knew her parents loved her and had tried to do the best for her and her siblings. She knew they tried to instill good values into her, especially the value of hard work.

So, exploring our stories is about understanding the undercurrents of narratives and scripts that unconsciously influence us, in some ways blocking us, but also in some ways giving us strength and resilience to forge forward.

Not all we inherit is bad, of course, but exploring our story sifts through what we want to keep and what we can let go off. We become aware of the parts of us that lie beneath our consciousness, the way most of an iceberg lies beneath the water, invisible to the naked eye. We do this by looking at, not only our own familial stories, but also the wider cultural narratives. Tina, like myself, was brought up with filial piety, a deep respect for elders. This is part of our cultural narrative.

The following transcript is what Tina shared with me in one of our conversations. She let me know she was ready to look at her issues, which were messy and stuffed away, like items in her linen closet. However, she was now ready to open that closet.

TINA

I carry a load of generational stress from parents, right? And their parents probably got it from their parents. So it's like the linen closet. The one that you start with good intentions, but then everything gets overwhelming.

You keep dumping everything in there. Yeah, it's a mess.

You don't want to open it. You don't want to look at it. Would you call that the self? That is a self.

It's like, that's the brain. That's what the inside of my brain looks like. I try to keep everything all organized, but then eventually it builds up. Then you simply chuck everything in. Until you have time, or you realize you can't close the door anymore, or you have to find something that you can't. You've got to bring everything out and bring out the labeller and label it. And put it in the right drawers or whatnot. And that's the processing and sorting through my experiences.

Often, there is unresolved grief as we start to unpack our selves, understanding the experiences we've been through. Sometimes the experiences we've gone through, like Tina's, diminish our sense of agency. However, as we continued, she was ready to take back her sense of control and choice, use the StoriCompass to navigate her life, and become the Agent of her story.

The *Agent* in the StoriCompass

In the StoriCompass, the Agent is you. You are the central element in the narrative structure. You are the main character and protagonist in your story. However, if you want to apply the StoriCompass to another context to work out what is going on with someone else, such as your team at work, then your team is the Agent. For example, if you run your business and want to use StoriCompass to gain clarity about your business's mission and story brand, your business becomes the Agent. This framework can be used in many settings or contexts—from therapy, to coaching, to organizations—to work through the unfolding story.

At the heart of this StoriCompass are two powerful elements: the Agent (you) and your Desire (what you're reaching for). This is your *Pathway of Pursuit*—the thread that carries you from both your past and present into your future, through choices, actions, relationships, and turning points: transitional life events such as moving to another country, getting married, having children, or gaining an educational degree.

The StoriCompass doesn't only chart your circumstances. It reveals how you position yourself in your story—the meanings you've made, the roles you've taken on, and what you're truly longing for, which we will cover in chapter 3.

When I asked research participants how they see themselves in their stories, I found that the responses often varied based on the person's culture and were tied to the language they used. For example, individuals in Western countries were found to use the pronoun *I* more compared to those in Eastern Countries, who use the pronoun *we* more.

I found that Australians with European ethnic backgrounds typically responded that the main person in their life stories was I or Me. They were the Agent of their own story, with a separate identity from the identity of their community or group. The Self was separate from others, and they pursued more self-motivated goals. They found meaning in *individual agency*.

On the other hand, for Easterners like Singaporean or Malaysian Chinese, I was puzzled to find that, for some, their life story wasn't even about themselves. They told me the main character(s) of their story were their parents. Some would include themselves but say, "myself and my brother" or another relative. They saw the Agent in their life story as a collective self. They found meaning in *collective agency*.

Knowing who you are in your story means you can start becoming the Agent of your life, whether that be through individual or collective agency. You can choose what plot twists you prefer and rewrite worn-out cultural scripts, or write a whole new chapter of your life. This is what some of the women I spoke with started doing.

Challenges in Becoming the Agent

Clara and Sanhydra live on opposite sides of the world, yet their struggles with their selves, identities, and life experiences show us that no matter where we are, our Agency can feel fragile. But we continue, which is what Clara had to do. As she moved from Belgium to Ireland, welcomed a second child, and grieved the loss of her professional identity, her story reminds us that cultural identity is most vulnerable during major life transitions.

Clara is a mental health practitioner in her thirties, from a French and Spanish background, married to a Spaniard. Her husband is in the corporate management world, which meant her life was on the move. We were introduced through a mutual contact and met on the Zoom platform. The following is her story verbatim.

CLARA

The moment that was hardest, for me, was when my husband was transferred to Ireland. I was ten days postpartum of my second child, and I had a two-year-old because my children are two years apart. We were moved to Ireland with very little notice.

The timing and all the rearranging around my work was very difficult. I didn't realize at that time; I think I only realized it now because I have gone through my own process of analyzing what I went through and how and why it was so hard.

I didn't have the time to grieve my professional identity. I didn't have enough time and wasn't prepared for the expatriation. I wasn't prepared for the relocation and all the changes in our dynamic that was going to come with it, like my husband having a much more demanding work position [and] me having a much more demanding motherhood position.

I have this conviction that every time you become a mother, you go through this process of transformation, of matrescence. It comes from anthropology, and it's this transition that women go through similar to adolescence because we have these physiological, chemical, and body changes that resemble adolescence.

Because it wasn't the same for me to be the mother of one child and to be the mother of another child, of two children.

I even had mastitis. I found my new baby kind of creating this barrier, I guess, for my first child. Yes. And I knew my first one, I already had this relationship with my first child. Then for this new baby taking so much space over my body. I couldn't cope with all these changes happening at the same time.

I cannot access my first child the same way. Yes. I cannot be a working woman anymore because we're moving abroad. And there was no kindergarten for my eldest, so I had to be at home with the two of them. I didn't have the time to properly grieve my loss of networks, my job, and everything I knew in my old home country.

These decisions that we were making, there were all these changes in dynamics, like my husband was out twelve hours per day.

So, it was a lot, like the culture shock, the weather; when we went to Ireland, it was January. So it was very cold weather in Ireland. Miserable. With a newborn and a baby two years old, it was a big challenge.

And it was awful to think that nobody was seeing the effort that I was going through. Like people around me were honestly asking me, why are you not happy? Like, you can stop working. You're going to be at home with your baby. Isn't that what every mom wants?

And I was like, I don't know. It doesn't feel OK at this moment.

I didn't have the time to properly grieve my life in Belgium, how everything was organized there, all my nest preparation there was for nothing because we recently moved, and we couldn't actually take advantage of this nest preparation process. So, there were all these things that I didn't have the time to prepare, to process, and I had no one around me supporting me and guiding me through the process with acceptance, with patience, with compassion, and with understanding; that was very difficult and complex.

It was very overwhelming because I think having a second

child in itself is actually quite difficult. And a lot of women go through postpartum depression because there's no more contacts, networks. I had a lot of isolation.

My husband had a very hectic job as well. And because of that, very long hours. You have to adjust in many ways, be the single parent in a way, [there] for your children without much support. Something that a friend recently introduced me to, solo parenting, right? Again, nobody explained to me then how to solo parent.

Nobody gave me the tools to say, OK, this is what you're going to be doing. Because I literally felt like a single mother. It was like, all right, I have the money but nothing else. He's not there, the family around us is not there. I am literally solo mothering and making all these decisions on a daily basis by myself.

For Clara and many other women who juggle families and children, it may not feel like you can be the Agent of your life story because the Agent is your partner; the one pursuing their career and the breadwinner calling the shots. Most women assume the role of supportive partner in the family home. However, within the context of each situation, acquiring a sense of agency and discussing with your partner how you can recover your agency for the benefit of the whole family is important. Clara wanted to be the Agent of her life story, but she felt lost and powerless after being displaced from familiar surroundings. She had to navigate life with more demands, cope with a new child, and settle her older child into new surroundings. She also had to grieve the loss of her professional identity, the identity of being a mother to only one child, and leaving Belgium to start life afresh in Ireland.

***

As women, we worry about our careers, our children, our families, and how we can ride the storms of life. For some of us, the storms of life can be ones we never recover from, especially when we lose someone we dearly love. This was Sanhydra's story, which continues to impact her Self and identity. Sanhydra is Indian, originally from Fiji, and a teacher in her late forties. The following is a transcript of her story.

SANHYDRA

I was born in Fiji. My grandparents were from India, from my father's side. And my mom's side, her great-grandparents were from Lahore, Punjab. I lived in Fiji till I was eighteen, then I moved to New Zealand to study. I went back to Fiji, worked there for a bit, then got married and moved back to New Zealand. My husband is also Fijian Indian.

In my own life story, the main character in my own life story would be my dad. Yeah, because I'm my dad's little girl, so it's my dad. I don't see myself as the main agent of my own life story. No, it's my dad. He passed away when I was twenty-one. I spent a lot of time with him. As I said, I was his little girl. I always looked to him, you know; he was my hero.

When he got sick, I just didn't, I couldn't handle that. Because I've always seen him working and, you know, doing things. Then he suffered a stroke.

After the first stroke, he was able to go back to work. We thought, oh, he's fine.

Then he had a second stroke, which was a brain stroke, so he couldn't walk or talk properly. He was bedridden for two years. We were back in Fiji with him. I was with him, so it was very difficult.

Tears formed in Sanhydra's eyes when she shared this deep loss of her father, and confessed she couldn't grieve his death. She still had not.

In Sanhydra's life story, the Agent was her father. He was her pillar. After his death, she wanted desperately for her father to come back to life so he could guide her.

Grieving and letting go can be hard but is important for each of us as we examine our life stories. Unless we face our loss, grieve, and let go of the past, it is difficult to make room for new beginnings, deeper healing, or the life waiting to be lived. The future remains clouded by what we haven't yet released.

Life Transitions

What Tessa, Tina, Clara, and Sanhydra shared is that within all of us, we can live between our past, present, and future selves, wanting to navigate life not only for ourselves but for our loved ones with whom our lives are intertwined.

Our identity changes through pivotal life points, such as moving to another country, becoming a parent, graduating from school, changing jobs, or losing a significant loved one. In these transitions, we absorb experiences and cultural values. Grieving change is vital at any pivotal point. Through different seasons of life, we need to work through painful memories from difficult experiences and understand how they impact our present, so we are not blocked from stepping into our future.

The women's stories I recount illustrate that across different cultures or within similar ones—racial, religious, community or national—we can be vastly different in the way each family navigates life.

Life is a matter of focus. What we focus on ultimately determines the outcome of our lives. To regain her agency, Clara needed to focus on embracing her new chapter, by grieving her losses, adapting to her new environment, and communicating her needs with her husband so she didn't feel like a solo parent. For Sanhydra, it was a realisation that she never grieved her deep loss and that she let go of the agency in her life to her deceased father, which allowed her to regain her agency and focus on her present. For Tina, she was ready to open the linen closet of her life and work through her issues to build agency despite the cultural and family background at play.

Building Our Lives from Our Values

When my husband and I started building our home, we focused on learning as much as we could by visiting many display homes to gather ideas. Collecting information about what each room would look like, the walls, the cozy interior, what features we would have. But all that amazing design and comfort counts for nothing without one crucial element. What's the absolute first, most essential part of any house? It's the foundation. Dug deep, often out of sight, it determines everything else. It provides stability and ensures the whole structure stands firm for years.

In the same way, core values are the unshakeable foundation of our lives. They are those deep-seated beliefs and principles—like honesty, compassion, integrity, courage, or community—we hold most dear.

As a house built on shaky ground or without a solid foundation will eventually crumble, a life lived without a clear understanding of its values feels unstable, directionless, and easily swayed by external pressures.

When life throws countless decisions your way—from career shifts and relationship choices to how you spend your precious time—your values act as your unwavering internal GPS.

Your values cut through the noise, helping you see what truly aligns with your core, not only what's expected of you or what seems easiest.

I've seen it time and again in clinical practice. Many individuals have led successful careers and accomplished much, but they feel a void, an emptiness they can't pinpoint or understand. That is because any accomplishments or achievement, when not aligned with who you are, what you value and want to become, will ultimately feel like failure. As if you are climbing the wrong ladder or the wrong mountain. You will never reach the peak of what you deeply value. The outcome then is not as gratifying as if you had climbed the right ladder to reach the destination that reflects the values you harbor and nurture within your inner self.

This was particularly true in Arianna Huffington's life. At the height of *The Huffington Post*'s success in 2007, she collapsed from exhaustion, breaking her cheekbone in the fall and receiving four stitches near her right eye. She was working eighteen-hour days, driven by ambition, but she neglected her health, sleep, and deeper well-being. This was a turning point in her life. When she re-evaluated, she realized she didn't want only achievement and influence. She wanted also health, wisdom, wonder, and generosity. Once she realized she was living her life in contradiction to her true values, she stepped back. She reprioritized sleep, mindfulness, and well-being, and eventually left her media empire. She founded *Thrive Global* to redefine success to include well-being, wisdom, and purpose.

In her speech to Smith College in 2013, Arianna Huffington exhorted the audience not to define success solely through wealth or status. She encouraged a broader form of success grounded in wellbeing, meaning, purpose, and contribution to others.

Learning for a Purpose

For me, education and learning have always been core values, so in all my pursuits of learning, my question has always been: *What do I do with what I now know?* Asking myself that question was a turning point for me; one of my core values is to use my learning to serve a purpose that makes the world better. If we only gain knowledge in order to show others how much we know, and that we know *more* than others, that's pointless.

My learning is to help others by empowering them to reach their own goals. That is my ultimate aim for you. My desire is to see individuals, families, communities, and societies thrive, to create cultures that are healthy, and to ignite each person to function at their optimal level.

At my deepest core, my makeup values human life, human dignity, and lifting up others. I want to bring healing, wholeness, hope, and joy. My values are why I do what I do. My desire to create positive change by helping people reach their potential is what makes me come alive and the reason this book was born.

Once you know your values, you gain incredible power to set healthy boundaries and make decisions that allow you to build a life in service of those values. You are empowered to say yes to opportunities that align with what you cherish, and a firm no to things that drain your energy or undermine your core beliefs.

When challenges arise during the storms of life, your values aren't mere guiding stars; they're your deep, unshakeable anchor. They keep you grounded, helping you stay true to yourself under pressure, and providing the inner strength to navigate difficulties without losing your purpose.

As houses need concrete, cement, and steel for reinforcements, you need clear values, identity, and knowledge of your cultural dimensions to keep grounded and anchored in life. Any architect or builder will tell you that without a blueprint, they would not have any idea how to proceed to build. Similarly, to build a life, we need our own blueprint.

The Cultural Identity Blueprint: CulturAlign™

The Self is not only a person—it's a cultural being, shaped by values, experiences, traditions, and inherited stories. That's where CulturAlign, the Cultural Identity Blueprint, comes in.

CulturAlign is the framework that helps you visualize, situate, and gain insight into your identity via your cultural background, values, and experiences. It's the blueprint to understand yourself so you can become the Agent of your life story, helping you explore how your culture influences you, how you show up in the world, and what you value. It captures what people perceive of you when they get to know you.

We each live with a time-traveling Self that allows inner dialogue between our past, present, and future selves. We have constant running conversation with ourselves, our self-talk. The I and Me are always talking in the mind's background.

Past: "She hurt *Me* before; I need to make sure she's not going to hurt *Me* again."
Present: "OK, *I* need to focus right now on *Me*. I've got this!"
Future: "*I* want to be free in *myself* and travel to Italy next year."

We not only have a time-traveling Self, but our identity is multifaceted, like a diamond. We all belong to a plurality of cultures. We live in communities based on our families, gender, ethnicities, workplace, hobbies, passions, and interests. These are cultural contexts, ways of forming groups so we feel a sense of belonging.

When Tina completed the CulturAlign, she reported that she could understand the facets of her life and how they influenced her journey, the changes within her, and her values over time; she was able to see it all in visual form. CulturAlign gave her perspective and knowledge about the woman she is now and helped her gain clarity about her identity and what she needed to work on to build the life she dreamed of, one that aligned with her values.

There are ten main dimensions to how we can be defined, the facets of our cultural identity:

* *Family and ancestry, which shape our values and how we see ourselves.* For example, Tina came from an East Timorese–Chinese family, with a collectivistic self but was influenced by Chinese, Australian, and multicultural views.
* *Language groups, which are the languages we use growing up and ones we learn later.* Tina was immersed in Chinese Hakka with her family when growing up but spoke English predominantly.
* *Religion or spirituality, which inform our beliefs and guide our values and sense of purpose.* For example, whether you identify as Christian, Muslim, Buddhist, New Age, or another belief. Tina was exploring her religious and spiritual orientation.
* *Age/generation or peer groups, which are the people you surround yourself with who influence how you think and act.* Tina had long-time school friends and a moms' group.
* *Gender and sexuality shape how we understand ourselves, form relationships, and experience belonging within our cultural world.* Tina identified as a heterosexual cisgender female.
* *Nationality includes the country where you grew up or currently live, which often shapes your lifestyle, worldview, and beliefs.* Tina was born in Australia and spent her life in Melbourne.
* *Political affiliations, which include views on policy, fairness, and leadership.* Tina did not report any political affiliations to a party.
* *Occupational responsibilities like work and study, which shape who we become through the time we invest in them.* Tina finished university and was working in IT/administration but thought of pursuing another, more rewarding role when her children grew up.
* *Race and ethnicity are central aspects of our background and cultural heritage. They shape how others perceive us and influence how we come to understand ourselves.* Tina considered herself an East Timorese–Chinese Australian.

* *Community and Locality, which include our neighborhood and community groups, such as cultural, arts, or sports groups, which shape daily life and connections.* They can also involve personal sports, hobbies, interests, and passions we pursue. Tina lived in the suburbs, went to her local gym, enjoyed her cultural arts festivals and music concerts, and interacted with her children's school.

As an example, Figure 2.1 shows The CulturAlign Blueprint that Tina completed, showing her many cultural contexts. This blueprint enabled her to capture in one visual form how she perceived the importance of each cultural context in her past, present, and anticipated future, and how that impacted her Self. From Tina's rating of the importance of each cultural context, we can understand whether it has high, medium, or low importance in her life. Your own blueprint will also capture values you had, have, and hope to develop. You can work through these cultural contexts and your values using CulturAlign, available through the QR code or here: **www.lidialae.com/readerhub**.

CulturAlign will help you gain an understanding of yourself as the Agent in your StoriCompass. It highlights which cultural dimensions are influencing your sense of identity.

www.lidialae.com/readerhub

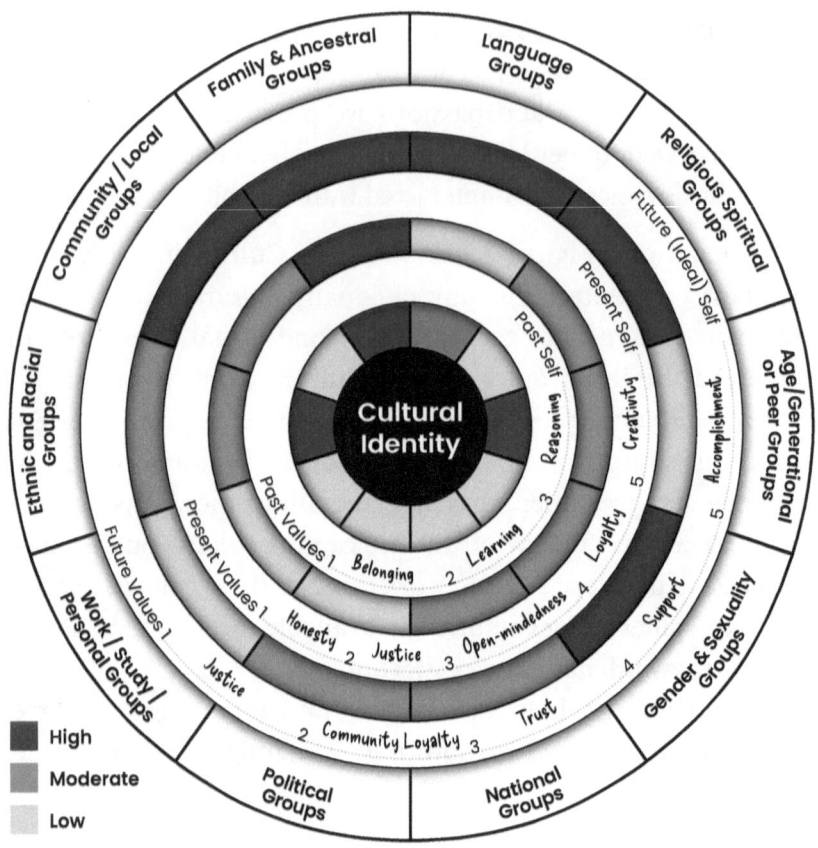

Figure 2.1 The CulturAlign Blueprint of Tina's life.

All these cultural contexts or dimensions contribute to how we define who we are, the way we saw how Tina's cultural identity is defined. When we get to know someone, we see them through the facets of their lives and relate to them based on their gender, the language they use, what ethnicity they are, what they believe, and how they present themselves, etc. These cultural dimensions also cue the *cultural frames* through which we experience others and the world we live in. Our cultural frames are the ways in which we see and interpret our experiences through the intersection of all the dimensions in CulturAlign and will be covered more in part 3. We are all precious like diamonds, cut differently, and can shine brilliantly.

Embrace who you are. We are each created unique, with diverse voices, colors, and idiosyncrasies. I relish that each person is unlike any other. It's time to start from a foundation of self-awareness to self-love: loving ourselves, who we are, and who we are created to become. That is the solid ground from which we can launch through life. This is where we tap into our *selves* as Agents in the StoriCompass.

Both CulturAlign and StoriCompass enable you to gain clarity about your Self and identity as you become the Agent in your life story. But being the Agent of your story is more complex and nuanced than we realize. We are also defined by what we pursue, what we desire. The key to activating agency, to becoming the Agent we want to be, is to define the desire(s) that motivate us to take action.

Key Takeaways

* The Agent in the StoriCompass is the main character and protagonist in your life story, who finds meaning in *individual* and/or *collective* agency.

* You can choose, act, and shape what comes next in your story by building a solid foundation based on your values.

* CulturAlign helps you understand how culture influences who you are, how you show up in the world, and what you value: past, present, and future in your temporal Self.

Deeper Actions

Reflect on the question: Who are you in your life story? Do you feel like you are the Agent?

To gain clarity about who you are and what you truly value and stand for, so that you can become the Agent of your life, work through the CulturAlign blueprint. To complete your own blueprint, please scan the QR code or go to **www.lidialae.com/readerhub**.

www.lidialae.com/readerhub

3

What Do You Really Want? (*The Desire*)

Go confidently in the direction of your dreams. Live the life you have imagined.

—Henry David Thoreau

Once we trigger an internal yes by affirming our truest goals and desires, the universe mirrors that yes and expands it.

—Julia Cameron

Pranjali paced in her student dormitory in Pune, India. Her gut knew; it always knew. Heart thumping, she took a deep sigh. What would her parents say? Especially her Amma who was so proud she got into dental school at her alma mater. But she was an adult now.

As the eldest of two girls, she had set an example for her younger sister. Her parents and extended family were proud. In her family, like many Indian families, dentistry was considered a "prestige career." It ranked high, alongside medicine. She had done well.

She thought of all the hours studying. Was she throwing it all away? Would she disappoint her Amma? But this nagging feeling that there was something better for her, wouldn't disappear. Her desire was to study the human mind, behavior, and philosophy, and psychology happened to be the perfect blend.

She agonized over the decision for months. In her early twenties, she knew she had to act. Without further hesitation, she called her father. A retired academic, he might understand.

They spoke and relief flooded her whole being as he listened to her heart: her desire was to study psychology. He gave her his blessing.

"My parents thought I would be a dentist. I studied for two years for dental school, but I realized I couldn't do it for the rest of my life. People assumed I should just continue because I had already invested so much. But I knew the cost of staying was far greater than leaving," she told me.

Pranjali was a bright and cheerful overseas student, completing a Masters in marketing when I interviewed her. As I listened to her, she felt heard. "I know you understand that because you're from an Asian culture too. There's like, this subconscious pressure that everybody keeps giving you. 'Oh, there's no money in this,' and 'How would you support yourself?' I just believed that if you're doing something that you love, you will be good at it, no matter what."

Pranjali's example shows that a deeply held desire which is aligned with your values and desired future, deserves action. Even if it goes against societal expectations. She didn't want to disappoint her parents. However, if she continued studying dentistry, she would disappoint herself, living a life that didn't resonate. Having the courage to break free from family and cultural expectations takes guts. Thankfully, she had an ally in her father, who was discerning of his daughter's true calling. That made all the difference.

With this new orientation to pursue her deepest core desires, her life took a drastic turn. She studied psychology, but when she realized she enjoyed marketing, which involves consumer psychology, the puzzle pieces came together.

The Pathway of Pursuit

When you follow your dreams, pursue the desires of your heart based on your core values, and build healthy steps to fulfill the dream, you are in the business of Self and identity transformation. This process of *becoming* is an exciting one. This *Pathway of Pursuit* is the relationship established when you, the *Agent,* pursue your *Desire.* In chapter 8, you will use the StoriCompass to map out your Pathway of Pursuit, but start to reflect on your Desire(s) now.

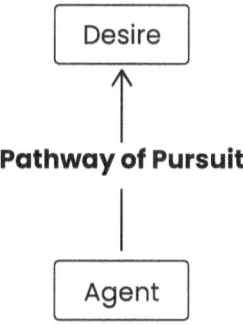

Figure 3.1 The Agent reaching for the Desire in the Pathway of Pursuit in the StoriCompass.

The Pathway of Pursuit lays the architecture of our lives. It gives us purpose and meaning, for we are all creators. Through pursuing what we want that aligns with our foundational values, we build meaning and purpose into our existence; we create our realities.

At this point in your life, your reality may feel far from ideal. You may be struggling with time to invest in your goals or desires, responsibilities that seem overwhelming, or insurmountable mental or emotional issues. Still, I want you to get crystal clear about your desire. What do you truly want in life? Your Desire pulls you through so you can experience a world of possibilities.

Values and Pursuits

We learn our authentic Desires through our values. Our values will always be a foundation that guide our every decision, including which desires to pursue. If we don't have a foundation, we run the risk of being tossed and turned by the waves of popular culture and following trends and fads that derail our lives.

When your Desire is rooted in deep values, it is a magnetic force that propels you into action and opens doors that lead to experiences you didn't think possible.

I know because I lived it. When I was a teenager, I journaled about my desire to travel the world. A year later, my parents sent my brothers and me on an overseas Chinese study tour to Taiwan, encouraging us to learn Chinese. Ba and Ma worried we were becoming "bananas" (yellow outside but white inside) or "chow mein" (noodles with a mix of everything)!

Soon after, when I started at the university, my traveling days kicked off throughout Southeast Asia and continued to the Middle East. When my boyfriend (now husband) and I spent time abroad working in Toronto, Canada, we zigzagged through more than thirty cities in America and Europe—from Prince Edward Island to New York City, from Rio de Janeiro to Paris—in one year! Nearing the end of our year abroad, we got married in Fiji. My desire to travel was rooted in my values—curiosity, learning and wisdom gained from others, and a love of diverse people and cultures.

This connection of joining core Desires with living a life aligned to deep values builds the life we have been seeking all along.

Our Desires are powerful. They speak of time, effort, imagination, and occupation of our internal states, our minds, and our hearts toward influence on behavior. Desire is like a magnet that draws people, places, and opportunities; it opens doors for us.

We need to be mindful of our Desires and learn to filter out Desires not aligned with who we are and seek to become.

The *Desire* in the Pathway of Pursuit

Desire is inherently built into our system from the day we are born. As babies, we cry because of our desire for milk or comfort. As toddlers, we desire to walk and talk, and as children we desire to know how things work.

Desire is the central element around which the narrative revolves, driving you as the Agent and structuring your story's meaning.

Values shape Desires, which shape actions, and in turn, build a meaningful life.

Desire is the innate drive to survive, and as adults, to thrive. This "wanting to know" or "wanting to be and do" pushes us to grow, develop new skills, and interact with the world. When we pursue a Desire, it defines us.

Think of it this way: What you pursue identifies you. When you pursue a Desire consistently, it shapes your identity. We see this unfolding in Taylor Swift's life when she picked up the guitar at twelve and wrote her first song, "Lucky You." From her initial pursuit of storytelling through country music, she continued her passion in different genres and is now an internationally celebrated artist. Attending her Eras Tour concert with my daughters, I got to see her identity phases—Fearless, Red, Reputation, Folklore—her story of becoming.

Likewise, from the moment Serena Williams first wielded a tennis racquet, her pursuit began to shape the girl into the woman the world would come to know. Her passion, consistency, and courage made her a global tennis icon. Over the years, Serena has made clear that tennis isn't just a career for her. She's used her platform for business ventures, fashion, activism, family, and advocacy. As a mother and entrepreneur now, she's voiced the desire to balance professional ambition with family and personal values. Both Taylor and Serena's identities were shaped by their Desire.

The Desire, whether tangible or abstract—wanting to own a home, gain happiness, or travel the world—serves as the motivation for the Agent, shaping the journey and defining the roles of other elements in the person's story, as covered in chapter 1, such as the core elements in our StoriCompass: the Guide, Beneficiary, Supporter, and Opposition.

The Pathway of Pursuit highlights deeper cultural, psychological, and ideological tensions, illustrating how desires and values shape experiences and storytelling. As we saw in Pranjali's example of her Pathway of Pursuit, the tension created by her pursuit of a career valued by her culture caused an inner psychological conflict when she realized it was not her true Desire. If her father and/or mother had been more adamant about her following cultural norms and hadn't accepted her choice to change her career focus, she may have stayed in dentistry and been unfulfilled in her life. Her parents may have occupied the role of Opposition (what gets in the way). However, they gave their blessings as her Guide (people who have shaped us) and released her to pursue her Desire (what she truly wanted). Perhaps in the hope that in pursuing her Desire, Pranjali would be the Beneficiary (who benefits), and then, perhaps even they would be beneficiaries as well, because no loving parent wants to see their child unhappy.

When you understand what you want, you won't only gain a clarity of self, reduced anxiety and inner conflict, and stronger emotional regulation, but also, as in Pranjali's case, you gain increased motivation, deeper meaning, and more joy. These play out in our external world, where we stop saying yes to everything and everyone.

Life becomes more intentional with focused goals and decision-making. There is greater alignment with our career and personal life. Stronger relationships develop. Pranjali felt closer to her parents because she was able to voice her inner desires and experienced their support.

Desire reveals what matters most. Pranjali knew what to protect and what to walk away from. She knew what she valued internally and how she was going to accomplish her Desire; she left India to pursue postgraduate studies in Australia. She aligned her deep passion with concrete goals; learning in a new culture and a place associated with the higher education she wanted to pursue. Having clear boundaries and knowing her parents were supporting her in the pursuit of her Desire, she is more likely to have greater success.

Pranjali's story shows how Desires have two levels: the internal and external, which I explored in my research as abstract or concrete. Abstract or internal goals are usually focused on meaning, motivational or emotional truth. For example, "I want to feel free, happy, loved, creative, safe, seen." These goals bring you to a desired state.

On the other hand, external or concrete desires are related to goals, actions, and direction. For example, "I want to launch a business, write a book, travel, build a home, study marketing", and so forth. External desires have concrete, tangible outcomes. They are desired outcomes.

When your internal and external desires align, your life feels coherent, grounded, and vibrant. However, if they do not, you might succeed outwardly but feel empty within, or feel emotionally whole but stuck in circumstances that frustrate you. Like getting a promotion in a corporate job, but where deep down you feel empty and would prefer to be a creative artist in a studio.

Knowing our heart's deepest desires and discerning whether they are aligned with our core values helps us build a foundation for a strong future. Unless we know what we truly want, it's difficult to set goals to achieve it. It is this Pathway of Pursuit—the Agent-Desire relationship—that ultimately defines our direction, and our lives.

This is what I wish for you and every other woman. When you truly know what you want and go for it, you lay the architecture for your ideal life.

What Is Your Desire?

We all have different Desires. Common Desires of women I interviewed include:

* travel
* romantic love
* new adventures
* making a difference
* having a family
* experiencing success
* buying/building a home
* freedom
* doing meaningful work.

My Canadian friend Colleen, a homemaker and former engineer in her late forties, had a desire to write about the transitions she has experienced to help other women, especially young mothers. As a young woman, Colleen was anxious to travel and explore the world. Following her husband's career allowed her young family to do just that. They lived abroad in Asia (South Korea) and in Argentina for stints of two or three years. This was exciting, and it also became exhausting, moving every couple of years with a young and growing family.

Her own upbringing had emphasized strong roots, stability and community in her hometown on the East Coast of Canada. Her grandparents arrived from England in 1949.

With Colleen's global experiences, she has now been shaped by many places and cultures, which give her new insights, meaning and purpose as a writer.

So often, it's when we reflect on our lived experiences that our passions, our Desires, emerge and enable us to reinvent ourselves, like Colleen.

COLLEEN

I've always journaled and used writing to process my thoughts. On our first job overseas, I was home with a preschooler and a baby while my husband worked long hours (sometimes, 80-hour weeks). I discovered some blogs that I found inspiring and helpful. That planted a seed. I thought, "I could do that. Write a blog. Help other younger moms."

For a long time, I didn't act on that. I thought I'd wait until life calmed down a bit. By the time we had our fourth child, we had moved internationally three more times and I realized life wasn't going to calm down any time soon.

For ten years, we joked that relocation was our only hobby. And it really was. It took up every spare minute, all the paperwork and packing and planning, and then there would be the tour to say goodbyes to friends and relatives yet again.

At this point, I felt like, I really need something that was my own thing. Not subject to relocation. Not focused on supporting the kids or the next move.

The first time I signed up for a writing course, I did it at 2 am. I'd waffled up until the deadline when a feeling of desperation kicked in. I needed to do something.

When I vent on paper, I can then summarize nicely what I'm upset about or frustrated with. As I've done that, I've become able to articulate the lessons I've learned through our transitions. I've begun to see the gifts so often hidden in the frustrations. When I share those things with younger moms, they feel seen and are encouraged. And that gives me motivation to continue even though my life still hasn't calmed down much.

So, the overall goal would be to take what I've been through and actually help younger moms with it.

***

Across the Canadian-US border, in the east coast of the United States, Tre, an African American woman in her late thirties, also navigated identity, cultural, and career moves. In our interview, Tre cheerfully shared she was proud of her background, which included Caribbean, specifically West Indian influence, and indigenous Native American influence. She told me she identified as a Black American woman. Her husband was from El Salvador. And so, their child is of mixed race and ethnicity.

Tre explained about her changing desires throughout the different seasons of her life, about wanting to be accepted as a newlywed in her husband's El Salvadoran family, to fit in, and then to be accepted for who she was at her workplace. Now as a mother and business owner, her Desires center on her son and making an impact in society through transformational leadership.

TRE

I'm an African American woman. I want to say we have some Caribbean, some West Indian influence in our bloodline. I know that we do have Native American indigenous peoples in our bloodline too. But I identify as a Black woman. My husband is from El Salvador. And so, our child is of mixed race, of mixed ethnicity.

So I think, I'm maturing in my own kind of professional

worlds and the circles that I'm in, and the work that I'm doing, and the relationships that I'm building, and certainly as a transformational leadership consultant, someone who's looking at culture-building and belonging, day to day. We've been together for almost twenty years. When we first got together, because [his family] they're also El Salvadoran, they need to know that I fit.

So that to me has been my experience with race and ethnicity. It's on the surface. You see what it looks like, right? You see the darker skin, you see the broader nose, you see the kinky hair, the coily hair, and so in your mind, you're wanting to place me and compartmentalize me into the spot that makes you feel comfortable.

But for me, much of the culture-building work that I do, and the belonging work, has very much to do with identity and understanding when you're in a workplace culture, in particular, which of your identities are affirmed and appreciated and accepted and celebrated. And which of your identities are you really pulling back? Right? Because you're not quite sure if you are vocal about who you are in that environment, will they support you and frankly affirm that.

Overarching goals for my life. My main goal now [is] and will always be to raise my son in a way, you know, where he can be a human being that contributes thoughtfully and in a positive way to his communities and to society. So that, to me, my greatest identity is mother, right? Raising him in a way that aligns to his family's value system and then gives him the opportunity to create the value system that makes sense for his life. That's a big deal for me. My greatest goals, I just want to be a kind, generous, and thoughtful person.

But I want to see success in my company. This is an endeavor that I don't take lightly. I've made many sacrifices to get to this point, and I want it to be something that I'm not just proud of, but that I'm also working really hard to make sure it's…something that outlives me. If that makes sense, right? I want it to be something that my son is very well aware [of]: Mommy has her own company.

My husband is very proud of the work I do, but I don't want it to be like a fly-by-night. I've built this, and I want it to be sustainable. I think another goal for my life is I really just want to lead with this positive mindset that, to me, has been such a game changer because I can't control everyone. Right? I can't control everyone's issues. I can't control everyone's problems. We have our own problems. I just can't. But I used to want to be the fixer and be in it and just fix. But see, that's where that faith came in. It's like, but you can't. Part of loving yourself is being able to let go of things that aren't serving you. That's been a big revelation for me and just standing in and being aware of the power of acceptance.

This authenticity of living a values-based life is what Tre wants to pass on to her son and live out in her own life. As a mother and social leader in the US, Tre has come to a life stage where she is letting go of things that are not serving her, aligning with her Desire, and accepting of who she is. This has given her movement to focus on what she can impact: her son, family, her community, and her culture, especially through her company.

Movement is what gets us to our goals.

Some of the women had to emigrate, like Pranjali and Colleen, to reach their goals or acquire the experience and knowledge to pass on to others. Others had to move across a variety of workplaces and cultures, like Tre.

Desires carry us throughout life. They lead us on pursuits, some good, some destructive. Your desires will lead you to places, destinations, and outcomes. Hence, the importance of understanding our desires.

What About Competing or Frustrated Desires?

As women, we juggle many things, always needing to work out which desires matter most for this season of our lives, without compromising our values. Desires can change throughout life's seasons. Let your most important values guide you. Once you've mapped all your elements in part 1, you gain more perspective and clarity to know how to work through competing or frustrated Desires and be empowered in parts 2 and 3 to realize your desired states and outcomes. Different Desires are unique to the various seasons of women's lives.

When children are young, they take precedence over our own desires. Being a mom, for me, gets prioritized over my ambitions. Sometimes it doesn't have to be either/or, but discussions and problem-solving with your partner or family are necessary so everyone is free to pursue their desires. Sometimes, unfortunately, it's women who put desires on the sidelines, prioritizing the desires of parents, partners, or children.

We met Sanhydra in chapter 1, who saw her father as the Agent of her life story. She was very close to him and never fully grieved his death even decades afterward. She carries heavy pain, even in her marriage, and frustrated desires.

SANHYDRA

I wish I can do what I want, but my husband is very different. Like, I want to go back to Fiji, but he doesn't want to. I want to go back to New Zealand, but he doesn't want to. He has his goals, which he does, but I'm stuck. The barrier is there. He's negative, but my girls are positive.

Every parent would want that, but to go past my husband, it's hard because every time I say, "Oh, can we do this?" He's like, "When we retire."

I keep telling him, I say, "I don't think I can...I don't think I'll last till retirement." I hope I do, but I don't know if I will.

So he's ticking his boxes, but I'm not.

He won't say it, but he'll be upset if I just do what I want. We call him Army General because he does an itinerary [of] where we have to go. And [when] we have to be ready. He'll tell us the night before that, right, "We're going there, six o'clock. You guys are going to get up, and we're going to move." So, we have to.

Now that the girls have grown up, they don't want to go on a holiday with us because of that. So I told him, I said, you need to give us a break. Not be regimented.

I think he's autistic too. I think he's on the spectrum.

It's his way or the highway. I think it's a cultural thing too. I mean, he is modern but not modern. Quite traditional still as well.

I've got two girls, and to date, I'm still told by his family that my family is incomplete because we don't have a boy. That's very traditional. And it breaks my heart because I've always wanted a boy too.

> There are times when I really want to walk out, but because of the girls, I can't do that.
>
> I just want that peace, [a] calm and carefree life now. But as I said, he's the main block...the huge wall that I have. And I need to find a way to break that wall. Once I break it, I can be free.

Sanhydra wants so desperately to have freedom as her Desire, but she is also staying in her marriage for her girls and trying to find a way around the block that is her husband.

Women who are mothers often don't feel like they have a choice to leave a difficult marriage. Even though they don't want to stay in unhealthy marriages, they still do it for their children. Children have a profound impact on women's desires. We visited Tessa's case in the first chapter. She was lost in herself, but her Desire to see her children have a better life prompted her into action for help. "My kids are my goal," Tessa told me, "to help them achieve what they want in their future." It is the same for Sanhydra; she wants to stay for her girls.

Many times, for women who have children, they find that it's their children who will motivate them to live a new life. Though it brings up many identity questions, our desires can restructure us and our new identity as a mother which emerges when a child is born. This period of being a mother cements the next several decades of life, until the offspring leave the nest. For the meantime though, Tessa's and Sanhydra's identity as mother precedes other identities, as they stay in marriages for their children. However, the confusion that was always there can resurface and is still something that needs to be addressed.

I have gained understanding of the complexity of these issues for women, as I have worked with many who feel stuck in their marriages. Some women have been brought up in cultures where divorce is frowned upon, where the man is the household decision-maker. Some of these women choose to protect their children by teaching them to adjust in a challenging situation. However, for other women, staying in a marriage seems more harmful to their children, so they choose to leave unhealthy marriages for their own and their children's well-being. If this is your story, know you are not alone. Your life still holds meaning and worth—whether you choose to stay, to leave, or to take small steps toward change. However, if you feel unsafe, reach out for help immediately.

Aligning What You Truly Want with Your Values

You may want freedom, but stay in an unhealthy marriage for your family's sake. This is a reflection of what you truly value, and the two differ. Values are *guiding principles* while desires are *wants or motivations*, emotional or physical urges that dictate your steps. They can conflict with your values, so know your core values first.

If you want something that deviates from your values and does not build on them, then you will eventually feel dissatisfied and misaligned. You will wonder why you become stressed, overwhelmed, depressed, or anxious. However, if you're clear on your values, you will understand the motivations behind your behaviors. For example, if you're staying in an unhealthy marriage, your reason may be cultural. Your identity as wife and mother may precede other identities; your culture may call on you to preserve a family unit. You know you deeply Desire to have an intact family, at the expense of your personal freedom. In this situation, mothers may feel torn between their Desire for the family they dreamed of and the reality of an unhealthy marriage. It can be hard to let go of an old dream and create a new life that may be different but far healthier. If you are in a tricky situation, it's important to seek professional help to work through these deep issues.

Go back to your values in chapter 2, to your CulturAlign

blueprint, and ensure you do the work. You will be empowered in part 2 when we cover how to break free from limiting cultural scripts. To live authentically, we need to know who we really are and what we stand for. People will also have more confidence in us as they relate to us. The message of our lives will have more clarity.

Our values become a magnet that guides Desires and draws others who value similar things. Communities are built around values by people pursuing similar desires. Goals and desires supported in a community of like-minded individuals have a better chance of being accomplished.

We are always evolving and becoming who we are meant to be. In Michelle Obama's book, *Becoming*, she shares her own life journey from being a girl in a humble Chicago neighborhood to becoming a law student, and from there, a lawyer and a wife, mother, and the first lady of the United States of America. She even opened up about her marital issues and how she and her husband, former President Barack Obama, went to marriage counseling. She shared that it was a turning point because she learned how her own happiness was her responsibility, not her husband's. Her desire to be the best version of herself allowed her to step into a position of great influence.

We sometimes feel like we don't have much control over what happens. We can't dictate when a romantic partner will arrive or whether we get a job promotion, but pursuing our Desires based on core values eventually leads us to our desired destination. It did for Michelle Obama, certainly, and now, she has added new identities built from her desires: international bestselling author and global changemaker.

You've now covered the first Pathway of Pursuit, the Agent-Desire relationship that gives life meaning and purpose. To go deeper, there are questions for you to reflect on your desires and motivations. So far, we have established that to own your life story, you need to know who you are as the Agent, what you stand for, and, what you really want. Without a crystal-clear vision of your Desire based on your values and cultural frames, it's hard to know where to aim to step into the process of becoming. To help you continue to map your story landscape and get to your destination, we embark on the *Pathway of Impact*, on your continual road of becoming.

Key Takeaways

* The Pathway of Pursuit is the relationship established when you, the Agent, pursue your Desire.
* The act of pursuing what you want in life that aligns with foundational values gives your life meaning and purpose.
* Be clear about your Desire(s) in life because when you consistently pursue a Desire, it shapes your identity.

Deeper Actions

Reflect on the following questions and feel free to journal your answers:

1. Think of a woman you admire who had to journey to become her true self. What about her story inspires you?
2. When you think about your journey to this point, what motivated you when you made major decisions? List as many motivations as you can think of, and be honest!
3. When you think of your desires, what obstacles have you encountered when trying to move toward them?

4

Who or What Guides You? (*The Guide*)

If I have seen further, it is by standing on the shoulders of giants.

—Sir Isaac Newton

A wise guide is more to be desired than gold or precious stones.

— Attributed to Thomas à Kempis

Her father was absent most of her life. He should have been her guide and protector, but he failed to be the kind of man she looked up to.

My heart went out to Sarai as I interviewed her in our Zoom session. Competent and composed, Sarai is a Zimbabwean executive now in her forties who runs a major health facility. Seeing her so confident and strong, I would never have guessed the pain and suffering she had endured. I admired her and felt for her at the same time. As she shared, I could see that her strength was rooted in her faith, which seemed to have guided her throughout life. This is what she shared in our interview.

SARAI

I was born in Zimbabwe. So by that time, when my parents met, my dad was working as a teacher. And my mom was actually pretty young, maybe fifteen years old. She fell pregnant with me, and she gave birth to me. The relationship with my dad didn't really last because my dad was like, well, you're not educated.

And by that time, he was kind of dating another woman who was also working as a teacher because it was such a respected profession back then.

After I was born, my parents decided to separate. Then, my mom was so young. When I was like two months old, my mom left my dad, and she had to go back to her family. She had to go back to school.

I was looked after by my grandma, my dad's mom. And I stayed with my grandma and also had support from my auntie, who is my dad's sister. So, they raised me up. I started receiving letters from my mom when I was in primary school. I didn't get to meet my mom until I was in year seven, going to high school. It was really hard for me when I finally got to really bond with her as a young adult...Then she passed away from AIDS.

[Sarai pauses for emotional release.]

My dad wasn't really there. He remarried. My grandma and my aunt, you know, they supported my schooling. My dad never even paid the school fees or took responsibility for anything. He was just somebody else.

So, the Guide, the authority figure in my life, it's my faith. You know, just believing in God, that's been very helpful, even though, like, I was really let down. But I always think, "What's the reason why I am where I am? I wouldn't have done it without God." You know, God has a good plan for my life. And that's why he protected me from so many things.

And I've witnessed a lot of miracles. When I was a young kid, like, I'm completing an exam, I would just pray and say, "God, I just want to get an A in this subject. Please, help me to remember the things that I have studied." And I've seen God coming through for me. And I remember lots of miracles, so I could spend all day talking about it, like the opportunities that kind of come seeking for me. Like the kinds of jobs I'll get. People would reach out and say, "I think you'll be the right person for this job." That hasn't happened once. It's happened multiple times.

So, I didn't have to, like, struggle and say, "Do I need to search for a right job every single time?" They've appointed me at the right time. You know, I've always seen the hand of God in my life. It used to be my grandmother, auntie, and my mom who guided me, but they've all passed now. I can definitely say, it is now myself and God.

Sarai's sharing about God as her Guide not only shows us how she makes sense of the losses in her life but how she accomplishes her goals, in her words, from the "miracles" she receives from turning to a higher authority in her life. She had role models in her grandmother, auntie, and her mom as Guides, but after they passed away, she looked beyond the physical to the spiritual realm.

Guides are usually authorities in our life, who or what we listen to for direction or counsel. After all, we start off requiring guidance from parents or authority figures. We know that those who acquire experience, knowledge, or skills are well-equipped to lead us in our own path, simply because they know more than we do. The types of people we seek for guidance varies depending on our own values. Some of us may look to religious leaders, some to teachers, some to family and friends, some to professionals.

In this chapter, we will explore the varied Guides who help us on our journeys toward our Desires and learn to discern those who may hinder us. We can also look at whether we are in the role as a Guide in anyone else's life, and how to offer wisdom that builds up others.

The Responsibility of the Guide

I do not take my role as a psychologist, mother, and leader lightly; these roles put me in a position of authority and as a guide to others.

I understand the importance of having the right guides or authority figures. Those who are wise, trustworthy, and invested in growth can shape us in profound ways. The right Guides see who we can become. They reflect this vision back to us until we believe in that vision. The powerful benefits of their influence include clarity and direction for our lives. Guides can help us gain wisdom and perspective; we benefit from the experience of our Guides without learning everything personally.

I am privileged to have my parents as continual guides in my life. They provided me with emotional grounding and the stability and encouragement I've needed in times of uncertainty. They have, at times, lovingly challenged my limits and held me accountable. At the end of the day, I would not be where I am without them.

As a child, I benefited from my parents' belief in my own potential. We need someone to believe in us in our process of becoming. This borrowed belief becomes part of our identity as we continue to evolve.

I remember the time I wanted to do an extra subject for my last year of high school—six instead of the usual five—and I couldn't decide what subject to pursue. My mother, though uneducated by some standards, was full of wisdom. She asked me how many balls I could possibly hold in my hands without dropping one. I looked at her. I found three sets of Baoding (meditation) balls and tried holding them with my right hand without dropping any. My answer was five! It was a brilliant way of helping me through my conundrum, and I completed five subjects well at the end of my final year to be awarded with the school's science prize.

Choosing the Right Guides

Guides help us discern the path. They offer perspective from lived experience. They hold space when we feel lost. They push us past limits that feel safe but keep us playing small. They reflect who we're becoming. The ideal Guide provides clarity, wisdom, stability, growth, and vision. However, as Sarai and others have shared, Guides can come in all forms. A Guide can be: God, a parent, ideology, books, institutions, or any other entity you respect.

Why is it so important to discern if we are listening to and guided by the right voices? Because who we follow means the difference between reaching our Desires and full potential, or not. Virtually all transformational leaders or accomplished individuals had someone or something that shaped, challenged, or directed them. They had Guides. In order for any of us to accomplish our goals or dreams, we need Guides. Especially if we seek to do something new. The right guides help you become what you desire. Release those that are counterproductive, and recognise their impact on your life.

The Pathway of Impact

In addition to the Pathway of Pursuit with the elements of Agent and Desire, as discussed previously, the StoriCompass includes the *Pathway of Impact* with the elements of the *Guide* and *Beneficiary*. These elements help us along our Pathway of Impact: the part of our journey where who or what we look to affects our lives (*Guide*), and we influence the world with our own knowledge, skills, and life experience (*Beneficiary*).

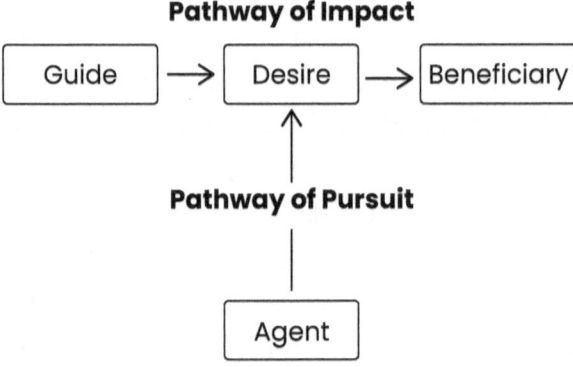

Figure 4.1. The Pathway of Impact with the Guide and Beneficiary, impacting on the Agent obtaining the Desire in the StoriCompass.

This pathway is the culmination of our values, Desires, and goals; the reason we have done everything up to this point; why we've pursued education, parenthood, creative inspirations, and relationships. We focus on the Guide in this chapter, and in the next, the Beneficiary.

The *Guide* in the Pathway of Impact

Oprah Winfrey often emphasizes how nobody succeeds alone. She has spoken about two prominent Guides who have a profound influence over her life. She considered poet, author, and civil rights activist Maya Angelou as her "mentor," "mother-sister," and "spiritual godmother." Oprah credits Angelou with guiding her through some of the most important years of her life and teaching her crucial life lessons. She also mentions her grandmother, Hattie Mae Lee, as a Guide who instilled a sense of purpose and faith in her from a young age.

History offers many examples of Guides—often parents or family elders—passing down wealth, values, and opportunity to future generations. Prominent families frequently cited include the Rockefellers, Carnegies, Waltons, Hiltons, and Vanderbilts in the United States; the Arnaults, Hermès, and Agnellis in Europe; and, in parts of Asia, families such as the Lees, Tatas, and Mitsuis.

The Guide Initiates the Journey and Plants the Seed

In the Pathway of Impact, the Guide is the entity that initiates a journey, an action, or plants a seed of Desire within us, the Agent, to pursue. The Guide instigates the Pathway of Pursuit for us, like Maya and Hattie did with Oprah. The Guide plays a crucial role in our life journey, offering direction: "Here's what matters. Here's what's next."

The Guide's influence can determine the difference between obtaining our Desire or not; how they impact us can influence the outcome of our efforts, but we always decide whether we accept it.

We may think of the Guide as the external forces, people, institutions, or outside influences that motivate and have authority over us. Indeed, external voices shape us from birth. Our caregivers taught us the first culture we experienced, the values and beliefs to adopt as we grow. However, during my research asking European Australians about who guided them in their lives, many answered, "Myself!"

This challenged my thinking as an Asian woman. I had thought of Guides as external, concrete people, like my parents, but I realize that many people with individualistic values tend to rely on themselves. They are their own authority as they become adults. They are their own Guide.

My research and experiences living in Western countries expanded my mind to consider that, perhaps, one of the most powerful Guides is the one within: Self.

The inner voice that decides from the time we realize our free will. Our inner compass that leads us to create the life we desire. The more we stay present within ourselves, become aware of internal states, we access this inner voice. Sometimes, it comes as a magnetic pull. I have felt the inexplicable need to attend a certain event, and when I did, I made the most remarkable connections.

This internal Guide can align us with our authentic beliefs and values, which we hear through inner convictions. Your inner Guide is your wisdom, intuition, or faith that sees the bigger picture.

Each of us is motivated by something or someone, a Guide, in our lives that legitimizes our quest.

The Guide(s) could be:

* **Internal**, our inner voice or convictions, beliefs, and values, which may have been passed down from elders or other influences and became internalized to help us make decisions to reach our Desire.

* **External**, an actual concrete person or entity, such as parents, mentors, teachers, professionals, institutions, spiritual leaders, etc.

* **Both internal and external**, sometimes we know something within (inner wisdom) that gets reinforced by external Guides.

For example, many people, including my research participants, see God as both an external Guide and an inner presence.

> *Guides can hold a position of authority and can wield enormous power and influence over our lives.*

It is this entity, force, and influence that aids us and, once we uncover and understand fully, ensures we know ourselves on a deep level. We become conscious of the impact of these influences on our lives and direction.

Understanding the Guide in Life Stories

To understand who might be a Guide in your life, it helps to see examples in others' life stories.

In my research, understanding cross-cultural differences between Easterners and Westerners, most Singaporean Chinese and Malaysian Chinese people report their parents are important Guides in their lives. However, this contrasted with Western self-narratives; many told me they tend not to seek out Guides because they were their own Guide, aligned with the island perspective in chapter 1. Their Self was their own authority and Guide. However, other Westerners also shared that, along with their Self, they had multiple Guides.

For one of my participants, a female Malaysian student, her Buddhist beliefs were the Guide. Her life revolved around wanting to achieve peace and have a harmonious family. This was different to my other female participant, who was Anglo Australian; her Guides were her God, her Christian church and her personal convictions which steered her to ensure she lived a life of meaning and significance.

Spiritual Guides

It is fascinating to me how many people make sense of life and turn to a higher power for comfort, guidance, and/or direction. In line with how William James, the father of American psychology, saw the inner life as the spiritual self, we see that, at their core, most people report primary caregivers and a spiritual tradition or entity as important Guides.

The majority of the world's population, according to the Pew Research Center, hold beliefs in God or a higher power, even if they are not religiously affiliated. My research highlighted one way faith and spirituality shape people's lives: how belief in God or a higher power becomes part of their life stories. Usually, it fits into their life story frame as the Guide helping them form identity.

Tre, who we met in chapter 3, shared candidly that she was clear about her authority and who acted as her Guide. In her own words, she shares about what guided her.

TRE

> Definitely God. I have these foundations of faith in God that were instilled in me as a child, and kind of moving into adolescence, into adulthood. You know, both of my parents did that right as we were growing up, when they were raising us. I look to those lessons, having those lessons from my parents. I am forming my own lessons that my son is now learning from. I wouldn't even say it's the person, I would say, it's the lessons that I've taken that have been instilled by those people.

A Network of Relationships

The ways in which our parents or caregivers seed, soil, and water us through their lessons enables the budding Self in us to form. If they show nurturance and love, we grow with a solid footing of self-confidence and self-love. If they are not able to support us in this way, we may struggle with seeing ourselves as competent and lovable. These first relationships are the most influential because they start us off in this life, and how they start us will affect our entire life. This is how the Self builds (or doesn't build) trust, as explained in Erikson's first stage of psychosocial development. From clinical experience, I have learned from clients that this primary relationship we have with our parents or caregivers influences whether we can fully trust in the higher power we cannot see.

We are all social beings, in a system where we were first under the authority of parents, then under the authority of teachers in school, and as adults, under the authority of supervisors. From childhood to adulthood, we are shaped by our life's voices—the voices of caregivers, elders, God, friends, partners, and work colleagues. And these relationships teach us further lessons about ourselves and the world.

Some voices are so deeply ingrained in our subconscious that we aren't aware or conscious of their influence. These voices come from authority figures, mentors, the cultural structure, family, faith, others we allowed into our lives, and even our inner dialogue. Some move us forward, while others hold us back, introducing and reinforcing doubts and fears.

Whether we are aware or not, we all have Guide(s)—forces that shape our ambitions, fears, and motivations. The key to transformation is not only identifying these Guide(s) but realizing their impact, then actively choosing which to embrace and which to let go. In doing so, we see clearly what directs our lives and why.

Evaluating the Influence of Your Guides

Most of us have walked more decades than we want with wounds and heartaches that need attention. We lost our innocence and woke up to the fact that not all Guides serve our highest good. Some are empowering, but others keep us stuck in limiting beliefs or old patterns.

I've been providing counseling for many years, long enough to recognize the power struggles and pain in families, couples, and organizations. Oftentimes, the wounds I have dealt with in my clients' lives, through the undressing of their traumatic experiences and/or bleeding emotions, have been inflicted by a Guide who betrayed my client's trust. Or worse, one who kept them in pain or who held them back because of malevolent motives.

One key skill to develop is knowing who to trust and allow into our inner sanctum. Especially those who we give the role of Guide in our lives.

The Guide is so important that we must learn to discern their likely impact on our lives. Choosing the wrong Guide derails our whole plot and changes the narrative of our lives so we no longer recognize our Self, let alone our story.

This skill of discernment can, unfortunately, come at a high price, after experiences of deep suffering and pain. This was especially true for Anna Mae Bullock, who we know as Tina Turner, the stage name given her by ex-husband Ike Turner. He played the role of mentor, musical director, and gatekeeper when she became lead singer in his band as a teenager. He introduced her to the music industry and launched her career, shaping her image, sound, and public presence.

Over time, under the influence of drug addiction, Ike's guidance turned into domination, abuse, and exploitation. He was physically violent, emotionally abusive, and controlling in both their personal and professional relationship. Without any control over her name, finances, and music, she reached the point of no return. After yet another physical altercation, Tina ran away from Ike with only her clothes and some loose change.

Free from Ike in her forties, Tina reinvented herself as a solo artist to become the Queen of Rock and Roll. Hers is a powerful narrative about what it means to reclaim agency after being trapped in an abusive, controlling relationship by someone who was initially a Guide in life.

Beware of those who try to steal your treasures and strip you down until you barely know yourself.

Recognizing your True Guides

How do you recognize those Guides who support you, and those who don't have your best interest at heart?

One way in which I developed a knack for understanding peoples' motives is to observe and listen to them. A lot can be picked up from the way people carry themselves, how they speak, what they say, how they treat others, and the feeling they leave you with.

Through these observations and that sense of the person, we can decipher who or what may be good for us. Your eyes may open to some Guides who inspire you to reach higher. But also, others may have unknowingly (or knowingly) instilled fear, self-doubt, or limiting beliefs.

The way you know if your Guide is enlarging your world or restricting it is by tuning into your body. When you think of the message and/or when you are in the presence of your Guide (whether it be a person, entity, etc.), do you sense an expansion of yourself? Or do you simply want to contract and hide? Are there knots or anxiety in your body when you think of, or are with, that person or entity? Often, when I am asked to do something, like making a decision, and I feel uncomfortable in my gut, I sense it's not for me. I have learned to be in tune to my internal state as a

Guide. This may not always be reliable, but I respect my internal compass and deep values as a Guide to help me make decisions.

When you are with people, try to get a sense and feel for them through their presence, actions, and words. Does this person give you space and time to speak, or are they cutting into what you want to say? These are telling signs. Trust yourself to act on gut instincts.

Guides who make you want to hide from others, from the world, and even from yourself are ones you need to run from, fast. They inflict hurt, doubt, and shame if you let them in. Trust me, they don't have your best interest at heart.

Good leaders embrace their position with humility, heart, and a desire to build up others. Too many workplaces, and leaders within these settings, unfortunately, have harmed others and created toxic cultures not psychologically or physically safe for employees or colleagues.

Sometimes it takes a breakdown for us to access the right Guide who can truly help, who leads to clarity in our lives. This was the case for Clara, who you met in chapter 2. Recall that she is the French and Spanish mother who left for Ireland for her husband's work with her eldest son and a newborn, and she never got the chance to grieve the loss of her professional identity. She continues her story to illustrate how finding the right Guide can make all the difference. This is Clara's account in her own words.

CLARA

> I have to be honest with you. I had a very, very big breakdown later when we moved back to Spain, eleven months later, because my husband did a really good job.
>
> I thought we were moving to Ireland for at least two to three years, and it was only an eleven-month move. And then we were repatriated to Spain. And that was too much for me, that was a very big, life-changing event.

In Ireland, when my eldest started school, I found myself alone with my youngest, and to have this time to discover what kind of mother I can be with him, what kind of child he was, not only in this dynamic of attention-seeking and fights with his brother, but rather, when you and I are alone, and there is no attention to fight for, and we can be together, as a mother. I got to check with him. How are you? What's your personality like? What do you like? What do you dislike? How do we interact? How do we connect? And so on. When everything started to be like that, we were repatriated, and everything started over again. Unpacking boxes, finding a school for my eldest again in Spain when we all moved. So, we were at it again, the three of us together. My husband was already at work.

So, it was very hard. And at that moment, I told my husband, "I need help. I am not well. I really don't feel well." I was having very dark thoughts, and it was very hard on me. And I really needed support.

So, I asked him to take me to hospital. We went to the hospital. And after very long hours of waiting, I got the help of a psychiatrist. She evaluated me. I had self-diagnosed myself with everything that was part of depression.

Yes. I was sick, maybe psychotic. I was like, "I am not well. Give me the heavy stuff because I'm not doing well."

And after listening to me, she said, "You're exhausted. Yeah, definitely."

And I was like, "No, no, no. You're getting something wrong. I'm going to tell you my story again. These are all the dark thoughts I have."

She said, "You are very exhausted. So, here is what we're going to do. You're going to leave your husband with the babies for a weekend, and you're going to go and sleep."

"What?!"

"And if you want, we can have a meeting after that. And you tell me if all of this craziness that you're describing is gone or is still there, and we can decide what we do next."

So, I came out.

My husband was waiting for me outside. He asked, "So, what did she say? Like, what pills do we have to go and get?"

I was like, "You know what? Funny enough, I don't need to be medicated."

He said, "No? Then how do we help you? Well?"

So, here it comes: "You're going to stay alone with the babies for the weekend. And I'm going to go by myself to get good sleep. OK? Whatever it takes."

I was surprised he was so supportive. He asked, "When do we do that? Go ahead. Take your time."

Excellent! So, I booked myself in a hotel the following weekend. It was seven in the evening. It's Spain. So, they were saying, "Should you order your dinner or something?" I was like, "You know what? No. I'm going to go to sleep right away."

I slept fourteen hours in a row. I was exhausted.

One of the symptoms I had was this fogginess. Yes. I would see everybody almost like in this fog. I would say everything started to go really dark when my youngest was four months old. And I think by the time I went to hospital, I think he was maybe fifteen months old. So that would be for almost a year that I lived with this fog.

After the long sleep, it was the first time I woke up and didn't see it. I have been feeling all these symptoms for a long time. I was like, "There is something really wrong with me. Every single diagnosis book would tell you I'm not doing well. That is huge. So that whole weekend, many symptoms lifted.

So amazing. I realized I'm highly sensitive.

To me, it was life-changing to understand that I needed time to rest. And resting was not sitting on a couch with babies playing on the floor. That was not it. Like I really needed to have full night's sleep with no awakenings in the middle of the night, with no alarm clock to wake up the next morning because there is breakfast to prepare or anything.

Sleep is a basic need for everyone. But for highly sensitive brain like mine, even more. And breastfeeding comes with a lot of sleep deprivation.

And then we started combining it with another understanding of myself, that I was also overstimulated by the stimuli that comes with young children. By all this unpacking and paperwork that comes with repatriation. Adjusting to this culture in Spain because reverse culture shock is really heavy.

And a reverse culture shock as a mother, because something that I realized is that I had never been in this country as a mother. Because I left, and I gave birth abroad. I went from Belgium to Ireland back to Spain. So, with all the changes, I was exhausted!

What a wise psychiatrist! For Clara, it meant the difference between sleeping in a nice hotel and getting restorative sleep, which improved her well-being, or spending time in a psychiatric hospital medicated and labeled with illness that wasn't really there. She learned she was highly sensitive and needed to prioritize more regular rest. We will hear more of Clara's story in the coming chapters.

Recognizing the Wisdom Within and Without

It's vital we listen to our inner voice. Clara acted on hers to seek help, and the psychiatrist acted on her professional experience to guide Clara's treatment. Even though it may have seemed she didn't initially validate Clara's concern, she instructed Clara to come back after she had slept.

Some have called the inner voice our intuition, sixth sense, inner compass, God, or other forms of knowing. Your *inner Guide*—your wisdom, faith, God and/or higher self—may be trying to guide you but is often drowned out by external noise. Go to a quiet area and listen to your inner Guide.

Ensure your inner voice aligns with your values.

Sometimes, it's picking up feelings in our gut, telling us not to get involved with a relationship, attend an event, or pursue a certain business opportunity. It's also important to get validation from external sources by seeking the wisdom of others who care deeply about you.

You are the receiver of many messages, but you also have the power to choose which messages you internalize.

This is your life. Your path. Your story.

What will you allow to motivate and/or guide you?

Your transformation begins when you consciously choose the Guide(s) that uplift and empower you, while letting go of those that don't.

Who is Speaking Inside You?

You can also choose which inner voice is always talking in the back of your mind, a positive one or a negative one. Become aware of your self-talk. When it becomes negative, try to understand why. Then make a conscious decision to stop the chatter and choose more positive self-talk. Journaling, affirmations, gratitude exercises, and other techniques help quiet the inner critic.

Your words ultimately build your reality, so beware of the words your central nervous system sends to the rest of your body.

If the voices around you keep you small, it's time to ask the ones you can't escape from (like your family) to speak with careful thought, or it's time to lessen your exposure to those unsupportive messages. But if there are voices you have no affiliation with anymore that undermine you, find new, supportive voices.

Read books that expand your perspective, surround yourself with people who support your growth, and seek wisdom from those who embody the life you aspire to live.

We develop wisdom from action and experience. It's important to have moments of stillness, to listen to wisdom within, and to have moments of movement. It's action inspired by the still inner voice in the quiet that moves mountains.

True wisdom is knowing who to listen to and who to ignore.

Wisdom is:

* Discerning which voices serve your growth.
* Knowing when to let go of old narratives.
* Recognizing that your inner voice matters as much—if not more—than external guidance.

Sometimes, wisdom comes from unexpected places: a chance encounter, a book, a moment of silence, an internal nudge. The question is: Are you paying attention?

If you want transformation, seek new sources of wisdom and motivation. Assess your Pathway of Impact and ensure your Guides motivate you toward your Desire so you can become the Beneficiary, which we will explore next in your story landscape.

Key Takeaways

* The Pathway of Impact shows the impact of others (Guide) on our lives as well as ours on theirs (Beneficiary).

* The Guide is who we listen to, usually a guiding force or authoritative figure. Guides can be internal (inner voice, wisdom, etc.) or external (people, entities, etc.) or both (God or a higher power).

* Be discerning about whom you see as a Guide. The ideal Guide provides clarity, wisdom, stability, growth, and vision, and seeks to release you to your Desire.

Deeper actions

Understand your Guide(s) by asking yourself these questions:

1. Who are you listening to? Who or what is guiding your decisions, desires, beliefs?

2. How have you collaborated with your guide to dream, grow, or believe in yourself?

3. Which of these Guides are helping you grow and move toward what you truly desire?

4. Which Guides feel less supportive? Are there any Guides you can let go?

5

Who or What Benefits from Your Success? (*The Beneficiary*)

> *We have not only to be responsible for ourselves,
> but for our influence on others.*
>
> — Attributed to Harriet Martineau

> *Tend your own garden and the world
> will bloom around you.*
>
> — Attributed to Sarah Orne Jewett

What keeps you going when you want to give up? When life gets hard, and you're not sure how you're ever going to fulfil your dreams?

Chances are, you'll think of someone or something that will benefit once you've obtained your goal or dream. This is the element in the StoriCompass called the *Beneficiary* or *Beneficiaries*, which is tied to your Why. Why do you keep going when the going gets tough? It's usually because of the answer to this question: *Who or what benefits when you pursue and realize your desire?*

This is what I asked Tre, the American transformational leader who you met in chapters 3 and 4.

TRE

> When I have accomplished my goals, who gets to benefit are my clients, my son, our family. I think, too, in a broader sense, I see myself as a stakeholder in the social good ecosystem. As a consultant that's working on transformational leadership, I believe the ecosystem gets to benefit because I am digging in and learning and making sure I have the right relationships and fostering those connections and nurturing those. But it would be my clients, my family.
>
> You know, in my ecosystem, that I very much see myself as part of, and then I think, too, when you're doing the things that are really enjoyable and making you happy, and that you feel good about, and you're thriving, I think your communities benefit, right? Because I'm happy with what I'm doing, right? For example, I want to go take a walk. I want to see my neighbors. I want to say hello. When I'm happy, I want to be engaged, right? And when that's happening, that brings me even more excitement to do the work that I'm doing. It impacts other lives.

Tre shares that once she obtains her Desire, her Beneficiaries are her clients, her son, her family, and even herself. This highlights an important truth, that the true measure of success isn't what we achieve, but who gets to flourish because we do. When we know who will benefit from our accomplishments, we uncover the deeper Why that drives our life forward.

This chapter will help you to uncover your source of motivation and why you are living your life, as much as it will give you tools to revisit your Why if it needs to be more compelling.

When you reflect on your journey, ask yourself: *Who or what benefits when I pursue and realize my deepest Desire?* This isn't merely a question of external validation or recognition. It's an invitation to examine the very core of your narrative. Recognize that your

Beneficiary unlocks meaning, purpose, and deeper connection in your story.

As women, embracing this perspective means acknowledging that our successes ripple beyond personal achievement, influencing not only our inner lives but also the communities and relationships that shape us. This question of "Who or what benefits from my success?" challenges us to consider who and/or what we are truly working for, and in doing so, it reveals the nature of the Beneficiaries in our stories.

When I felt like giving up, when the overwhelming pressure to write and summarize my research findings got the better of me, I would go back to who would benefit. Once I received my Desire of a completed thesis, who were my Beneficiaries?

Doing so deepened my purpose beyond my Self. My Desire became purposeful, not only personal. I moved from thinking, "What do I want?" to "What will this make possible for others?" The *collective self* motivated me. If there are others involved, my mind and heart go into action. When I know I am doing it for others, I am less focused on me and my limitations. I have a message to give, and so, I work harder to overcome my self-consciousness and fears.

Knowing with clarity the Beneficiaries in our life story strengthens our motivation and follow-through, enabling us to persist against the odds because we're not doing it only for ourselves. We'll be more committed and resilient when things get hard because we know others are watching or waiting for us.

Understanding who benefits from your growth also reveals who doesn't, or who might resist because they feel threatened by your success and joy. You will see where relationships align with your becoming, or where they conflict with it. This helps you set healthier boundaries or invite people into your growth. Because the truth is real transformation creates new relational patterns, not simply personal shifts. It opens doors for new relationships when your identity shifts. For instance, becoming a writer and wearing this identity has allowed me to develop meaningful relationships with other writers.

Remember, we create new relationships and realities when we start owning our life story.

The *Beneficiary* in the Pathway of Impact

In the StoriCompass, the Beneficiary is the entity for whom the journey is undertaken—whether that benefit is tangible, emotional, or symbolic. It is the reason the journey is undertaken. In your life narrative, you can view the Beneficiary from the following perspectives:

* **Internal**, the part of you that craves fulfillment, growth, and self-recognition.
* **External**, the individuals or communities that draw inspiration, support, and tangible benefits from your achievements.
* **Both internal and external**, as many of the benefits we derive from a realized Desire benefit ourselves and others too.

By understanding your Beneficiary or Beneficiaries, you gain clarity on the true aim of your endeavors. Rather than chasing success solely for external accolades, you see success as a process of giving and receiving—where every achievement nourishes your inner Self, enriching your relationships and those around you.

A widely circulated quote—often attributed to Winston Churchill although its original source is uncertain—says, "We make a living by what we get, but we make a life by what we give." These words highlight that being clear about the Beneficiaries in our lives shapes identity; we become who we are through what we give, not only what we get.

Your Beneficiary reveals what part of yourself you want to serve—whether as teacher, healer, protector, liberator—because you can see who benefits when you have these identities. It taps into what Erik Erikson proposed in the seventh stage of psychosocial development: that we go through the stage of generativity (versus stagnation) where we seek to leave something meaningful to the next generation. This is essential for healthy adult identity development, especially in midlife. This element in the StoriCompass is concerned with legacy.

Ultimately, knowing your Beneficiary links your personal story to the larger cultural story we all write, merely by breathing and living in this world on a daily basis.

Your story becomes a gift to others, not only self-discovery. For example, if your Desire is "The power to speak your truth," your Beneficiary might be "other women whose voices have been erased." Clarity about the Beneficiaries in your life anchors your life in intergenerational or communal meaning and purpose. You take your role not only in self-authorship but also cultural authorship, because you're shaping what becomes possible for others. This was one of the motivators for me to write this book. I could see how it would create possibilities for my girls and every other girl who learns to craft a meaningful story from struggle and hard work. I hope it plants a seed in their minds: *If she can do it, I can too!* That is the message I want to instill. If I can achieve what I and others thought impossible for a refugee girl with parents who didn't complete high school or speak English, so might others achieve their dreams.

Cross-Cultural Differences Found in Beneficiaries

In my research, I found that the Why and Who can be very much tied up with the Desire. For example, many Singaporean and Malaysian Chinese shared that they wanted to work hard and earn enough to look after their parents in retirement, or to be able to care for their family. The Desire was to nurture, care for, and afford a comfortable living for the most important people in their lives, their families. Their Desire was so deeply connected to their Beneficiaries that it structured their whole life story. In my doctoral thesis, I labeled this a *family enhancement pathway*. These Easterners sought to enhance their families' well-being and actively sought success in order to benefit their families.

Why many people in Asian contexts pursue certain goals (Desires) often comes down to Who the beneficiaries are in their lives. The Why of their lives is really, "Who gets to benefit?"

Reflecting on author and inspirational speaker Simon Sinek's thesis about starting with your Why instead of What or How, while I agree that it is deeply significant, I realize for many people, including myself, as a product of Eastern beliefs and philosophy, the Why is not as powerful as understanding the *Who*. Who I live for is what guides my Why. Why do I do what I do? It's because of the most important people in my life—my family, my two girls, and the people I serve. They are the ones Who get me out of bed each day.

My larger Why also is that I want to leave a legacy for the next generation, for all women to know they are, in essence, the very heart of every culture. They are of great value and worth.

For many women, their children and family are the Who in their lives. They go to great lengths to work hard and stay afloat for them. It's the Who that gives the reason for the Why.

My new take on Simon Sinek's thesis in his book *Start with Why* is that behind the Why is really a Who. So, I am thinking instead, "Start with Who!"

Who is the source of motivation for your life? For me, I couldn't tap into my Why for finishing the PhD until I connected with Who it was going to benefit. As it turned out, my two daughters were the primary beneficiaries—through role modelling—and the research also benefited my clients and many others.

With this in mind, I propose adding another inner circle to the golden circle Sinek outlined in his book; before the Why, the innermost is Who. The Who is as, or more, powerful than the Why, the How, and the What in our lives. This is because the Who is behind the Why, giving clarity to What and How we approach anything. This I believe applies not only in business but our personal lives too.

Our greatest goals find meaning in the lives they touch. Who our work serves is the heartbeat of Why.

Many self-development books emphasize self-actualization, self-acquisition, or self-enhancement. However, that doesn't resonate deeply with me. Nor does the emphasis on the Self ring true for me. What is true for me is that whatever I do, it's not only about myself, it's also about others. It's about how my family, community, and others can benefit. For me, family and people in my circle are an integral part of my very Self and my values. It's why I do what I do because as much as I've been Westernized in a Western culture, I discovered in my doctoral research that I still have a family enhancement pathway consistent with Easterners, instead of a self-enhancement pathway that was seen in most Western self-narratives. In simple words, whatever I do in my life is to enhance the collective, my family, and my community, instead of only myself. This is not to say Westerners merely follow the self-enhancement pathway and ignore family and community, but in the sample in my research, most Western self-narratives referenced the Self more so than others.

Exploring Your Personal Why and Who

At the heart of every powerful narrative lies a compelling Why and Who. This Why and Who is not simply a goal or ambition; it is the deep-seated purpose motivating every decision and action. This personal Why often intertwines with our experiences, values, and dreams—elements honed by both societal expectations and personal triumphs.

Taking the time to explore your personal Why and Who involves:

* **Self-reflection:** Understanding the moments that defined you and the aspirations that drive you.
* **Authenticity:** Honoring your inner voice even when external pressures push you in different directions.
* **Integration:** Merging your inner needs with external realities so your purpose is not fragmented but whole and vibrant.

When your Why and Who are clear, they naturally direct you toward the right Beneficiary—those who resonate with your truth and who can both reflect and amplify your success.

This was the case for Aylin, whose story shows her upbringing to become who she is now, a very successful fifty-year-old finance executive. After a marriage breakdown in her late twenties, she became a single parent with a toddler. Out of desperation and sheer hard work, she has climbed to a top senior-executive position in a traditionally male-dominated field. Her Who and Why were established through the values ingrained by culture and family.

AYLIN

I was born in Melbourne, Australia, but raised by Turkish parents who migrated in the late 1960s. They didn't know about Australian culture, and hence, they tried to safeguard us. So, in effect, we were brought up the way Turkey was when they left it in the 1960s. But what they didn't realize was Turkey was evolving as well, and they forgot about that so, you know, we experienced strictness, the rules. They were trying to survive while bringing up their children in hope that they'll return to Turkey.

As my parents best described it, before they knew it, the kids were all older and started putting roots here in Australia.

So, what it meant to me was the struggle of trying to be accepted with my Australian friends, what they could do or say, and then make sure that I don't force my strictness on my child.

My parents had no idea; they didn't understand. We used to have to resort to lying to our parents. We would go on excursions and forge their signatures because it was easier. We also had a language barrier. My brother and I, we couldn't really talk Turkish to them. So, when we tried, we got ourselves into trouble because we were using different, wrong words, and we had no idea. Despite that, I guess what was instilled is an awareness of our culture, and we knew what our values were. We grew up respecting our elders, which I wouldn't compromise.

My mother was brought up in what was a man's world, and it was the man's right. And so, I had two sisters and two brothers. So, the three of us were treated differently. My dad, however, was of a different perspective. He was like, the boys will get a job anyway and be independent, but he allowed us as well. For me, by the time it came to me, so to speak, because I was the youngest daughter, I think I had a bit more leniency with my dad.

I think I see a lot of Turkish in me, and yet I see a lot of Australian in me, too, and other cultures, because I respect everyone. There are things that I love about other cultures. So, I think it's mixed with my community. They all come from different backgrounds. So, it's all about respect and understanding. I think you become almost any culture that you find some similarities with because you connect with those people.

I am a Shiite, while we weren't practicing Muslims. I reckon I didn't even think my dad was practicing until he got very ill, and so sick that he was sort of bedridden. It surprised me, actually shocked me, that he was frail and prayed privately.

The Sunnis from Turkey practice it, praying. They're much more strict on the household. They don't assimilate. Whereas the Shiites, which I am, we're a lot more secular, so to speak. We're always a minority in Turkey. But what I realized was what Dad was teaching from the Koran, like empathy. You would say, "Don't put your hand out to someone else's bread." I interpret that as if you want to succeed, you never step over other people's successions or their thing, and you know, you've got to own it yourself. These and other things, Dad taught me.

My dad left a legacy for me, and now I am thinking about what I desire in life. It's more of a legacy, a desire to be true to myself, my beliefs. I do push boundaries. Perhaps I'm at an age where I don't really care about what other people think of me. I am fifty now.

I wouldn't have been pushing boundaries before because I needed to survive, and I wouldn't want to speak up in case I jeopardized my career. I feel like I can now. I am privileged to have walked the path, so to speak. I want to build my legacy, as we speak, and that is to give back. Giving back my knowledge, giving back to my friendships, giving back and bringing people into the community, whether it be my finance committee, whether it be in my friendship community, whether it be women in the finance community, I want to give back.

I haven't always been in the finance industry. My career pathway dropped into my lap when I was at a very low point in my life. It was out of desperation for me and my son. I was a single mom; he was about four years old. I had to leave my husband. I started in real estate because, you know, I couldn't do it full time. And then I got to a point after a couple of years where I needed a salary. In those days, positions were still advertised in newspapers, and I remember circling a bank teller position. I literally simply walked into the bank. Now, I knew nothing. I remember selling myself in desperation in the interview because I had no experience. Then my boss, who is a dear friend to me now, took a chance on me.

I climbed my way up. It was hard, but I wanted to achieve because of my Why. If I achieved my goals, I thought, all of us—coming back to it—is everyone in the circle, the broker, me, the company—you know, everyone—gets to benefit. Personally, I'll grow, and I learn things all the time.

Aylin's story highlights the cultural background and values instilled into her, especially by her father. He enlarged her world, and the struggles of being a single mom did not deter her from reaching her goals. She has a growth mindset. She is constantly learning and has confidence that what she strives for makes a difference, not only in her life but in the lives of others, because she seeks to give back and benefit others. The Beneficiaries were herself (because she will grow) and people in her circle (her son, friends, finance committee, and people in her community). Her Who and Why are powerful in motivating her, propelling her forward without limits.

Identifying Your Beneficiaries

When we come to identify who or what our Beneficiaries are, we may find there are inner Beneficiaries. In Aylin's life, she tuned into her fearlessness of pushing boundaries for personal growth, recognizing she was in a learning process. She also had external Beneficiaries, like her son, community, and many others in her orbit.

The *inner* Beneficiary is the most intimate and transformative component of your narrative. It represents the Self that not only experiences success but is also fundamentally changed by it.

This inner dimension is about:

* **Self-compassion:** Recognizing your achievements and your struggles with equal kindness.

* **Internal validation:** Celebrating progress regardless of external applause because you are of worth and value by being your authentic self.

* **Personal growth:** Allowing your internal life to evolve as you do, absorbing lessons and insights that shape who you are.

For many women, embracing their inner Beneficiary means breaking free from confines of perfectionism and societal norms. It's about creating a safe, nurturing inner space where you acknowledge your ambitions and emotions as valid parts of your journey.

I shared that while my inner Beneficiary grounds me, my goals and ambitions show me that I can achieve great things, even though I came from humble beginnings; the *external* Beneficiaries—my children, family, colleagues, clients, and you, reading this book—serve as mirrors and motivators as I work toward my goals. External Beneficiaries motivate us powerfully, the Who.

These include:

* **Family and friends:** The trusted circle that champions our victories and supports us through setbacks.
* **Mentors and peers:** Individuals who inspire us by sharing wisdom and encouragement.
* **Communities and networks:** Broader groups that provide both a sense of belonging and platforms for shared growth.

External Beneficiaries energize our path by offering diverse perspectives and resources that propel our mission forward. Their feedback and recognition validates our journey and provides the practical support needed to navigate challenges. External Beneficiaries include family, friends, mentors, communities, and work networks that celebrate our life's victories along with us, but that also contributed to these successes, so any success—and benefit—is mutual.

The reason we strive is rarely for the milestone itself—it's for the people Who will be better off because we reached it. That's when our Why comes alive.

When Beneficiaries Create Pressure Instead of Purpose

It is important to recognize that not all Beneficiaries serve our higher purpose. Sometimes, the expectations and demands of Beneficiaries become a source of pressure, leading us away from our authentic journey. This pressure might manifest as:

* **Unrealistic standards:** External demands that push us toward outcomes that do not resonate with our personal Why. For example, maybe you're pushed by your spouse or mentor to take on a high-status promotion because it "proves success," even though your real purpose—your Desire—is to have more time for family and creative work.

* **Misaligned values:** When the values of those around us conflict with our inner truth, leading to turmoil. For example, you may feel pressured to stay in a stable but unfulfilling job because your family values security, while you value creativity and risk-taking.
* **Over-dependence on validation:** Relying too heavily on external affirmation can sometimes erode our self-confidence and obscure our true path. For example, only feeling confident in your work when others praise it, which makes you chase approval instead of pursuing what truly matters to you.

Understanding when our Beneficiaries are exerting undue pressure allows us to recalibrate our focus. It empowers us to differentiate between supportive influences and those that may distract or diminish the authenticity of our narrative.

Letting go of external expectations and undue pressure can be liberating.

When we release the weight of imposed standards, we allow our purpose to shine through clearly.

This process of releasing external pressures not only preserves our creative freedom but reinforces the integrity of our life story, ensuring we write each life chapter with deliberate purpose.

Strengthening Your Commitment to Your Why and Who

Reaffirming your commitment to both your personal Why and the Beneficiaries who genuinely support you is a critical step in owning your life story. Here are some strategies to strengthen that commitment:

* **Set clear boundaries:** Protect your inner space by defining what expectations or requests are constructive and what are not.

Boundaries, like saying "no" when you are overstretched or when a request is not constructive and healthy. Please, set them.

* **Regular self-assessment:** Reflect periodically on whether your Beneficiaries align with your personal Why. Nurture the Beneficiaries who do and let the others go. Evaluate why you're doing what you're doing—and for whom—at least monthly so you strengthen your commitment to your life goals and dreams.

* **Celebrate small victories:** Acknowledge incremental successes that validate both your internal growth and the positive impact on your external Beneficiaries. These celebrations motivate you to realize your wildest dreams and cheer you on when the going gets tough.

* **Cultivate supportive networks:** Engage with communities and mentors who encourage authenticity and personal empowerment. They bring clarity to your Why and may even become your Beneficiaries too.

By fortifying these aspects, you create a resilient framework that not only sustains your journey but ensures that your narrative remains true to your values and aspirations.

Your Why and Who Holds the Power

Remember: Your life story is ultimately yours to author.

Your Why and Who holds the power for you.

By understanding the Beneficiary in your StoriCompass, you are empowered with a tool to evaluate and shape your narrative. Whether it's nurturing your inner Beneficiary or aligning with external Beneficiaries who uplift you, this element offers clarity on where true validation, meaning, and purpose lie.

As you continue to craft your narrative, let your purpose and values be the compass that guides you. Embrace those who genuinely resonate with your journey, and do not allow external pressures to dictate the terms of your success. In doing so, you not only honor your unique story but inspire others to own theirs with courage and authenticity.

Your journey is a masterpiece in progress—one where every success, lesson, and relationship contributes to a rich tapestry of self- and other-empowerment. And in that tapestry, your Why and your Who, the Beneficiaries in your life, are the threads that hold it together. Your Beneficiaries will remind you every day that you are the author of your story, despite the forces in your life that may help or hinder you, which we explore next.

Key Takeaways

* The Beneficiary is the entity for whom the journey is undertaken, the reason Why you pursue the Desire.
* Beneficiaries can be internal (self-growth, self-realization, etc.) or external (individuals, communities, etc.) or both.
* Knowing your personal Why and the Beneficiaries who genuinely care about you are a critical step in owning your life story.

Deeper Actions

Reflect on and journal about your Beneficiaries using these questions:

1. Why do you do what you do, in terms of your larger goals like work or chasing a dream, beyond the goal itself?
2. What would be lost—for the Beneficiaries and for you—if you didn't obtain your Desire?
3. Draw a circle and place yourself in the middle. Around it, list every person or group who benefits from your well-being and/or success.

6

Who or What's Assisting You Forward? (*The Supporter*)

No act of kindness, no matter how small, is ever wasted.

—Aesop

Alone we can do so little; together we can do so much.

—Helen Keller

Cristina fell into a fetal position on her sofa. She sobbed deeply, as if releasing years of pent-up pain, anger, confusion, and helplessness all bundled into a mess of knots in her gut and chest.

Startled by the emotional outburst, Cristina's mother, Bianca, ran from the next room and embraced her firstborn. Although Cristina was now in her late forties, she needed her mother's support more than ever.

Bianca sat in silence and absorbed the pain radiating through Cristina's body. Cristina had always been the one who held their family of three together, especially when her father—Bianca's husband, Mihai—had left them. He escaped communist Romania in the 1980s, and then sponsored the three of them to reunite with him in Australia. Yet he never truly settled into the Australian way of life. He fell into depression, drank excessively, and wanted to return to his family of origin, to what felt safe and like home to him, in Romania. Bianca understood the heartbreak Cristina felt when her father left them to return to Romania immediately before she started university, abandoning his role as husband and father. This kind of abandonment kept repeating in Cristina's life. Bianca had also held her daughter when Cristina's first husband left, telling Cristina he did not love her anymore.

Now, holding Cristina close to her once again, she understood the torment of Cristina's grief during the latest trouble with her second partner, now her ex. They had been together many years. Bianca was shocked to learn of the gravity of psychological, physical, emotional, and verbal abuse Cristina suffered at the hands of this man, and his gaslighting left Cristina a shell of herself. He undermined her reality and manipulated her to suit his needs. Bianca barely recognized her daughter once the relationship finally, mercifully, ended.

Cristina recounted her story to me. She was picking up the pieces of her life and owning her life story, strengthened by the support of her mom. As she recovered from the heartbreaking moments of the relationship ending, she focused on building her catering business while maintaining her professional role as a schoolteacher. In our interview, she talked about her mother's role in her life.

CRISTINA

My mom taught me independence. She helped me pay my uni fees. She was my rock during that time. Yeah, she is amazing. Massive role model.

My mom is still my rock; like, I couldn't survive daily without her because she looks after my dog, and she just helps me a lot. I can call up on her and go, "Mom, I'm working tomorrow. Can you do this shopping for me?" She'll just go and do it. So, I actually rely on her quite a bit because I don't have anyone else to help me at the moment.

What Bianca provided over the course of Cristina's life as a Supporter in Cristina's StoriCompass included letting her daughter know she was never alone on her journey. Her steadiness fostered in Cristina a sense of belonging and trust in relationships, and in life itself, even when Cristina's father—and her partners—were absent. She brought structure and completeness to Cristina's story, helping Cristina understand that despite the pain, they were both seeing progress in their life journeys. They weren't stuck there, being abandoned by men. Not only through personal willpower, but through listening, empathy, grace, and timely intervention; they provided each other the safety and nurturing they each needed in order to heal. Research by Dan McAdams has found that coherent self-narratives that include others are more emotionally grounding and hopeful; when we understand others' roles in our stories, when we truly fathom we are not alone in our struggles, we do better.

Cristina's gratitude for her mom as the Supporter empowered her to keep moving forward despite the pain. Instead of focusing solely on her hardships, wounds, or disappointments, she was able to also celebrate her triumphs and accomplishments with the help of her mom, and this helped her grow and learn from her experiences. Gratitude has been found to be strongly associated with emotional well-being, resilience, and relational depth.

Borrowed Beliefs Provide Strength

Parents and caregivers model how to interpret life and build our systems of meaning. As mentioned before, they give children nurturance, an interpretative system to make sense of life, and borrowed beliefs. It is these borrowed beliefs that become internalized. Therefore, over time, the Supporter shifts from being external to internal. We internalize the parts of our caregivers' stories that have given us strength and wisdom, so that we can rely on that same strength in our journey. We realize we have internalized qualities like courage, faith, or perseverance through what we have learned from our role models: our Supporters.

When we can see this kind of wisdom within ourselves, we strengthen our self-concept and increase confidence in our capacity to face challenges; we become our own Supporter.

Once we understand how this deep support shapes our growth, we're more willing to seek help when needed. We're more likely to offer help to others. This contributes to a healthy reciprocal model of interdependence that is wholesome and culture-building. Over the long term, having Supporters and being a Supporter nurtures humility, community, and emotional maturity.

We never have to do life alone. And we shouldn't.

The Pathway of Forces

The last pathway in the StoriCompass is the *Pathway of Forces*, which is influenced by elements of the Supporter and the Opposition. In this pathway, two conflicting influences act on us (as the Agent), helping us reach the Desire as a Supporter or inhibiting us reaching the Desire as an Opposition.

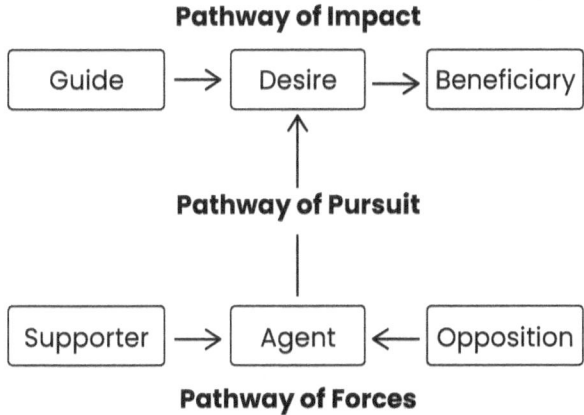

Figure 6.1. The Pathway of Forces with the Supporter and the Opposition in the StoriCompass.

Depending on the strength of support or opposition, we are either going to obtain our Desire or not. For example, in Cristina's case, her Desire in her words was "to be financially free and feel comfortable in who I am." She has both elements acting on her. Without her Supporter, her mom, she admitted she would have struggled to get back on her feet after the oppositional force, her ex-partner, not only eroded her sense of confidence and self but also robbed her of the funds she had invested in their joint business. The pain she went through could have crushed her, held her back, but with her mother's support, she looked ahead to rebuilding and obtaining her Desire.

The *Supporter* in the Pathway of Forces

Every woman's story grows with both guidance and support, sometimes from others, sometimes from within. The element of the *Supporter* in the StoriCompass facilitates progress; removes obstacles; and provides encouragement, tools, and/or insights. Without the Supporter, the Agent might remain stuck or uncertain, perhaps halted from obtaining their Desire.

Similar to the Guide, the Supporter can be both internal, external, or both:

* **Internal:** Our self-resources like grit, perseverance, compassion, patience, courage, and beliefs that remind us we're already enough and we can reach our Desires.
* **External:** An actual concrete person or entity, such as parents, friends, community support, books, etc. The external Supporter provides empathy, strength, knowledge, insight, and more when you feel stretched.
* **Both internal and external:** God, and sometimes we need to be our biggest cheerleader and show self-compassion, seeking out people or communities to help us to our desired state and/or outcome.

Sometimes the same person can be both a Guide and Supporter, like our parents. However, how they differ is that the Guide provides wisdom and motivation in a more directive role about where you're going and why. They take more of an authoritative stance. In contrast, the Supporter helps you keep going and remember who you are along the way. Guides and Supporters many times don't take the same role. For example, I used to look to my teachers as Guides and my friends as Supporters.

In my research, I found both Westerners and Easterners reported similar Supporters, but Westerners reported a higher number of Supporters than Easterners. This could be because of research findings that Westerners engage in a more elaborate self-narrating style and provide more information than Easterners. So, Westerners may simply talk more than Easterners, on average.

The most common Supporters, reported by both Westerners and Easterners, were "self, parent, mother, father, grandmother, sister, brother, extended family, friends, teacher, mentors, and partners."

For me, during my PhD journey, it was my husband, parents, and my mom-in-law who often stepped in to help with my children whenever I needed babysitting. My supervisor was a Supporter, as well as a Guide, empowering me along with the research. He is a world authority in my field of study, so he took that role as a Guide in teaching me, but he also supported me in terms of providing resources and being present to me as a supervisor. That is why he's both a Guide and Supporter in helping me reach my Desire to become a graduate scholar.

As I write this book, it's now my writers' group, supportive family and friends, editors, self-help books, and Julia Cameron's *The Artist's Way* that act as my Supporters. This book helped me reclaim momentum in writing daily, exactly as it helped Elizabeth Gilbert in her creative journey. Cameron's book helped me form a contract with myself to complete my Morning Pages and have Artist

Dates, along with having an accountability group of writers who were on the same path of becoming authors. My global gathering of creative friends who meet online most Thursdays have inspired me to continue with this book. Group members champion one another as we metamorphose into new identities as authors!

Every main character, whether in fictional or nonfictional works, has Supporters. If we turn to fiction, in the classics of literature, every plot had a protagonist with their supportive aides. In Jane Austen's *Pride and Prejudice*, Elizabeth Bennet had her sister Jane Bennet. In Charlotte Brontë's *Jane Eyre*, Jane had Helen Burns, Miss Temple, Diana and Mary Rivers. In Harper Lee's *To Kill a Mockingbird*, Scout (Jean Louise) Finch had her father Atticus Finch, and in J. R. R. Tolkien's *The Lord of the Rings*, Frodo had faithful Samwise Gamgee.

Even in real life stories, we see the same patterns. In Michelle Obama's *Becoming*, she had her mother Marian Robinson and her famous husband, Barack Obama. In her books, *The Gifts of Imperfection* and *Daring Greatly*, Brené Brown credits her therapist as well as her husband Steve as key Supporters in helping her on her path. She also has a sacred circle of friends. The poet and activist Amanda Gorman attributes her mother, Joan Wicks, her teachers, and community programs as her Supporters. There are important people and entities that have supported each of these significant figures in their lives to achieve greatness.

If you want to do anything great, the golden rule is make sure you have the right support around you, and also, make sure to be a Supporter for someone who needs help. However, many people struggle to ask for help and support, let alone accept it.

Why We Struggle to Accept Help and Support

Are you blocking your breakthroughs by not accessing support?

No one can really know if we are in need unless we open up and ask. Remember how Clara, in chapter 4, struggled so much with sleep deprivation that she went to see a psychiatrist? When she finally sought help and followed the doctor's advice, her brain fog lifted, and she gained an understanding of herself, which not only improved the quality of her life but also of her family. Yet, she struggled for almost a year before she sought help and support.

Why is it so hard for many women to ask for help? It may be because we fear rejection, or fear that we will be perceived as weak, or look like we're not coping. Or it could be we don't actually know where to turn. Whatever the reason, we all need Supporters in life. Supportive people, helpful beliefs and habits, and tools to help us gain knowledge that aids us in overcoming obstacles and moving closer to obtaining our Desire.

Cultural Viewpoints on Seeking Help

There may be cultural elements at play. Research shows the more individualistic someone is, the more self-reliant they are. People in individualistic cultures like the US, UK, and Australia tend to value independence, autonomy, and personal responsibility. They've internalized beliefs like, "I should handle it myself," or "Asking for help is a weakness." In Australia, we often say, "She'll be right, mate," and let women carry these heavy loads all by themselves, when it's not right.

On the other hand, collectivistic cultures encourage members to rely on each other for help. It's a way of life that gets so ingrained. I grew up like that in East Timor, when we all lived in a community, and in Portugal, in commission flats.

Our community helped each other. Our extended family were

always in each other's pockets, giving advice or physical support whenever there was need. I love that about our culture, and our elders still encourage that. Unfortunately, the longer we've lived in the West, the more I can see each of us, especially younger ones, becoming more individualistic and looking after our nuclear families. We become more hesitant to reach out to extended family members and rely on friends who we've built our communities around.

Asking for help is not a sign of weakness but a show of strength. It shows we have the courage to admit we have come to the ends of our means and we need external support.

In many Western cultures, we have come to accept that seeking help from anyone—including professional mental health workers such as myself—is not weakness, it is a strength. Unfortunately, this is still a challenge in some Eastern collectivistic cultures like mine, where seeking help for psychological problems is often stigmatized: "Problems should be kept in the family, not spread out in the world to strangers!"

In some Eastern cultures, like Sanhydra's, mentioned in chapter 2, there is also a narrative glorifying self-sacrifice, especially for women. She shared her sense of isolation with me and the expectations she felt as an Indian woman and mother: "We're supposed to be the caretakers, the ones who prioritize other's needs over our own, so to ask for help may be like a failure to fulfil our expected role."

Handling It All

We may worry that if we seek help, we will be perceived as incompetent, weak, or overly emotional. Especially professional women. However, Sheryl Sandberg, author of *Lean In: Women, Work, and the Will to Lead*, asked women to push forward by enlisting support to navigate leadership, motherhood, and corporate life. She advocated for women helping each other, particularly in male-dominated environments.

The fear that reaching out for help may damage credibility or career prospects is very real. Accompanying this is that many women have internalized the belief they should be able to "handle it all," which is a result of perfectionism and high expectations we've placed upon ourselves. The "Superwoman" image that some women project may be their undoing because it becomes harder to admit vulnerability when one needs help. Sandberg pointed this out in her book, *Lean In*, the "do it all" mentality and expectation is unrealistic and harmful, leading to burnout, guilt, and self-doubt.

Deep down, some of us women may not have trusted people. Nor do we feel safe around, let alone feel we can be vulnerable with others. Or we may have experienced rejections, so we don't want to be in that situation again. We'd rather suffer alone and get through it by ourselves.

Taking the Chance to Trust

It's important to realize that not all people are the same; past experiences may not repeat. We can take another chance. We can't change anyone, so we might as well not try to.

It's better to invest energy and effort in changing our Selves.

Even when changing ourselves, it's better to enlist each other's help. We can and are able to carry each other's burdens. I believe we have been naturally designed this way. That being burden-bearers is a wonderful way of showing we are all interrelated and need each other. It is a web of mutual support and encouragement that enables the strength of the individual and of the group. That's how communities thrive. We all have unique skills, knowledge, and expertise. When we work together, contribute to the web that connects us all, we are much better for it.

Identifying and Enlisting Your Supporters

What do you need to get to your desired state or outcome? What support do you require to achieve your life goals? These two questions help you clarify the Supporters you're seeking. Feel free to make a list of internal, external, and/or both. Is it a mentor or supervisor to help you upskill in your work? Is it a babysitter so you could have more free time to work on projects you want to accomplish? Is it a friend who you need emotional support from? A therapist you need to help you work through underlying issues? Or is it that you need to speak to yourself in an uplifting and kind way to encourage yourself that you can do it?

Write down the support you require to fulfil your deep core needs and be on your way to obtaining that lifelong goal, those desires you have been seeking. For example, in writing this book, I needed beta readers and editors. They are people with experience and skillsets that guarantee I will meet my goals of completing this book well. How did I go about this and how did I know who to turn to, especially when choosing the right editors? I reached out. For beta readers, I asked friends, family, and colleagues for time and support. I've always lived with the mantra, "If you don't ask, you don't get!" To find good editors, I asked professionals in the field, authors who have already published. I did due diligence in researching. I googled suggested editors and read reviews about them. It was important to vet out whom I thought would be an appropriate fit for me in my nonfiction genre.

Through this process, I developed a simple approach to identifying and securing the support I needed:

1. **Know** what support I need to get to my Desire.
2. **Research** what is available.
3. **Identify** from the research who could be the best fit.
4. **Trust is key.** Do I have the confidence they will support me? (This is when I rely on my internal sense of intuition and external research of the credibility and quality of support.)
5. **Ask for help.** I made my needs known to people, and I was so surprised at how willing they were to help.

To ask for the right kind of support, it's important to be clear about what you want and when you want it. Then, give the person or group clear instructions on how you want them to help. Be specific, so they and you know what the support looks like and when everyone will be satisfied. Because to offer and receive help and support are the most important relationship-building exercises we can all engage with. Fostering connections meets a core need in every one of us for relating and finding significance. We all need meaningful connections.

When Support Is Not Support

Each one of us needs to recognize the signs that someone's "support" is holding us back rather than lifting us up. We sometimes sense this in our gut, pick up on some kind of injustice or get a feeling that something's not quite right. Maybe, you can't even get a sentence in any more in a conversation, or this person doesn't listen to you in favor of giving you unsolicited advice. Your feelings, your ideas, are not heard or validated. The whole narrative or focus is on the person supposedly meant to be your Supporter, and it's no longer about helping you reach your Desire. When you reach that point, pull away. Politely decline the support and know that you're better off without it!

As a mother and therapist, I am always mindful of the ways parents enable codependency in their children. Children can feel so helpless and frustrated that, by adulthood, they have not launched. They are not independent. Unfortunately, they haven't been given freedom to explore and experience the process and steps to learn and steady their own two feet toward independence, if parents shield their children from learning the consequences of their behavior. For example, if children do not do chores or remember what they need for school without any repercussions, then they never learn that actions, or the lack of them, have consequences. Children need to experience these consequences and make their own mistakes so they can learn from them in a loving environment and grow into healthy adults.

We need to shift from dependence to *interdependence*, building self-trust while still valuing support. All help should point us to interdependence. Whenever a Supporter offers more dependence on them, you're sure to find yourself eventually developing codependence. The help they provide should ground you in your interdependence and eventual independence.

Whom Can You Support?

Another question is: Are we also meeting others' needs? Being there for people as their Supporters? Reciprocity and the universal law of sowing and reaping is important. Unless we are sowing kindness, goodness, care, and love, it's hard to reap these same rewards in our lives. Others won't be as willing to help if we aren't a Supporter for them. The best way to assess whether we're supporting others enough is simply to ask if they feel supported and, if not, what else could help them feel that way.

You Don't Have to Be and Do This Alone

For so much of our lives, we can live in loneliness and feel unloved. We can feel there are walls around us, and it's hard to penetrate the barrier that connects us vulnerably to others. We feel helpless to know what to do, angry that nothing really changes in our lives, and powerless to break through barriers that stop us from reaching that place of plenty, of abundance, of love, of acceptance, of freedom. That is what our Desire may represent: a symbol of worth, of freedom, of being valued deep within our core.

We don't have to be or do life alone. As Cristina, Clara, myself, and others have found, Supporters are around to help us reach our Desire.

Life is more meaningful when we are in relationships, in connection, and offering each other our gifts of support.

If you're stuck anywhere in your life right now, think whom you can enlist as your Supporter. Think of what kind of help you need, exactly, to move closer to obtaining your Desire.

Sometimes, it's simply another pair of listening ears, or a shoulder to cry on, someone or something to help you recharge. Sometimes, the mere presence of the other person who is there for us is enough to connect us again with our strength, knowing we aren't alone in this. We have support. It's time to move forward and tackle our obstacles!

Key Takeaways

* The Pathway of Forces shows the influences that help us reach our Desire, as the Supporter, or inhibit reaching our Desire, as the Opposition.

* The Supporter facilitates progress, removes obstacles, and provides encouragement, tools, and insights.

* Supporters can be internal (grit, perseverance, self-compassion, etc.) or external (individuals, communities, etc.) or both (God).

Deeper Actions

Reflect (and if you like, journal) on the following questions:

1. Who are the Supporters in your life right now—the people, communities, and networks that genuinely help you move toward your dreams, desires, and goals—and how are you showing up as your own Supporter?

2. When you look back to the times you achieved something meaningful, which Supporters made the biggest difference, and what inner strengths or qualities did you draw on within yourself?

3. If you fully stepped into being your strongest Supporter, what would you be saying to yourself, doing for yourself, or putting in place to help yourself succeed?

7

Who or What's Standing in Your Way? (*The Opposition*)

The obstacle is the path.

—Adapted from Zen teachings/traditional proverb

Be like water. It flows around obstacles, not against them.

—Adapted from Bruce Lee

Aylin experienced more obstacles than most women did as a single mother. Yet, as she reflected in her interview with me, these difficult circumstances forged strength and passion in her life.

We met Aylin in chapter 5, when it was hard for her to share her story. Brought up traditionally Turkish, she had borne her share of pain and struggles. Losing her father was monumental during her teenage years. Later, she ran from the toxic relationship with her husband to build her life as a single mom. She never expected it would be other women who tried to block her success. Then more obstacles followed. This is what she shared in her own words.

AYLIN

It was out of desperation. I was a single mom and had a four-year-old. I started in real estate first. Then the bank. Then I moved up very, very quickly. But that's where I had my first encounter. Funny enough, it was actually the women that stood in my way, women who didn't make me part of a team because I was doing better. They were very threatened, to the point where I said to my manager, "Please don't put my scores up; please don't. Don't say how well I've done in front of the team. I just can't do that anymore." And it's because I was trying so hard to be accepted.

For me, it just comes naturally, but I was hungry. I wanted it, to earn my little bonuses. I could remember getting a parking ticket, and I remember crying my eyes out. After the fine, there was only a dollar to spare for two weeks. And I thought, "What the hell?" I remember crying. Those things, you know, don't leave you.

I was at the bank for seven years, but throughout, I just got promoted and promoted. I mean different areas, to the point where I went "OK, I might try something else," and I went and did finance brokerage, and then I got picked up by another company.

I knew my stuff inside out, never once did a broker go, "Oh, you said this would go through, but it didn't; it got declined."

In those seven years, I felt like I earned their respect. Even today, I get people reminding me of how awesome I was. So, you have to be a standout in your job, and I think growing up, I learned that you have to be a standout.

I got headhunted to be a state manager for another position. Now, this is the next level, so to speak.

It turned out to be a horrible, horrible experience. My manager, I suppose, was a narcissistic, horrible, male chauvinistic show-off. They hired me because I had built my brand up. And then it was so hard under him. He started to chip away at my personality, "Oh, that's not the way to talk. That's not the way that we do it." He eroded my confidence.

The place also was very institutionalized, and to the point where I was always looking behind my shoulder. I was self-conscious. I started questioning myself. I was saying I wasn't good enough. I'm, you know, all this sort of stuff. I held out there for about a year and nine months, until something else fell in my lap. Again, that was because employers called around, looking for someone, and apparently my name kept on popping up.

I accidentally bumped into my current company CEO at a session, and he offered me my current job just because of my personality on the spot. No interview. Nothing.

He knew my track record. He loved my go-getter attitude. He loved that. He said, "I see you walking, your energy, everyone's like trying to push through people to give you a hug." You know, because that's the person I've become now.

Through her tribulations, Aylin echoes in this chapter the insights of both Carl Jung, the Swiss psychiatrist and psychologist, and Maya Angelou, the American memoirist, poet, and activist: you will face setbacks that may feel like defeat, but they have no power to define who you are.

Adversity merely introduces you to yourself, and in that moment of choice, you decide who you will become.

In this chapter, we cover the Oppositions in our lives and learn how they teach us wisdom and build strength. Aylin is now a very successful corporate executive directing teams of hundreds in the finance industry. We learn from Aylin's life that, despite the hard stuff—the other women threatened by her success, the insecure manager who undermined her, the toxic institutional culture, and her internal worries that she was an imposter who would be found out—she persevered through the pain and struggles. She continued to stand out, to build her personal brand, to connect with others in her industry. She is now in a position where she feels valued and seen for her talents. All those tears, they had not been shed in vain. Her life shows us that to get to the top, we need to build the strength to climb over various obstacles along the way.

The *Opposition* in the Pathway of Forces

In the StoriCompass, the element of *Opposition* is a vital part of the narrative. It's not necessarily a villain, but it is any force that gets in the way of the Agent obtaining their Desire.

Like many of the other elements the Opposition can be internal, external, or both.

* **Internal:** What is internally produced such as limiting beliefs, self-doubt, fears, etc. It could also be painful memories from trauma that creates resistance or obstacles for the Agent to overcome in order to obtain the Desire.

* **External:** Circumstances and life events from outside of us over which we have no control, like the loss of a loved one, job loss, war, famine, natural disasters, etc. It could also be people or organizations, such as a toxic boss, an unjust system, racial discrimination, or cultural expectations, etc.

* **Both:** Internal Oppositions that might be introduced and/or reinforced by external ones. For example, limiting beliefs and self-doubt may be sustained by a toxic boss and unjust system, as in Aylin's example.

Becoming aware and identifying the sources of our internal and external Oppositions can mean the difference between a successful outcome—obtaining our Desire—and an unsuccessful one, in which we are stuck in an ever-repeating cycle of stagnation.

Each of us needs to expect Opposition. It is part of the flow of living, and whatever life throws at us, we can adopt the mindset that we have the capacity to cope. So far, we have all survived trauma, pain, and struggle. New situations are no different; we will survive.

Research on Oppositions

In my research, participants reported a breadth of Oppositions that included self, family, parents, siblings, girlfriends, school teachers, limited finances, death of a loved one, marriage breakdown, social issues, and conflicts within cultures or communities. What is interesting is that events can also be seen as Opposition, especially when they are negative, such as a breakup, health problem, or injury.

I found that the Opposition was the least-mentioned element of the life story structure in the interviews, possibly because people may find it hard to disclose personal conflicts in their lives. There was also a cultural difference in that Westerners reported Self as an Opposition more than Easterners. Westerners often expressed themselves as a hindrance to obtaining their goals.

In self-development, the Opposition often symbolizes the narratives we've inherited that keep us stuck, internalized oppressive beliefs such as "I'm not enough," or "They'll think bad of me." Unconscious habits or fears blocking growth, such as fear of success or an avoidance of opening up to other people.

In the StoriCompass, the Opposition enables you to understand yourself better through the challenges and hurdles that you face on your journey. The Opposition shows up in several ways. In Aylin's work situation, her Opposition initially was the threatened women, but when she got the parking ticket and realized how close she was to not being able to support herself and her son, her concern about her coworkers' reactions left her. She understood there was a part of her that wanted to be accepted by them. However, once she was able to name the real situation—that those women were jealous of her success and would likely never accept her as long as she continued to do her best—this clarity transformed her pain into focused awareness on her most important goal: succeeding for herself and her son. What the jealous women thought was not relevant to her priorities, but it took her feeling the discomfort of their opposition to realize that.

Oppositions in our lives often reveal core values and inner tensions. For instance, navigating family conflicts may expose competing identities. Our identity as a loyal and dutiful daughter and/or partner may conflict with our identity as a hard-driving, successful businesswoman with personal financial and career goals. Or our experience with burnout may show us that working long and hard at the expense of our mental and physical health is not actually a priority for us; a different life where we get to enjoy a calmer, peaceful, simpler way is more important to us.

Aylin experienced inner tension between wanting acceptance from her team and needing to succeed and shine in order to provide her family with security. She also realized security was more important to her than being accepted by the coworkers who couldn't support her success.

Understanding our Opposition sharpens our sense of self.

---

*Conflict is often a mirror, showing us
who we are becoming.*

Embrace the Oppositions in Life

Oppositions give shape to our story. Without resistance, there's no transformation. Every plant that ever bloomed had to push through a whole lot of dirt; a caterpillar has to go through metamorphosis to become a beautiful butterfly. The friction we all go through is what gives the landscape of our lives texture and depth. Acknowledging the Opposition helps us frame adversity as meaningful, not random suffering, but a necessary tension in the arc of becoming. Think about it. Every compelling narrative—whether it's in movies, books, or real life—includes opposition. If there is no opposition, there is no triumph.

Naming an Opposition ignites purpose and fuels motivation. Many people find their life's mission in the thing they once had to overcome: transitions, injustice, shame, exclusion, etc. Like Colleen found her purpose in helping young mothers navigate life transitions after she had survived many of her own. The Opposition becomes not only an obstacle, but the force that forges our calling. It can turn wounds into sources of drive, resilience, and meaning, as it did in my life.

Finally, understanding the Opposition in our life helps us to stop over-functioning, people-pleasing, or avoiding conflict simply to keep the peace. Aylin found her attempts to please her female colleagues undermined her more important goals of providing a good life for herself and her child. She identified her main priority through the tension she found at work. Our conflicts teach us boundaries, strategy, and discernment. We begin to set better boundaries after we've been hurt, and we engage with more emotional intelligence. Even when the Opposition is self-sabotage, perfectionism, or an unhealthy system, once we tackle it, awareness leads to better strategies and choices.

Redemptive Stories

According to psychologist Dan McAdams, in his research on life stories, when we experience a challenging situation, perhaps a place with so many obstacles we can't even see the way forward, but we eventually overcome our challenges, these are called *redemptive narratives*. Redemptive narratives link to greater achievement, health outcomes, and well-being. In other words, if we can see our redemptive stories, we do better mentally and physically than if we see the negative parts of our stories.

Why do we love stories of redemption, of overcoming odds? From my perspective, these stories give us hope and inspiration. To create our redemptive story, we need to identify the Opposition in our lives. With this in mind, we can work out the underlying issues and obstacles that operate in our lives and think of them as redemptive stories rather than tragedies.

Who or What Are Your Oppositions in Life?

It's the hard stuff that prepared Sarai, who we met in chapter 4, for her role as a director of a large health facility. She also fled her marriage because her ex was abusive. As a single mother, she leaned into her faith and hard work to overcome hurdles. She is now one of the leaders in her field. This is her story of Opposition.

SARAI

As soon as I got there, I met up with the man I would marry. We had met back in Zimbabwe. He also moved to the UK, and you know, I fell pregnant.

My firstborn son came during my first year of college. But I kind of carried on with university. I wanted to do geography and environmental science, but then you had to pay school fees. I had some of my friends there; we were quite lucky that they all moved to England. The majority of them were like, you know, if you do nursing, it's better because you get paid for bursary. And I'm like, no, I don't want to do that because I don't want to deal with blood and everything. I was like, well, I can do mental health nursing. Psychiatric nursing is pretty different. So anyway...I decided to do mental health nursing. I did three years at the university. And luckily enough, when I finished, I was able to get a job, but obviously I was married then.

Trying to juggle parenthood, university, and working, you know, having a mortgage as well. So, in terms of my married life, there was a little bit of an age gap... eight years or something like that. But there was a lot of domestic abuse—that's what I experienced quite a lot. There were moments I even wanted to divorce him back in the UK. It was hard. When you're kind of caught up in the cycle of domestic abuse, sometimes you don't realize how extensive that was.

It was pretty difficult, and there were two occasions...like, police involvement. And my son was quite young and probably kind of witnessed the violence. Back then, I did endure because I wanted to have an intact family. Because coming from a broken family, I really wanted to make sure my kids grew up with two parents together in a loving environment and everything. But yeah, my ex-husband just struggled with a lot of impulse control. He was just triggered by little things.

So, in my early years of marriage, back in England...there were cycles of serious domestic abuse, either resulting in blood, bleeding gums, or all sorts of police involvement. But then, you could call the police, and they'd say, "OK, do you want us to charge your husband?" And I'm like...you think about the kids...and I said, "Oh, please, don't charge him." So, you get plugged back into that cycle.

So, there were a lot of these times.

My mom was still alive back in Zimbabwe. And I would call her, and she would say, "You need to leave that man." Because when I reconnected with my mom, it was really good getting to know her. She was a smart lady because she went to high school, university, after having a child, got married. She got an amazing job—a very, very smart woman.

So, it was nice, being able to speak to my mom and correspond with her. It was in my young adulthood. This was after Year 12. That's when I kind of met her, and then we were spending time together.

So yes, she knew this was happening, but she was very supportive. She said, "You need to leave your husband. You need to leave him. It's not OK."

But again, I would just say, "OK."

Then again, I've got, like, uncles back in the UK, and I remember they would come and just try to resolve things. But you know, like our culture—coming from Zimbabwe—sometimes people don't realize the impact of domestic violence when that's happening. And they don't look at it like there's a justification to say, "You know what? I'm leaving this relationship because my mental health is struggling."

My uncles just said, "Sometimes it happens. You just need to hang on and see. You'll be fine." But anyway, I kind of suffered through it, and he'd just apologize like, "You know, I just lost it," or something like that. And then the cycle would repeat again.

So, I kind of endured, and then I finished uni. I remember I got a job straight away. And it was really good because I was able to get a promotion in terms of stepping up into a senior role, which he didn't like. So, he would just come up with obstacles. If there was an opportunity for me to step up into another job, he'd be like, "Oh, if you do that, what's going to happen to the kids?" or something like that. Then he would say, "We can support each other. We can do this." So anyway, I kept on.

Usually, they say you have to be very careful of the person that you marry, or they can be a hindrance to you, when I was growing up. It's true. I'm a grown-up now, finally I can make my own decisions, so I need to be better at setting boundaries.

So, after a while, the abuse started again, and I couldn't stay anymore. I used to feel like I was in prison. We divorced.

What stopped me for years, you know, was my marriage situation. My ex-husband was a hindrance. He was a stumbling block and telling you reasons why things couldn't happen. We have a better relationship now in terms of coparenting because he has moved on, so we still support each other with looking after our boys, even though they're a bit more grown-up. So, it's helping each other to do that, which is good.

At the moment, I'm just trying to be strategic. I'm a single mom. My young son, he's finishing school next year. So, I'm in a full-time demanding job, working as a director. We've got so many responsibilities, so obviously it takes a lot out of me. Even when you're not at work, you're really at work. The buck stops with you.

Sarai's difficult beginning and her entire life has been a real struggle. Her ex-husband was an Opposition for many years in their marriage, which unfortunately was sustained by her culture's expectations to stay in the marriage, especially from her uncles. Yet, despite the domestic abuse and pain she endured, meeting her and seeing her resilience and strength, I can attest she now embodies joy and success. Against all odds, she has climbed high. Her journey reinforces the truth of an African proverb: "Smooth seas do not make skillful sailors."

Our Oppositions come to all of us like a double-edged sword.

On one side, they can cut us—cause pain or discomfort, force us to face internal resistance, or point out those who don't support us in our journey—but on the other side, they can release us by offering options for choosing how we want our life to go, and for meeting these internal and external hurdles. Facing our Oppositions can be challenging, but it can also give us the tools and strength we need to reach our goals.

Research by McAdams and his colleagues has found that those who choose the redemptive path—stories that reflect the journey from challenge to triumph, bad to good—are better adjusted, with life success. Those who tell their stories as stories of tragedy, not acknowledging the triumphs along the way, have poorer outcomes.

We never get a choice about our life; we are born into a time and place with the families we have. However, once we have the faculties to make decisions, the choice is ours to make regarding how we live our lives. Like Aylin and Sarai, who chose to keep standing out and building a better life and future for themselves and their children.

Identifying Your Internal and External Oppositions

Women over the years have faced enormous challenges and endured much. Despite our long suffering, we are still the heart of every culture. As women, we hold and give birth to new life, new ideas, and new ways of thinking and being in this world that ultimately create better futures for each person. That is my hope, my dream.

In order for us as women to realize our dreams, we need to identify what is stopping us from obtaining our ideal selves, goals, and desires. Is it limiting beliefs, gripping fear, lack of awareness of ones' values or drive? Or is it external, such as an insecure manager or structural, cultural, and/or social barriers?

One of the most powerful tools all of us have is the capacity for self-awareness. Self-awareness is the key to any change. Without an awareness of where we are blocked, what our limiting beliefs are, what we truly fear, or what our underlying issues are, it's hard to know how to face our Oppositions and step out of them and into solutions.

Once you identify which Oppositions may be at play, it's easier to make informed decisions about how to tackle your situation. Whether that is to form an alliance with other women to tackle structural, cultural, and social barriers; to change industries or roles; to choose one's family structure accordingly; or to lobby at the government level. Change is possible.

In 2011, Saudi Arabia still expected women to be subject to male guardianship, limiting their mobility, freedom, and legal rights. They had one of the world's most restrictive policies against women, a ban on female drivers. However, then–thirty-two-year-old Manal al-Sharif became internationally known after a video of her driving in Saudi Arabia was posted on social media in defiance of the ban. She was arrested and detained for nine days, drawing global attention to the issue. Her act catalyzed the #Women2Drive movement in Saudi Arabia. Although she was initially vilified by conservatives and exiled from her country, she continued to speak out globally.

In 2018, Saudi Arabia officially lifted the ban on women driving, which was a significant and practical victory.

It's important for women to uphold and support each other to expose the biases that undermine who they are, for women are the heart of culture.

Biases are deeply ingrained in society and are perpetuated by men and women alike.

Racial bias, unfortunately, is still a significant issue. I've tasted its poison, as have other colored women like Tre, who shared how

Black women in the United States are characterized, and which she had to persevere through while working in many toxic corporate cultures. Sarai also shared about the racism she experienced while living and working in both the United Kingdom and Australia.

Breaking Free

Some of our darkest traumas and ugliest experiences and memories become the parts of us that want to tie us to the past. However, there comes a point in each of our lives where the desire to move forward, to obtain what we want, is so great that we break free. We can find strength in our stories about facing challenges. And this strength—and reframing those negative or undermining messages from past experiences—helps us take action toward our Desires.

Desire, when it is in the forefront of our conscious and subconscious mind, gives us the power to seek fulfilment, as our subconscious seeks resolution for the tension between our Desire and reality. Think of a time when you've wanted something so badly that you've worked hard to attain it. That is because we are designed that way; our subconscious mind seeks tension resolution. How can you obtain this Desire so your tension is lessened? When we experience blocks to attain this Desire, we need to identify the blocks—the Oppositions—so we understand how to tackle obstacles. Thus, we move towards tension resolution.

Breaking free involves making the decision to act and taking consistent action each day, putting one step in front of the other even if we feel scared or insecure. Even though at times we may get knocked down and feel like we've moved backward more than we've moved forward, we use our stories of resilience to give us the strength to get back up. Life is like that. We may feel like giving up, but we persist because we know our values, and we know what kind of life we want. Eventually, the forward steps we take bring us to our Desires.

Learning from our Mistakes

Some of us have made wrong choices and decisions, which cause regret, loss, and pain. Whether that be financial, relational, or career choices, your poor decisions may present as an Opposition in your StoriCompass in obtaining our Desire. However, we can all learn from these mistakes and still overcome them.

Acknowledge the mistake for what it was. We all make mistakes. But from this day onward, you can decide not to keep making it. What have you learned from this mistake? Write down the mistake or wrong choice and what you learned from it. Promise yourself you have taken the lesson to heart. Pick yourself up. Dust off every negative thought or feeling associated with that mistake. Arm yourself with that experience, and it will now be wisdom in your guidebook. It will be the wisdom gained through your experiences that guide you to overcome pitfalls when you see them, and even to help others avoid the same pitfalls.

Build a community of Supporters to ensure you don't repeat the mistake. Raise your head high. Then take a step forward. You are wiser, smarter, and more experienced from this day. This is what Aylin and Sarai learned through owning their life story. There is no failure if there's learning. Your mistake is now part of your redemptive story!

Key Takeaways

* The Opposition is any force that gets in the way of the Agent (you or me) from obtaining what is desired.
* Oppositions can be internal (limiting beliefs, self-doubt, etc.) or external (negative life events, people, etc.) or both.
* Expect and embrace Opposition because it is part of the flow of living; Oppositions shape our stories and character.

Deeper Actions

Reflect on (and/or write in your journal) your answers to the following questions:

1. When you picture your dream or deepest Desire, what inner voice, doubt, or belief immediately tells you it's not possible, and where do you think that voice comes from?
2. What people, systems, or circumstances outside of you make it harder for you to move toward your dreams, and how do they influence your choices?
3. If neither those inner voices nor those external barriers had power over you, what would you dare to do differently today?

8

What Does Your Life Look Like? (*Your Story Frame*)

> *I want, by understanding myself,
> to understand others.*
>
> —Katherine Mansfield

> *Life can only be understood backwards;
> but it must be lived forwards.*
>
> —Søren Kierkegaard

In the late 1990s and early 2000s, neuroscientist Marcus Raichle and his team at Washington University School of Medicine in Saint Louis were studying task-based activity using functional MRI (fMRI), a machine that scans people's brains while they perform a task, like solving a problem. Researchers used the brain scans while the subjects solved a problem and compared those scans to periods of "rest" where they stared at a fixed point.

While analyzing fMRI data, Raichle noticed something odd. Brain activity didn't drop to zero during rest, which scientists expected. Instead, certain brain areas were consistently more active when the subjects were not engaged in a task.

Puzzled by these findings, Raichle and his team started to ask why certain brain regions were showing more activity when their subjects were not performing a task. Could the brain have a baseline mode of functioning, rather than simply going "offline" during rest? What kind of mental activity happened during these so-called "resting" periods?

These questions led them to be the first in identifying the brain's baseline mode of functioning, which they called the Default Mode Network (DMN), and uncovering that the brain is never truly at rest. It's always constructing meaning, reflecting, simulating, and remembering.

Published in 2001, their landmark findings redefined how we understand consciousness, showing that the brain has a natural tendency to generate narrative, meaning, and identity when left to wander.

They found that the DMN is a network of interacting brain regions which include core regions like the medial prefrontal cortex (mPFC) (involved in self-referential thinking), posterior cingulate cortex (PCC) (involved in autobiographical memory), precuneus (which plays a role in various cognitive processes like visual imagery, self-processing, and consciousness), angular gyrus (involved in language and meaning), and the hippocampus (involved in memory formation and retrieval).

You can think of these regions of the brain—the DMN—as your internal narrator; it's the part of your mind that asks the questions "Who am I? How did I get here? What do I want? Why did that happen to me?"

It runs in the background like an internal film editor, constantly sorting through your life experiences and trying to make a story out of them. Whether you're replaying an old memory, imagining a conversation that hasn't happened, or wondering what life means, that's the DMN at work.

In this chapter, you will learn how the DMN and StoriCompass can work together. Your DMN and the StoriCompass are powerful in giving you insight into your life's landscape. As the internal narrator, the mind tends to follow recognizable story frameworks or arcs that make sense of experiences. Seeing your life as a story structure or frame with all the different pathways and elements enables you to understand where you are at each of the pivotal points of your life. It enables you to gain a bird's-eye view to navigate forward. Having mapped what your life looks like, you can proceed to move beyond your cultural script and then create the life you want to live, with joy, meaning, and legacy. First though, it's important to understand how your DMN works.

How the DMN Works in Real Life

To illustrate how the DMN works, think back to Aylin, who we met in chapters 5 and 7, the Turkish Australian single mom who forged a successful career by climbing the corporate ladder. If you recall, before she changed careers, she felt unfulfilled in her real estate job but didn't know what she truly wanted. During this ambivalent period of her life, she read books, updated her resume, and attended webinars about career-change, but nothing clicked. Her task-focused brain connected with her networks, but she still felt stuck, disconnected from deeper motivation.

Frustrated one day, she took a walk. She asked herself, *Why am I doing all this? What have I always loved?*

As she walked, her medial prefrontal cortex started reflecting on her values and identity. Her hippocampus pulled up childhood memories of counting money for her mom and visiting the homes of Turkish community members with her dad, a leader in their community, to offer assistance and support. Her precuneus imagined a life where she helped people sort out their finances. Her posterior cingulate cortex made the connections.

"I've always found meaning in helping people by lending them a hand with their finances."

Her DMN did its work unconsciously, not through force but

through quiet, internal story weaving. Neuroscientists have found that most of the internal narrative construction by the DMN is automatic and unconscious, but when we use deliberate self-reflection and narrative thinking, ideas emerge into our consciousness.

One evening, it hit Aylin: "I don't just want another job. I want to do something worthwhile in the community by helping others build their financial futures." That insight resonated deeply within and gave her a new vision for her life. Later, she saw an ad for a job at a bank, and she applied. She got the job, which led to starting afresh in a career that utilized her interest in finances and in helping others. She worked hard, because she found a career she genuinely enjoyed, and rose in the ranks until she reached her current position as an executive. Back then, her DMN helped her align her memories, values, identity, and imagination into a new narrative, which she is now living.

The DMN works best when we're not forcing it. Breakthroughs come to us in rest, reflection, and creativity, not when we're grinding harder, but when we relax and give the inner narrator a chance to speak.

Oftentimes in my life, I get wisdom or "Aha!" moments when I am driving on the freeway alone, showering, running, swimming, or housecleaning. When my mind is at rest doing mundane chores or activities, creativity strikes. Ideas, words, insights for writing my stories or about my life float up from the corners of my mind. Purpose and meaning build. I trust the inner wisdom within and without.

My DMN incorporates all my lived experiences, values, beliefs, and faith to provide those insightful moments and allow me to build a sense of myself as a creative person, and as the creator of my life story.

How the DMN Varies in Each Person

One of the many roles in my psychological career, which I still enjoy very much, is assessing people's learning. I work with neurodivergent children and adults who have diagnoses of autism spectrum disorder (ASD), attention-deficit hyperactivity disorder (ADHD), depression, learning disorders, and more. They constantly amaze me with their abilities and resilience despite their learning and emotional struggles.

Scientists have found the DMN functions differently between neurotypical and neurodivergent brains, especially in conditions like ASD, ADHD, and depression. These differences affect how people experience self-awareness, social connection, imagination, and internal narrative.

In neurotypical people, the DMN activates at rest, for example, when daydreaming or self-reflecting. It supports autobiographical memory, sorting out identity and moral reasoning, simulates future scenarios, and enables a continuity of self. It deactivates appropriately when we shift to external, task-focused activities; like writing an email, known as task-induced deactivation.

In contrast, in neurodivergent brains, such as those on the autism spectrum, scientists found reduced connectivity within the DMN, especially between the medial prefrontal cortex and posterior cingulate cortex. This means neurodivergent people may have challenges with self-reflection, imagining others' perspectives (what psychologists call "theory of mind"), and narrative coherence. The airport scene from the movie *Rain Man* captures this beautifully. When the autistic character Raymond fixates on exact times and airline-safety rules (insisting they can only fly Qantas), can't name how he feels, doesn't infer that his young brother Charlie's goal is to reach LA quickly, and recounts the situation as scattered details rather than a clear, cause-and-effect story.

People on the autism spectrum also find difficulty switching between the DMN and task mode. Therefore, in ASD individuals, it's as if the internal narrator is less integrated or synced with the social world, making self- and other-reflection more effortful or fragmented. Their brain processes information differently, with strengths in visual detail and spatial reasoning. Temple Grandin, a prominent animal science professor with ASD, shared that her thinking is primarily visual, and that language comes to her second.

The DMN works differently, as well, for individuals with attention and hyperactivity issues. People with ADHD often have an overactive or poorly regulated DMN, even during focused tasks, which leads to mind-wandering, difficulty sustaining attention, and distractibility. They experience challenges in inhibiting internal thoughts when external focus is needed. Someone with ADHD may need to do a task for work but find themselves being continually distracted by thoughts and unable to sit down and focus on the task. This is why many with ADHD, such as Olympic gymnast Simone Biles, have turned to medication for help. When her medical records were leaked, she responded by telling the public that there was no shame in having ADHD or taking prescribed treatment, and that she refused to hide it.

In people suffering from depression, findings show hyper-connectivity and ruminative overactivation of the DMN. There is an excessive focus on self-critical thoughts, past regrets, and negative thought loops. Hence, depressed individuals have difficulty disengaging from internal narrative to act in the present. It's as if the person is stuck in a past time. In depression, the narrator becomes a relentless critic, playing the same negative messages over and over in an endless loop. Billie Eilish, the Grammy Award–winning singer, has been open about her struggles with depression. In a *Rolling Stone* interview, she described a particularly dark period when, in her journal, she wrote that even though she knew she was fortunate, she still felt deeply unhappy. This reflects a common experience of those with depression: achieving external success but feeling trapped by unhappiness and negative self-talk.

Where DMN functions differently in neurotypical and neurodivergent individuals, scientists are finding that a person's cultural background can also have an influence on how their DMN operates. In fact, culture plays a powerful role in shaping how the DMN activates, because the DMN is deeply tied to the self, memory, imagination, and social thinking, all of which are culturally constructed.

It's a question I have thought about extensively since I completed my PhD research. How do the cultures of our classrooms, schools, and workplaces shape both neurotypical and neurodivergent individuals? How can school and family cultures support children to develop healthy selves and DMNs, to grow up to be resilient, engaged adults?

These questions emerged from understanding cultural neuroscience research, which shows that individuals from different cultural backgrounds exhibit distinct patterns of DMN activity, particularly when engaging in self-reflection, thinking about others, moral reasoning, and narrative construction.

Through listening to hundreds of life stories, I suspected that these DMN patterns are linked to people's self-narrating styles (the way we talk about ourselves), which are influenced by whether a person's culture emphasizes individualism (the US, Australia, Western Europe) or collectivism (China, Japan, India, many African and Indigenous cultures). For example, research has found that people in individualistic cultures use first-person pronouns like "I" more frequently, while those in collectivistic cultures prefer first-person plural pronouns like "We". I have often wondered how our local cultures—family, schools, community groups, and workplaces—shape our DMN patterns as ethnic and national cultures do.

Neuroscientists, using neuroimaging, found that in individualistic cultures, the DMN, especially the medial prefrontal cortex, shows stronger activation when a person thinks about their Self as an autonomous individual. In contrast, in those from more collectivist cultures, the same brain regions activate similarly when people think about the Self and their connection to close others, like family.

What these neuroimaging results show is that Chinese participants—Chinese culture being collectivist—blur the boundary between Self and others in their DMN responses. Because the DMN supports creation of personal stories, cultural differences influence how an individual structures their life stories, whether the narrative is linear versus cyclical, and whether the narrative is focused on individual stories or stories about interconnectedness. It could also lead to different emotional responses to life situations, such as prioritizing personal achievement over harmony in relationships, as well as different meanings for success, failure, and growth. These findings highlight culture's influence on our lives.

StoriCompass: The Landscape of Our Lives

Each and every one of us, like the women whose stories you've read, has unique life challenges, whether we are neurotypical or neurodivergent, from Western or Eastern cultures, or have other influences. Our challenges and lived experiences deepen the terrains of our individual story's landscape. Some terrains are rougher than others, but each is special in its own right and adds to the richness of diversity in our world. The Default Mode Network is unique to each person's story landscape, the life each of us is creating and living.

Knowing the DMN is the brain's story builder that links past, present, and future to create a coherent sense of Self, we can use the StoriCompass tool to see the structure of our life story, which becomes the frame of our lives. As values are the foundation of the house, the elements of the StoriCompass are the frames that give our life stories form and shape. We can use the three pathways and six elements to explore internal scripts and recurring patterns to deconstruct and re-author our personal narrative. Later in the chapter, I'll include a graphical representation of the StoriCompass and provide examples.

Each pathway of the StoriCompass activates the DMN to encourage deep narrative processing. The Pathway of Pursuit—with the Agent-Desire relationship—prompts the DMN to reflect on personal goals, agency, and identity. The Pathway of Impact—with the Guide-Beneficiary relationship—explores formative experiences, cultural inheritance, motivations, and memory, as well as invites moral reasoning, deeper purpose, and future vision. Lastly, the Pathway of Forces—with the Supporter-Opposition relationship—activates autobiographical memory and emotional meaning-making to enable reframing of life experiences, social connections, and limiting beliefs.

To illustrate this, let's look at Tessa, whom we met in chapter 1. When she mapped out her Pathway of Forces with the Supporter and Opposition in her story, she began to notice a disturbing pattern: "Why do I keep gravitating to my mother and husband for help and casting myself as my own worst enemy?" That question arose from within her DMN, which helps her integrate everything she's experienced and everything she knows about herself. And when she asks, "What is my Desire now? What do I really want besides seeing my children succeed?" she is engaging in future self-imagining, a core DMN function.

The StoriCompass provides the *life frame* (the story structure of one's life), and the DMN supplies the content and emotional resonance. Understanding this, we can appreciate how both allow us to access, observe, and ultimately rewrite our internal storylines to better serve our values.

As a recap, here are the elements of the StoriCompass:

1. **Agent:** the central person(s) (the *I* or *We*). Know who you are. The central character or person(s) in the life story who has agency. An essential question to ask is: Who is the main agent or character/protagonist of my life story?

2. **Desire:** the goal, dream or desired state/outcome. What the Agent seeks, such as freedom, belonging, identity, success, love, healing, or any other Desire. Important questions to ask are: What is desired? What am I or our family moving toward? What is my vision of a fulfilled life? What does the Agent (I/We) really want?

3. **Guide:** the motivator or call to action. The Guide is who we listen to, usually a guiding force or authoritative figure, and it can be both internal or external. Internal Guides could be our inner voice, intuition, while external Guides could be God, a mentor, cultural norms, institution, etc. In life stories, the questions to elicit Guides are: Who is guiding me or who am I listening to? What pushed me to change? What made me question the status quo?

4. **Beneficiary:** who or what benefits if the Agent succeeds. Remember our Beneficiaries are deeply intertwined with our Why and Who—those that benefit when the Desire is obtained. Often this can be the Agent themselves, but can include family, community, or future generations. Reflective questions to determine the Beneficiary are: Who am I doing this for? Who or what does my healing/success story impact? What is my why?

5. **Supporter:** those who assist the Agent. Supporters can come in all sorts: friends, mentors, faith, education, books, inner strengths, ancestors. In eliciting Supporters, ask yourself: What resources, people, or parts of myself are helping me grow and to obtain my Desire?

6. **Opposition:** the obstacle(s) that prevents the Agent from

obtaining the Desire. The Oppositions in our lives can be internal, such as self-doubt, trauma, fear, and so forth. They can also be external, like racism, patriarchy, poverty, cultural expectations, or people who stop us from reaching our Desire. Interestingly, some of the women who shared their Oppositions were frank in reporting that their Opposition was their intimate partners. To understand Opposition in your life, ask: What stands in my way? Who or what do I wrestle with?

These essential questions arising from the six elements act like guideposts that not only frame our lives and activate our DMN but also provide a map to unpack a life, so we can discern our internal landscape. We've explored each element separately in the previous chapters, but in this chapter, we're finally going to bring all these elements together so you can see the different life frames that operate in people's lives. Then, you'll do your own work on your personal narrative using the StoriCompass tool.

Our Life Story in Visual Form

As a lifespan psychologist, I know that we all have different learning styles. I am a visual learner, the type who loves to see the big picture, so mind maps and diagrams suit me. That is why I developed the StoriCompass. Through the StoriCompass, we can see the entirety of a life captured in graphic format. In figurative form, we view more clearly and explore areas of our lives needing attention, where to intervene, and where to put our focus.

Sooner or later in each of our lives, we come to turning points, which I will cover in chapter 9. When these turning points appear in our lives—life-changing decisions about our career, marriage and family, where to live, etc.—we need to understand what kind of life we want to build, what frames to build to house our Selves, and what things we need to change in order to get to where we want. We can use the StoriCompass to activate our DMN so it works for us, giving clarity and control to make decisions that enable us to live life on our terms.

With this tool, we work out how our story fits our dream, the shape of it, where we need to make changes, and the patterns that emerge so we can shift the ones that need to change. Take decisive action.

Clarity precedes strategic action.

In *Narrative Means to Therapeutic Ends*, the book that gave birth to narrative therapy, family therapists Michael White and David Epston described how problems are culturally and linguistically constructed, and how people should not be blamed or pathologized for them. Instead, they emphasized *externalization*—the process of separating the person from the problem—which is the core philosophy of narrative therapy.

In narrative therapy, the issue is located in the problem itself rather than in the individual, so the person can rewrite their story. It is a shift from "I *am* the problem" to "I *have* a problem that affects me."

In line with narrative therapy, the StoriCompass can help untangle the elements in your story so you can see your Self not as the problem but as a solution. To gain clarity, I would like to ask you two questions: In the landscape of your life, what does your story frame look like? What does it reveal about you?

Inside our internal stories, the structure or frame that holds our Self is similar to the bones that give form to our bodies. The frames enable our lives to take shape and reveal the elements in our story.

We all have hidden life stories. Painful memories. Conflicting emotions. These are hidden within the structures of our lives. Like the shame I endured for many years, not wanting to be visible in the public arena, because of my experiences of being shamed for my Chinese features, my accent, and other ways that I was different from my peers. Racial bias had contaminated my sense of Self. It kept me invisible for years, a silent struggle that stopped me from claiming my voice. Until now.

Perhaps it is like that for you too. Like these brave women who shared their vulnerable stories with me, they sometimes found it difficult to unpack their stories. Or their shame. Some cried, admitted that they had never grieved their deep loss—about not being seen, about feeling out of place, about losing their loved ones, about struggling to reach their goals—but, after some exploration, they realized they had always held on to a higher purpose, even when they weren't in touch with it consciously. They discovered that, in exploring their life stories, they could find their path again and reclaim their voice. Their life.

The last variable in the StoriCompass is context. The context is the circumstances or conditions surrounding your StoriCompass, as shown in Figure 8.1. For example, it could be the context of pursuing a specific dream or goal like becoming a writer, or the context of a work or career trajectory.

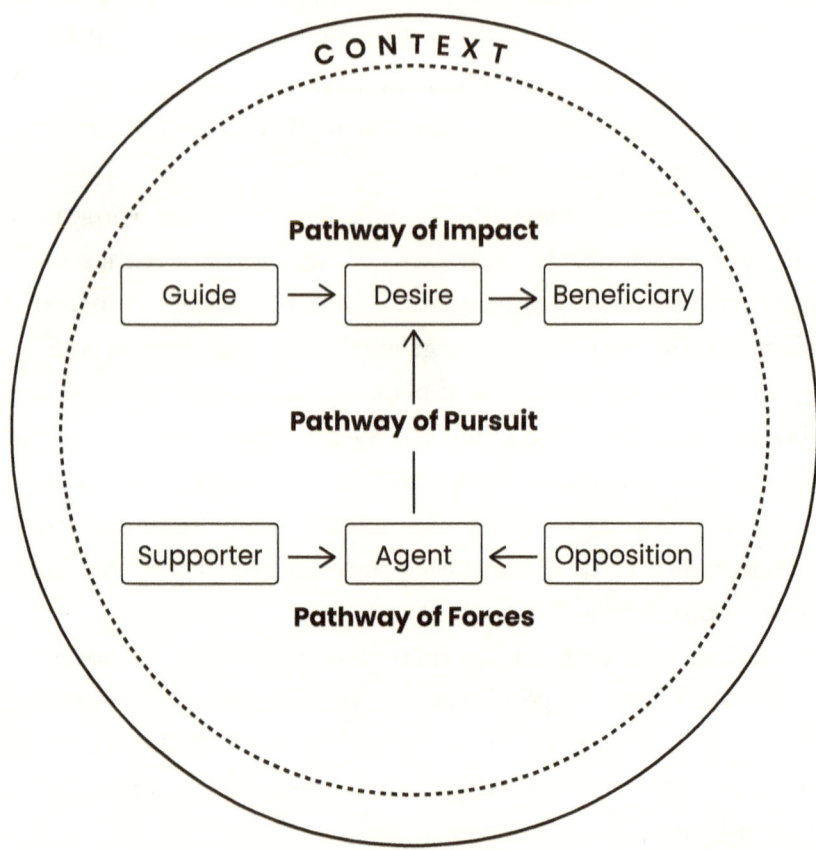

Figure 8.1. The Context of the StoriCompass with Three Pathways and Six Elements

So far, we have mainly referred to the context of an overall life and how each of the six elements form the narrative landscape of your life, once you work through it for yourself. The StoriCompass can be used across the different contexts of life and work. You can also use it to look at specific aspects of your life to analyze different situations, exactly as I did when I tried to figure out why I was stuck in my PhD.

The StoriCompass in Action: Tessa and Self-Sabotage

To put the StoriCompass to work, let's return to Tessa's life story. Remember, Tessa struggled with her biracial identity throughout her life. This is what she shared when she went through the StoriCompass:

TESSA

> My life story is about Me. I want to be the Agent in my life. My Desire and priority now is my kids. Mainly, it's my kids' health and happiness, which are my goals. I'm committed to helping them achieve what they want in their future.
>
> My Guides are my husband and my mom. I listen to them most. The Beneficiaries are my children, family, and people who would benefit once I've made sure my kids are successful.
>
> My Supporters are my husband and mom. My Opposition is "me". I feel like I'm my own worst enemy.

Tessa's Desire centered on her role and identity as a mother, which is very common for moms with young children. Her two Guides—her husband and mother—were dominant figures, and she sometimes felt torn in her loyalty between them, yet she allowed them to guide her life decisions. It's interesting to note that her children's health and happiness were both her Desire, and that they would be the Beneficiaries once she helped them reach their goals. In her mind, the collective family and others in her life would benefit from seeing her children thrive. Her main Supporters were her husband and mother, while she reported that her Opposition was "me" (herself).

After sharing her StoriCompass, she elaborated that she often felt like her own worst enemy in her goal to give the best to her children. For example, she struggled to stay organized for their appointments or keep a tidy home. She frequently felt overwhelmed by tasks and by the "mess" in her mind, and she was often critical of herself, engaging in negative self-talk.

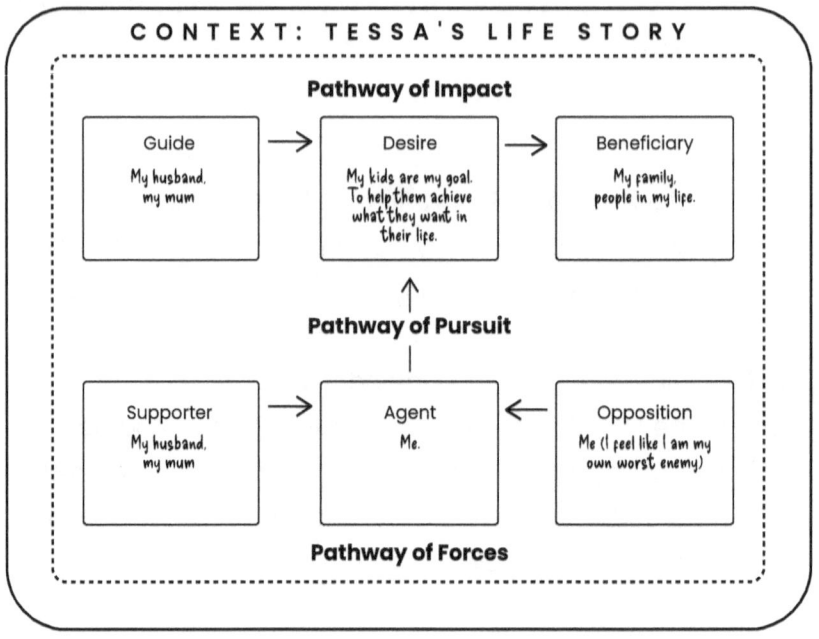

Figure 8.2 Tessa's Life Story Frame Using the StoriCompass

Tessa's story (illustrated in Figure 8.2) shows that she does not appear in any of the elements as someone who can help herself (Supporter) or as someone she can listen to (Guide) or have goals (Desire) that improve herself. Her why (Beneficiary) is other people. She only saw herself as an Opposition. While it may sound noble to be so other-focused, without seeing yourself in other dimensions of your story landscape, it creates sabotage in your life. Tessa readily acknowledged that her life story currently was one of self-sabotage. She was "her own worst enemy."

Without having to explain much, when Tessa saw her life story structure mapped out, she understood immediately what was going on. She had framed her life story as one of self-sabotage. She realized that she needed to develop her inner confidence, so she could have goals that not only fulfilled her children's needs but also her own.

Tessa saw that moving her Self from the Opposition to other elements in her narrative could help her self-development. She realized she could start to help herself as Supporter and listen to her inner narrator as the Guide, instead of letting the voices of her husband and mother drown hers out. She could shift the Guide role to herself. She could be a Beneficiary of her success alongside her family. However, she also realized she needed goals for her life so she could derive meaningful self-fulfilment.

Though wanting to see our children thrive is a common and noble desire for many parents, without following our own desires as a person wanting internal growth, it is hard to meet our deepest needs and Desires.

Children often derive confidence and a growing self-concept from observing the adults in their lives. If they see Mom growing as a person, it gives them permission to do likewise. They then have a template of a healthy life to follow and live by. We teach more through our actions than through our words alone.

If Tessa were content with this life frame and her life were supported by her culture—say if she lived in China where her mother is from, and her peers lived similar lives—she may not experience such internal conflicts. However, Tessa lives in a Western culture where agency and autonomy are valued, in contrast to the way her own mother was brought up and raised her. Her life feels empty because she's unsure how to exist in this world; her two cultures are in conflict. Then she also must contend with the cultural expectations of her strong Greek Australian husband. Her life story structure reflects the lack of her own solid identity.

If we cannot find our true identities in the goals we pursue, we may sabotage ourselves in ways that stop us from creating a life where we are our own Agent. If we don't see the ways we can help ourselves, if we don't listen to our internal compass, to our Why, and don't find fulfilment in our dreams and Desires aligned with our values, we may struggle with our mental health and feel frustrated, resentful, and stuck.

Our lives are a balance between Self and others. How much do we allocate to self-care and how much to caring for others? It is never easy, and we may find this aspect of life becomes unbalanced, especially during the period when that symbiotic relationship between mother and child is still in formative stages; between the ages of birth to around age eight. However, we can make wiser choices when we are clear about our cultural identity, which cues the frames we adopt (covered in chapter 12), which not only benefits ourselves but others, like our children and family.

The StoriCompass helped Tessa activate her DMN to give her clarity on how to make choices that would help her get to her Desire. She explored ways to develop herself by inserting Self into the StoriCompass as Agent (establish self-development goals and understand her cultural identity), Supporter (by speaking more kindly to herself in her self-talk and showing self-compassion), Guide (listening to her internal narrator and being in tune with her internal compass), and Beneficiary (by seeing how she could benefit from pursuing goals that not only met her children's needs but her own).

Relational Conflict: Tina's Life Story Frame

When we use the StoriCompass, we can also see the dysfunctional relationships in our lives and explore ways we can shift those relationships. For example, Tina, who we met in chapter 2, complained about her unfulfilling relationship with her husband, due to his lack of engagement with the family. She talked about him as an Opposition, but then realized he was sometimes a

Supporter too, because if she asked him directly to help, he would. Her frustration was that he didn't take initiative. This dual role he was occupying—as both Opposition and Supporter—spoke of their conflictual relationship, the tensions simmering under the surface. When she looked at her StoriCompass, she found herself thinking, *Where is the spark we once had?*

Tina asked herself the essential questions and worked through mapping her story landscape. She explored why her husband was an Opposition and dug deep to understand the reasons behind feeling constantly angry with him. She realized their communication deteriorated when the children came along. Tina and her husband were so exhausted they had little time to talk through how they worked as a team and how to meet each other's needs and wants. They were busy meeting their kids' needs, so they buried their own. They stopped sharing with each other, both of their Desires left unfulfilled. Their hurt and lack of intimacy appeared as a sense of frustrated helplessness simmering under the convenient emotion of anger. Figure 8.3 shows what Tina's StoriCompass revealed.

When Tina looked at her life story landscape and spent time journaling, her DMN was activated. This led her to identify what she could do to help the situation, including how she might enlist her husband more as a consistent Supporter. She started opening up to him again, hoping this would encourage him to open up as well. It worked. He is now more involved in household tasks and duties; she told me he is more willing to help with the kids and more present in the family and their relationship.

Often, the solutions to life problems are within us, we only need to see the puzzle pieces of our lives clearly so we can move toward healthy relating and well-being.

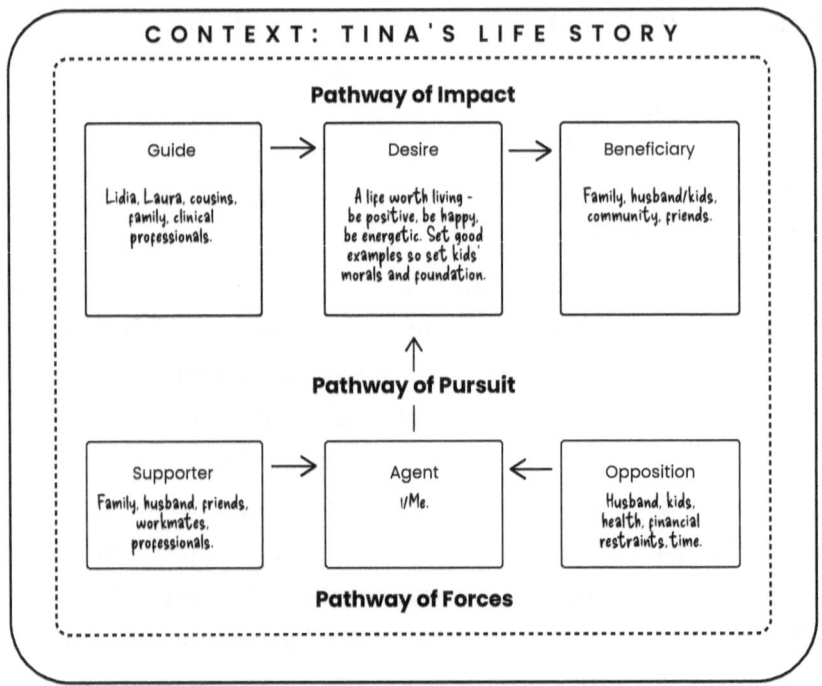

Figure 8.3 Tina's Life Story Frame Using the StoriCompass

What Does a Healthy Life Story Frame Look Like?

Tre, whom you met in chapter 3, has a life story frame that contrasts with Tessa's. Though they have somewhat similar Desires that include children, Tre's overarching goal is for her son, wanting him to grow up to be a thoughtful person. What contrasts Tre's story to Tessa's is that Tre does not see herself as her worst enemy but defines her Oppositions as societal expectations of Black women, combined with others' lack of understanding in how to help her in the tasks she wants to accomplish. Figure 8.4 shows Tre's StoriCompass structure.

Tre has externalized her Opposition. She deals with this in her words by "keeping my own goals in mind and in motion, but making sure that I'm being kind and listening, and having a positive attitude, but not sacrificing my own needs."

While Tre's life story frame is also "other-focused," it doesn't include self-sabotage. Tre prioritizes her own needs and desires. This is healthy and important for our growth and change. Too often, women sacrifice themselves for others, but a woman who has owned her life story no longer sacrifices her needs nor her deepest desires based on core values.

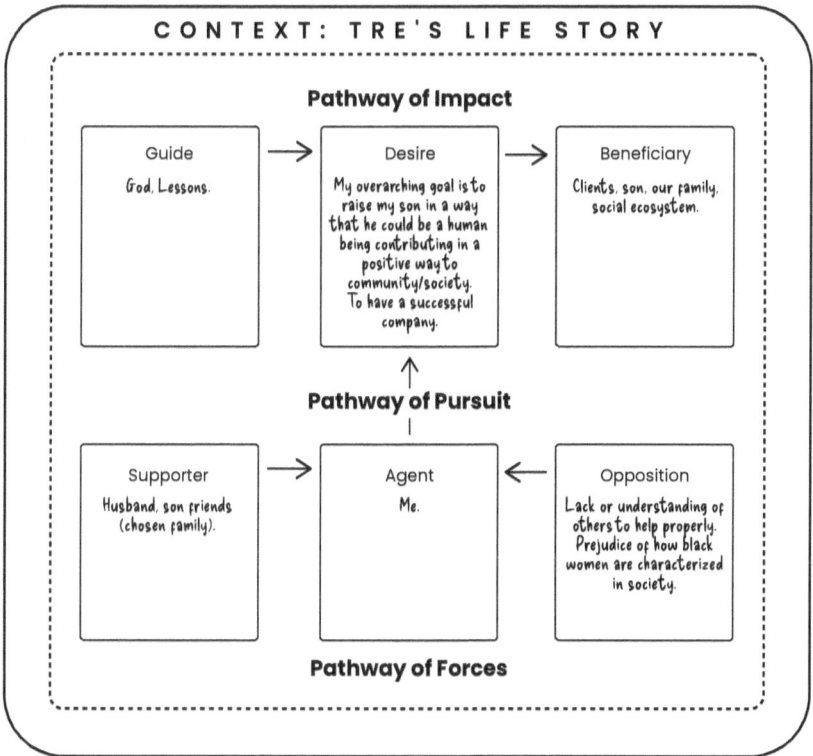

Figure 8.4 Tre's Life Story Frame Using the StoriCompass

Life Story Frames can change. We may have a healthy story frame today, but at any point in our lives, these frames can shift. We never know what life may throw at us; a major event can rearrange the frames of our lives. We may lose an important Guide or Supporter, which can feel like a major frame has been uprooted to unsettle us. I felt like that when my Poh Poh passed away. Poh

Poh left a gaping hole in my life story frame as she was a pillar who held up our whole extended family. A matriarch who was a staunch cornerstone for many.

I come from a line of strong yet gentle women who are my Supporters and Guides, who add structure to my life. Although my Poh Poh has passed away, what she taught me remains and lives on in my mom and me.

The StoriCompass helps us make sense of our lives. We naturally may feel lost when we don't have a sense of ourselves as an Agent, or a clear Desire or Beneficiary, or maybe our Supporters and Guides have been taken from us due to life's circumstances. Or life's Oppositions become overwhelming. Our StoriCompass can enable us to see the changes in our lives when we are trying to make sense of it all. One of my clients, after she remarried, could not understand why she returned from her honeymoon feeling anxious and overwhelmed. She told me she should've felt like she was on cloud nine, drunk with love, but instead, she felt like a spiderweb in a storm, stretched thin, barely holding.

We mapped her StoriCompass frame before her wedding. Then we mapped it after her honeymoon. She saw the reason behind her anxiety and overwhelmed state: Overnight, her life story narrative had exploded! Indeed, her feelings of being stretched thin came from her new reality. Her web now had to carry more than only herself. The Agent of her story was no longer just *I*, it included her new husband. Even her Desire, along with other elements, now intertwined with his, and she enlarged her tent to embrace his five adult children. Suddenly, with her five children, they had become the extended modern version of *The Brady Bunch*, the 1970s sitcom featuring the comedic trials of a blended family.

Once she understood what happened internally, with the elements in her life story restructured due to her marriage, her brain no longer tried to juggle disconnected or confusing data. This understanding strengthened connections between her prefrontal cortex (reasoning, insight), her amygdala (emotions, fear), and her hippocampus (memory, context). Her comprehension translated to acceptance as her emotions became less charged, allowing coherence to quiet down her amygdala's alarm signals. She then focused on navigating how to accommodate her new family instead of focusing on the disconnect she felt between her old and new lives.

Making sense of our experiences begins with connecting fragmented thoughts and feelings. Our brain's DMN weaves these pieces into a coherent self-narrative, while the StoriCompass offers a map and structure—helping us identify roles, obstacles, and desires within our personal story. Together, they guide us from confusion to clarity.

It's now time to gain the clarity you need to move forward. Once you work with the StoriCompass, you'll be able to see how you can map your life stories, how the terrains of your life have shaped your story landscape, and the pathways and other elements that operate in your life. With the StoriCompass and CulturAlign, you have the map and tools to situate yourself in your story and navigate your life. These give us the understanding of how we have framed our lives, which will be the focus of part 3.

Many of our ailments and mental health issues may be traced back to or born of interpersonal conflicts, causing tension and unrest within. If we feel our wings are clipped by another, how can we take flight? When we map out our lives with the StoriCompass, our DMN is activated, and we can identify other factors clipping our wings. It helps us make sense of our lives.

Or we can think of it as swimming. When there are invisible forces of culture operating in our lives, it is similar to when we're expecting to swim in calm waters but undercurrents catch us by surprise. These undercurrents can cause us to lose our bearings and increase our risk of drowning.

In the next section, we'll explore how to work with StoriCompass and your cultural scripts to rewrite your script so you can master the waves in the ocean of your story.

Key Takeaways

* The Default Mode Network (DMN) is a network of interacting brain regions that function as an internal narrator and editor, constantly sorting through experiences to weave a story out of them.

* Each person's DMN is unique and deeply tied to the self, memory, imagination, and social thinking, which are all culturally constructed.

* Our StoriCompass provides the life frame and can activate and work with our DMN to unpack our life stories and help us make sense of our experiences.

Deeper Actions

To use the StoriCompass and map out your pathways and elements of your story structure, please scan the QR code or go to **www.lidialae.com/readerhub**. Work through the questions and download the visual map that gives you clarity on the elements you need to work through.

www.lidialae.com/readerhub

PART 2

Moving Beyond the Cultural Script

We are all bound up together in one great bundle of humanity.

—Frances Ellen Watkins Harper

Five oceans flow between and around the seven continents of our world. These seven continents are home to diverse cultures, each shaped by geography, history, language, and belief. Africa has over three thousand distinct ethnic groups, while Asia, the most populated continent, holds thousands of deeply rooted traditions and religions. Europe has many countries and cultures, each with a long history. In North and South America, there are Natives and people from other places, creating a vibrant mix of cultures. Oceania includes Australia, New Zealand, Fiji, and many more islands, where Indigenous people have strong traditions and connection to the land. Antarctica is unique; it doesn't have Native people, only scientists from around the world who work together and develop their own collaborative international culture.

Even though the many cultures around the world are distinct by geographical separation, they are also connected and can be as fluid as oceans. People move, travel, and share ideas through the internet, books, and music. This means cultures are always changing and growing. While some people stay close to their cultural traditions, others mix old and new ways. Our cultures help shape who we are, but we also share about our Selves with people around the world, reshaping cultures in what I call the dance between culture and self co-construction.

In our modern times, we are readily exposed to many cultures. We glean so many forms or ways of living. In fact, we search for templates, narrative forms to live by. More than ever, we have access to different life stories that inspire and change us. These stories challenge our limiting beliefs. They let us see that our story fits within a larger story of culture. In part 2, we uncover how outdated cultural scripts limit us so we can break patterns that hold us back and live more aligned as we step into the power of personal authorship.

9

Breaking the Patterns That No Longer Serve You

A people without the knowledge of their past history, origin and culture is like a tree without roots.

—Marcus Garvey

*Every day is a fresh beginning;
Every morn is the world made new.*

—Susan Coolidge

What is the family you were born into? What is your family's cultural heritage? How has your cultural heritage shaped who you are? Whether we like it or not, our family impacts every part of our lives.

When I was a child, I used to question why I was born into *my* family. Maybe you did too. Mine was a Hakka family. The term "Hakka" (客家) literally means "guest families." According to research, we are Han Chinese, originating from the Yellow River Valley of China's central Henan and Shaanxi provinces, who may have been on the move since the fourth century. Five major migration waves later, the Hakka diaspora now spans the globe.

I've read that there are about eighty million or more of us scattered around the world, most live in China in the Guangdong province, and in Taiwan. Being Hakka is my cultural heritage. Although my blood is not pure Chinese Hakka, as there is still a running debate within my family about whether our mother's maternal great-grandmother was half Dutch or Portuguese, and half indigenous East Timorese. My Poh Poh, before she passed away, told us her grandmother was half Dutch, but according to Poh Poh's sister, she was half Portuguese. Then on my father's maternal side, his grandmother was of indigenous, brown-skinned West Timorese heritage.

Today, after many mixed marriages, my extended family looks more like the United Nations. Yet, the Hakka spirit remains. Linda Lau Anusasananan described it beautifully in her Hakka cookbook, writing "like a dandelion, a Hakka can land anywhere, take root in the poorest soil, and flourish and flower."

This dandelion analogy rings true in my family's life. We may have arrived in Australia with only our suitcases and started at the bottom of the ladder with nothing, but we embraced the opportunities this great Southern Land offered. Through sheer hard work, we planted seeds in the arid soils. In due time, we assimilated into the Australian culture. Then, we blossomed, through educating ourselves and becoming contributing citizens.

No matter what culture you may be from, the process of growing from a seed to a flourishing, blossoming flower is similar. We all need to ensure that our seeds and roots get the right conditions and nutrients to thrive. Every seed contains the blueprint of what it might become, but whether it flourishes depends on the soil it's planted in and the environmental conditions it experiences.

Like seeds, we all carry inherited beliefs, behaviors, and ways of coping. And like a seed sends out roots to anchor itself and survive, we, too often unconsciously, develop early emotional and behavioral roots: our coping mechanisms, belief systems, identity scripts, and family roles. But roots that first kept us safe can later hold us back.

In this chapter, it's time to look within as we dig into the past, into our family's plot, to understand the medium in which we're planted and the environmental conditions surrounding us that affect our growth. So the dandelion in you can also flourish and flower. The seed in each of us needs rich soil to reach toward the light. Unlike plants, we get to choose what we remain rooted in; if we find ourselves in barren soil, we can work to create a better environment for growth.

Discovering Cultural Scripts that No Longer Help

As storytelling expert Michael Margolis has often taught, the stories we tell about ourselves and the world shape our reality; therefore, to change our world, we must first change our story.

As much as I am proud to be Hakka and love my family to bits, it hasn't always been easy growing up between and within different cultures, as we Hakkas seem to find ourselves.

Growing up in my family, my parents were not afraid of hard work; they were frugal and saved every dollar, so we moved into our home three years after arriving in Melbourne. Being a homeowner meant we could put roots down and not worry about eviction from landlords.

Ba and Ma so wanted us to succeed that they worked hard to foster a spirit of excellence and drilled a growth mindset into us, so eloquently explained by psychologist Carol Dwek. Dwek highlighted that the growth mindset is the belief that a person's abilities are not fixed but are instead developed directly through effort, strategy, and perseverance, not simply raw talent. This growth mindset is part of the seed that wrapped around me, as it is for many Chinese families.

I remember coming home one day during primary school to share math test results with my parents. Math was highly valued in our household, which I suspect is true in most Asian households. There is a pecking order of subjects and professions; math is prioritized because doing well in math helps young people get into good professions like medicine. The stereotypical Chinese mentality is that you've really made it in society if you become a doctor! That day, I came home not at all disappointed with my 99 percent result. I was eager to share it with the family, to show off my hard work. Ma and Ba took in the news. Ma smiled and looked at me with love and encouragement in her eyes. She wanted to set the bar high, so she innocently asked, "What happened to the 1 percent?"

The pattern of excellence was set. That idea seeded and germinated within me, reinforced by my various cultural messages, so I grew up aiming to close the 1 percent gap. I didn't always succeed, but I did try.

Like most Chinese families, this concept of giving 100 percent is deeply rooted in our thinking. It traces its roots to the Confucian tradition—self-cultivation, filial responsibility, and striving toward the utmost good—later reinforced by the imperial exam culture in China. In my family, Ba and Ma role-modeled this by working day and night to improve our circumstances.

***

Fast-forward about two decades. I was knee-deep in trouble, not making any progress with my PhD. I didn't understand how the powerful grip of self-doubt and imposter syndrome was tied to the 1 percent gap. I procrastinated on my thesis, blaming my unrelenting schedule, my children's needs, our social calendar, all the housework I needed to do. The list went on. I thought my consulting work, the administrative tasks, and everything else that comes with running your own business also halted my progress. But these weren't the real causes for my delay.

Sure, all these factors meant I was constantly distracted by others' needs and my endless to-do lists. But what was really at the heart of my problems?

As I shared in the introduction of this book, once I admitted to my supervisor that I was overwhelmed and stuck, he suggested I use the model on myself. I heeded his advice.

In 2015, I found myself in front of my advisory committee in a university classroom. I had to explain myself: Why hadn't I made any progress in three years, with multiple absences after having two kids? I was armed with explanations, ready to present my PowerPoint presentation. The stakes were high. Would my supervisor and other professors let me complete my research?

I showed them the slide with my life story frame, feeling the butterflies in my stomach, I started to talk and heard my voice quivering.

LIDIA

I can summarize how useful this model is for real-life narratives using my life story. I am the Agent of my life. It all began when I was sixteen and first learned about what a PhD is. Neither of my parents completed high school. My mother was from a family of eleven children and was expected to give up schooling to look after her siblings when she was a teenager. My father was an orphan after his father passed away from tuberculosis, and my father witnessed his mother's attempted suicide. We were all refugees after the Indonesian invasion of East Timor. My parents drummed it into my brothers and me that education was our path to building a better life. So, when I found out about psychology and the PhD, I wanted to do something worthwhile with my life and help others with it.

My parents are probably my biggest help and Supporters at present, volunteering to look after my daughters and encouraging me to complete my PhD. I think they are vicariously living this dream with me as well.

What's opposing my desire to finish the research is self-doubt and lack of time...I do feel stretched as I ponder how

I can be a good mother and also help my family. I still need to carve out time to complete my PhD. I think I will gain more time in the near future.

Who has guided me foremost is Yoshi, he has been so supportive and patient. He has helped me map out a realistic plan to finish this PhD. And you, my advisory committee: Nick and Lisa, my future is really in your hands. Will you allow me to continue my PhD research so that I can obtain my Desire and also be the Beneficiary of it?

But really, it is not only I who will benefit from this achievement. It is also my family. My parents and husband will be proud, but I am now completing this for my daughters. I want them to dream big and to know that anything is possible if they put their minds and hearts into their pursuits. When I have had fleeting thoughts about giving up, I think of the implications for them. I can't give up—it's far too important that I show my girls what's achievable.

And I believe this research will benefit the wider community; this model is so useful for working with real-life narratives. It's a framework that can advance research into narratives and can help counsel clients and others to gain clarity about their lives and the pursuit of their dreams. I love working with this model, and I'm excited to present my research to you and to the wider world. Please, give me the chance to continue my research and complete my PhD.

I remember that day clearly. Nervousness pulsated through me, but I managed to somehow speak coherently. I remember the relief I felt afterward. Did they let me continue? You already know.

But what was my Opposition? I had initially put down "time constraints" and "self-doubt." But what was truly behind those?

It wasn't only self-doubt but also imposter syndrome; behind both were deeply rooted limiting beliefs, such as, *I can't do this. Do I have what it takes to pull all this off? I'm not sure I can absorb this amount of knowledge and come up with something new, something novel and innovative for my thesis. Will I have the strength to persevere and juggle all that is on my plate?*

It was a constant scrutinizing of my capabilities. It was a crisis of ability and identity.

This questioning process enabled me to gain awareness. I wasn't only doubting myself and my abilities, my thoughts were undermining my every move; it was fear that paralyzed me and caused procrastination.

I had arrived at my own story loop, the story that drove my self-doubt and imposter syndrome.

What Is a Story Loop?

In our life stories, unresolved "loops"—regrets, traumas, events—can stick with us longer than we realize, until we're able to find closure. These are emotional or psychological narratives: a moment, memory, belief, or identity that has never been fully processed, understood, or integrated. It's something we keep circling back to, consciously or unconsciously. It can be a painful memory that still shapes how we see ourselves. For example, we might have the old story of "I still don't know why my father left when I was ten. Maybe I am not worthy of being loved."

It could be an unfinished dream or "what if" that lingers in the background. For example, "I can't stop thinking about the job I turned down. Was that the right choice? What if I've made a mistake?" This kind of thought may especially come up when we feel stress at work. We might remember other choices we had in our careers and wonder what might have been different.

It could also be a defining moment when a decision or lack of closure created internal conflict, such as a relationship that never resolved. For example, "I always wonder what would've happened if I'd said yes to him."

In our life stories, we may have questions such as:

* Why did this happen to me?
* What does this mean about who I am?
* How do I make sense of this loss/failure/change?

These open loops in our life stories create emotional rumination and fuel anxiety or regret. They also reinforce limiting self-beliefs like, "I'm always overlooked," or "I fail at relationships." They keep us stuck in past identities, so we find it hard to imagine or step into new ones.

Story loops are powerfully linked to the Zeigarnik Effect, discovered by Lithuanian Soviet psychologist Bluma Zeigarnik in the 1920s. She found that waiters in a café remembered unpaid orders better than those that had already been paid. Like all our memories, when the bill is settled, the memory seems to fade; there is closure. This was replicated in the lab where participants were twice as likely to remember tasks they didn't finish compared to the ones they completed. Hence, the Zeigarnik Effect is this:

We tend to remember unfinished or interrupted stories better than resolved ones.

When I started to examine my story loops, my mind illuminated. It dawned on me that my strong family cultural value to complete what we started as best we could, giving 100 percent, limited me in my process of becoming a scholar.

My procrastination came from an unresolved story about whether I could achieve my PhD. Experiences like grief, trauma, change, or a moral dilemma all engage the brain's Default Mode Network as we mentally revisit, rehearse, and reconstruct the events in our lives. The DMN is where we ruminate and retell our stories. But an unresolved story loop—such as a story that gets stuck in procrastination, pain, chronic shame, or identity confusion—can trap the DMN in endless replays, contributing to anxiety, depression, or fragmented identity.

As I used the StoriCompass to look at my experience, I realized my aim to close the 1 percent gap had served me well before by helping me strive for excellence. But it was now debilitating my progress, as I began to understand through journaling the story I was telling myself. Why was I so stuck? How would I close this story loop and move toward completion?

How Do You Close a Life Story Loop?

We can resolve these story loops through questioning, reflection, and often with help like therapy, writing, spiritual practice, meditation, or other interventions. Working with our DMN can help us find narrative coherence—a sense that our story "makes sense" and has continuity. And we can engage our DMN to help us close our story loops.

These are the steps through which I closed my story loop and stopped procrastinating.

Name the Loop

First, you need to name the loop. What is the unfinished business, memory, or belief that stops you from moving forward?

My story loop at the time of being stuck in my PhD research was this: *I'm not smart enough...to complete this research.*

What is yours? Together, we can identify what it is keeping you stuck, going around in circles, not making progress in your life.

Being able to question your limiting beliefs and explore the deeper meaning behind the blocks in your life is essential.

Question the Limiting Belief

When you can name what it is, you can question the limiting beliefs and explore the meaning behind it. This is the second necessary step. Meaning is what gives us narrative coherence. The gestalt moments of our lives, where the parts make sense as a whole. Conversely, it is also the meaning we give to our experiences that keep us stuck. But once we grasp the negative meaning behind actions and beliefs, we realize we can do something about it.

Like turning on a switch, I could finally see that I developed a story not only that the 99 percent wasn't good enough, but that I wasn't good enough. Therefore, the work I did wasn't enough. Deep down, what I wrote didn't make the mark. It stunted me in writing my thesis. I saw my "Not good enough" thinking linked to the "close the 1 percent gap" subconscious experience. Every time I wrote my thesis chapters, I would trash it, thinking it was awful. This debilitating story loop hijacked my progress!

I realize how powerful this script, story loop, had lodged itself into my subconscious mind. Even while writing this book, this story loop still reared its ugly head.

It took on another insidious lie: *I'm not qualified enough...to complete this book.*

I had to do a reality check. Many authors who have not acquired professional qualifications nor clinical experience write books that impact people. I had to reinterpret my stories about my perceived limitations. If people without my qualifications write books that help people, I can certainly write a book that helps people!

I realized this story loop could take on many forms in my subconscious mind, depending on the situation I was facing and who I was becoming:

"I am not smart enough to complete this research."

"I am not qualified enough to write a book."

"I am not fit enough to run this marathon."

"I am not... enough to..."

These types of story loops can literally rob years off our lives. It undermined at least three years of mine as a graduate student as I stayed in the procrastination/"too overwhelmed" loop. Don't let your stories rob you of your time any longer.

Reframe, Re-author, and Choose

Thirdly, to close the story loop, I had to reframe, re-author it, and ask myself: *What new interpretation or action can I choose now?* I developed a cognitive strategy the way I did when I got over the fear of swimming in my late teens, using the wisdom of Susan Jeffrey's book, *Feel the Fear...and Do It Anyway*. This book helped me develop my cognitive strategy to reframe and overcome the fear of drowning.

Back then, before I jumped into a pool, I would tell myself, "If I drown, I die, but I will die anyway." I faced my fear of death by drowning. I know it sounds morbid, but it literally cured me of my fear of swimming and drowning. Many times, we need to face fear head on.

My cognitive strategy at the time when I wrote my thesis chapters was: "It may not be good enough, but it will do. Besides, I can edit what I write, but I can't edit what I haven't written." That unfroze my writing paralysis.

Integrate the Lesson

Lastly, we need to integrate it. Let the lesson be part of our current identity. Our story loops are not wounds; they become wisdom for us. Every time I am becoming someone more or stepping out of my comfort zone to grasp a new identity—becoming a mother, or becoming an author, becoming a speaker, a marathon runner, a leader—I tell myself, "I don't have to be enough. I need to be *me*. Even 'imperfect me' is sufficient. Just keep showing up!" I can re-author and integrate all parts of me because I choose to close my story loop with a new meaning. I choose to live from a different frame, which will be covered in part 3.

What are some story loops you may be dealing with in your life? Some of the common ones I've heard women share with me are:

"I should have chosen differently."

"I lost myself somewhere along the way."

"I can't be who I want to be and still belong."

"I'm not enough, or too much, for the world I'm in."

"I am losing my mind."

"One day, I'll start living my real life."

"I have a story, but who would care?"

There are more, and it's important to keep questioning what keeps you stuck so you can uncover your story loop. Once you do, go through the above four steps to release yourself from its grip so you can keep moving forward. If you do, you can come to a turning point in your life.

Turning Points in Our Lives

Closing my story loop was a turning point in my life. A turning point is a moment of unforgettable change in our life stories. It stands out in our story as a major transition. It is a specific key event that causes a *deep shift* in self-understanding, direction, and/or identity.

With my turning point, I could finally release my mind to focus on completing my research. It was through examining more deeply the element of Opposition in my StoriCompass that I recognized my story loop and closed it. I stepped out of a stuck identity of a procrastinating student into a graduate and realized my dream of contributing something original to world knowledge.

I no longer had to be 100 percent! I simply had to show up, understand parts of myself that were restricting me, and integrate them as part of my story with a new meaningful twist.

It was the internal work I had to do so I could be of service to others. We all have different meaning systems; how I see something may be different to how you see it. We have varying worldviews and perspectives. Different life frames. It's what makes us unique. However, if how we attribute meaning holds us back from our best life, we need to reframe our meaning systems so we can be free. Our story loops offer powerful entry points into what the DMN already works on: "What's unfinished? What hasn't been integrated yet?"

New positive meaning-making activates our Default Mode Network and is a known predictor of post-traumatic growth and identity development; it usually leads to turning points.

This was the case for Clara, when she went through a difficult time after the birth of her second child. We followed Clara's story in chapters 2 and 4, as she struggled with moving from Belgium to Ireland with young children while her husband worked long hours. She had to make sense of her experiences, noting that "every time a new child is born, a new mother is born, too, because you never mother your children the same way." This is a second identity development that happens with motherhood, which she said no one really talks about. She highlights her turning point by accepting herself as a "struggling" mother, shedding her expectations of being an "ideal" mother.

CLARA

Every time, you have a new child, I thought, "You know what? I've mothered one, I just have to do it again. It's like, just doing the same thing again, and I'll be fine." But this baby is completely different. This baby needs completely different things, different timing. He was even being breastfed in a different way, sleeping in a different way!

Nobody guides you through this process of rediscovering yourself as a mother. And it changes the way you mother your second one. But the moment the second mother is born also changes the way you mother your first one.

You don't have the same time availability or neurological calm. There's all these changes that all of a sudden you have to confront this grief.

And probably the best advice my mother gave me ever was one day, I still remember, the boys were both napping in the car. We had just come back from the playground, and I just had this breakdown, and I called my mum and I said, "Mum, how did you do it? How could you do that?" Because we were also highly mobile children, right? And my sister is just twenty-three months younger than me. So, she had a very similar situation. And I said, "How did you do it? I have the feeling I'm nowhere. I'm not a good mother to my eldest. I'm not a good wife. I'm not a good mother to my youngest. I'm not good to myself. I'm completely neglecting myself. I have no time to even get a shower. How did you do it?"

And then she gave me that wonderful advice, and she said, "You know what, Clara? There are going to be days that are going to be for yourself. There are going to be days that are going to be for your eldest, and he's going to be the spotlight of that day. There are going to be days that are going to be for your youngest, and they're going to be days that are going to be for Dad, for your husband. And this is how life is going to go on. There is never going to be this perfect scenario where everybody gets what they need, exactly how they need it, the time they need it."

That, I think, really helped me to start seeing things from a different perspective and taking my youngest on my lap in this baby carrier and saying, "Today's your brother's day, and you're going to be in here." Or to my eldest, "We're not going to be stimulating you much today. You're just going to be hanging in there while we play with your brother." And just making that peace with the ideal mother that I had created in my head and coming to terms and acceptance of the mother I was able to be.

Clara's turning point enabled her to embrace motherhood again and accept her limitations as well as her ability. She closed her story loop of "I'm not good" and believing the lie she needed to be the ideal mother and wife, and she changed it into "There is never going to be this perfect scenario..." and accepting her limited attention and time could still be distributed to everyone, including herself. Her mother's advice guided her to make new meaning out of her struggles, where she made "peace" with the ideal mother. She reframed her life.

Personal Growth After Turning Points

Each of our lives take different shapes and forms, so our turning points will be unique. Cristina—whose father left the family to go back to Romania when he couldn't assimilate into the culture of his adopted home of Australia—was confronted with her turning point when her abusive relationship ended. She asked herself, "Is there something really wrong with me that men continue to leave me?" She realized her whole family had a pattern of divorce. Her grandmother divorced, so had her mother, and now it was her turn. She was at a point where she needed to go deeper and use her understanding of her family history and personal story to create a positive turning point through her relationship breakdown.

Cristina asked, "Why do these patterns of my life just keep playing out this way?" To understand the unhelpful patterns that run unconsciously until we name them, Cristina glued the pieces of her life together, gathering the threads of her major turning points to weave her life story. Her DMN is always "on" in the background, but her deliberate act of self-reflection enabled her to use the stream of internal memories provided by her DMN and identify the damaging patterns in her relationships, making it possible to break the cycle.

Cristina arrived at her story loop when she recognized that her dad's departure left a hole in her life, and that she had internalized the narrative "We're not good enough for him to stay." This pattern has unfortunately impacted her life since. This was what she shared.

CRISTINA

> I felt abandoned by my dad obviously...I don't know if I've ever spoken about it to people. My mum didn't hate my dad when he left, but she was very heartbroken. Because he said that he was going home to his family. So, he didn't consider us "family." I don't know. He just couldn't assimilate in Australia. Romania was always his home.
>
> So, my mum was, in a way, happy that he left because he was miserable when he was here. And he used to drink a lot, but when he drank a lot, he just cried, and he was very depressed. He wasn't a violent man or a mean drunk; he just felt sorry for himself. And yeah, Mum was sort of relieved that he wasn't around to make her feel like he did.
>
> I felt abandoned, you know? My dad left. So, then I met

Trent, my first love, when I was in my fourth year at uni. We fell very much in love. We were very, very happy for a long time. And then, things fizzled on his behalf. He loved me a lot. Towards the end of our relationship, I didn't understand why he didn't love me anymore. We ended up divorcing because he fell out of love.

I wonder if it goes back to that internal thing with Dad: that it's like we're not good enough for him to stay.

After that, I was looking for a rebound to get over Trent, and I just wanted to feel loved by someone, and I thought, "I'm just going to have a little fling with this man, Matthew." We ended up starting a business together. I was on cloud nine.

But…slowly, very slowly, a bit like torture…he started manipulating, controlling lots of little tiny things. Over twelve years of being together. When he and I split up, I was a shell of myself. So, everything that I had worked for with Trent—and Trent helped me become this confident woman and the person that I was—Matthew took it all away, like all of it.

Cristina realized that her father's abandonment was her first turning point; it was the first core relationship with a man that imprinted on her other relationships with men. Her first marriage was another turning point: finding love with her first husband, Trent, who showed her she was important and valued. However, their divorce was another turning point, bringing in doubt again about her value. And unfortunately, at that vulnerable time in Cristina's life, she unknowingly made an unwise choice to feel loved and valued again by thinking she'd have a fling. As so many of us have discovered, dating when we feel vulnerable and in doubt about our worth can lead to poor choices about who we let into our lives. We may inadvertently send signals that attract the wrong partner.

Regrettably for Cristina, at this low point, working through the

StoriCompass, she asked herself, "What role am I playing in the love stories of my life? Who gave me these roles? What unconscious beliefs have I inherited through my generational line?"

She dug deep, comprehending that it wasn't only cultural scripts she inherited as a Romanian, but also the scripts developed as someone who's carried the burden of being provider, caretaker, and sustainer of the family. She had to move beyond personal and cultural scripts to understand her unconscious, habitual story loops and identify narratives behind her dysfunctional patterns.

Eventually, Cristina was ready to disrupt her default storytelling. She was ready to identify the story loop that ran subconsciously, the narrative of "I'm not good enough for men to stay." She is re-authoring her script, reconstructing her Self and internal sense of who she is. She is enough; those men's decisions were about them.

Turning points are opportunities for personal growth, times to engage our agency and reframe life.

Cultural Differences in Turning Points

When I asked the research participants about their turning points, I was fascinated by their experiences. Westerners—such as European Australians—shared turning points that reflected more self-agency, for example, realization of their need to change their own behaviors, or pursuing self-interests like traveling, learning new skills, attending university, etc. The Easterners, like Singaporean Chinese, shared turning points that were more reflective of their shared relationship with others, such as the birth of a sibling, growing closer to a special friend, joining the army to serve their country, etc. Their responses revealed cross-cultural differences in turning points.

This shows how we experience turning points—how we interpret, narrate, and assign meaning to them—is shaped by our cultures. Different cultures emphasize different values, life paths, and markers of success or identity. For many, breaking a personal and/or cultural script becomes a turning point.

Looking at Our Personal and Cultural Scripts

Turning points change us. For myself, Clara, and Cristina, our turning points reflected values deeply embedded in our relationships to our Self and with others. Here, we look beyond simply the Western or Eastern cultural contexts; it is the way in which each cultural context captured in CulturAlign shapes us.

Many of our turning points relate in some way to our family's cultures: the unique norms, sets of behaviors, and experiences we were brought up with. My parents' way of instilling a culture of excellence in me became debilitating when it turned into a story loop that got me stuck in my pursuit of my PhD, but then led me to understand myself more fully. Clara reaching out to her mother during a crisis moment, and her mom sharing wisdom from her own experience with parenting, grounded her in the family's cultural values. Cristina's loss of her father when he abandoned them to return to Romania impacted her relationships with men, until she was able to see through the story loop that she wasn't valuable enough for a man to commit to.

Free From Unhelpful Cultural Expectations

When I talk about culture, I'm not just talking about ethnic culture. I'm talking about all the places and communities that exert cultural influence on us, whether family, workplace, or the nation we live in. I discussed this at length in chapter 2. There are always social expectations that impact our lives, and there's also intergenerational transmission, family scripts we carry, that we unconsciously live with, which can stop us from living a fulfilling life.

To break free from outdated or unhelpful patterns, we must explore these patterns and consider whether or not they serve us. These scripts are cultural expectations, which we may not be aware of. They also influence internal story loops that hold us back from creating our dream life.

For all of us, any group we're part of includes a culture of expectation. We should become aware of culture's influence on us so we own our life story and make decisions based on our values, dreams, and goals rather than the goals of others.

From my perspective, Clara's mother's advice is golden: *There will be days for each member of the family.* There are some days for each of the children, some for my husband, then there are days for myself so I can pursue my self-development.

Having friends to check in with and work through cultural and social expectations has been helpful. Sometimes, with cultural expectations pressuring us, we don't always feel we truly have control over our lives. Connecting with others who feel similar pressures can be helpful in shifting our story loops.

For some of us, it can be hard to let go of life's painful turning points. For others, it's about understanding how the cultures of our communities influenced us to think and behave. Whichever situation you find yourself in, be conscious of whether you're letting invisible forces of culture, circumstances, and other people take the reins of writing your life's script. Close your story loops. Stay aware of how doing this brings about significant turning points that open paths to new opportunities. Now is the time to break unhealthy patterns and become the author of your life.

Key Takeaways

* Cultural scripts are the cultural stories, sometimes unknown to us, that shape our personal stories.
* Story loops are the unresolved emotional and psychological narratives never fully processed, understood, or integrated, which can keep us stuck.
* Close your story loop by:
    1) Naming the loop;
    2) Questioning the limiting beliefs and exploring the meaning behind them;
    3) Reframing and re-authoring the story;
    4) Integrating the reframed story as part of your identity.
* Turning points are specific key events that cause a deep shift in self-understanding, direction, and/or identity.

Deeper Actions

Work through these four exercises to break patterns and scripts that no longer serve you.

1. Name a Family or Cultural script that causes problems in your life right now. If you have more than one, go through this step in the coming weeks when you have shifted one script first.

    Complete the following:

    ✧ "In my family/community, a good _____ must _____."

- ✧ "We never/always _____."
- ✧ Keep one rule, retire one, rewrite one as a single sentence you can live by now.

2. Identifying a Story Loop. To uncover this, ask yourself, "What is the unresolved issue I have in my life that keeps me stuck from fulfilling a dream, a goal, or an outcome I desire?"

   Dig deeper to the belief that keeps this story loop running. Write a truer belief that fits your values today. Use this formula:

   - ✧ "I believe_____about_____" or "When I experience _____ I believe _____."
   - ✧ and then replace it with the new belief:
   - ✧ "When_____happens, _____is true," etc.

3. Identify the Change Required for Your Turning Point. Pinpoint the old cultural/family script (in Step 1) or the story loop (in Step 2) you're wanting to close. Write an *If–Then* plan:

   - ✧ If _____ happens, then I will _____ for 90 seconds, then choose. (Example: If I feel pressured to say yes to a request, then I will pause, breathe, and reply tomorrow.)

10

Becoming the Author, Not Just a Character or Victim

The beginning is always today.

—Mary Shelley

I dwell in possibility.

—Emily Dickinson

I couldn't contain my excitement. A present! From my teacher too. The classroom was full of noise and activity on our last day of school. The bell rang to usher in the summer holidays. I thanked my Grade 1 teacher, telling her in my broken English that I loved being in Australia, being in her classroom as her student. I was so grateful for making new friends over the past six months. She returned the warmest smile.

I clutched the precious box while I rushed out to meet my grandfather, Goong Goong at the school gate. I excitedly told him we needed to get home right away so I could open my present. He looked amused, flashing his beaming white teeth with one golden filling. That afternoon, we all walked home faster than usual, with my brothers chasing each other to see who would get there first. Everyone was eager to see what was in that box.

We arrived home to the three-bedroom house we all lived in: me, my brothers, my parents, my grandparents, aunties, and uncles. Poh Poh met us at the door and asked what the commotion was. When she saw my box on the coffee table, she joined the rest of the family waiting eagerly for me to open it.

Lifting off the lid, my eyes lit up. Little books, some of them I had read in the past months, were neatly arranged together. I couldn't believe my teacher's generosity. She had given me what I loved and what she nurtured. Books she knew I would love. The excitement quickly wore off for my brothers, who thought I might have received toys. They hurried to the kitchen for a snack.

Goong Goong, a book lover himself said, "Well, you'll be entertained during the summer holidays."

Indeed, I nodded with excitement. I couldn't wait to open the pages and transport myself into the stories. Thus began my love affair with books, one that persists today.

During my primary school years, I started making books. Writing short stories, little fairy tales, then adding pictures to go with the stories. I would staple them together and read them to myself with delight. Even at that tender age, I dreamed of one day becoming an author.

Along with being an author, all those hours playing "Moms and Dads" as a toddler taught me that I wanted to be a mother and have a family. As a child, I held on to these dreams quietly, not knowing how I would obtain them.

Becoming the Protagonist

What dreams and desires did you have as a child? Who or what did you want to become? Have these dreams and desires happened yet? Or are they still brewing in you? Or have you abandoned them?

This chapter is about becoming the author of your own life. Not only a character, not a victim, but the protagonist of your story. What does this actually mean? It means instead of being defined by your past roles or by others' expectations, you let your authentic calling, desires, and values—your true self—define you and contribute to your story. You stop being "the one who always holds it together" or someone's rescuer or doormat. You choose who you become, not only who you've been. You make conscious decisions rather than default reactions. You stop living under inherited or imposed stories.

When you're the author of your own story, your life reflects your internal compass, not merely external demands. You shift from playing a part in someone else's script to co-creating a new kind of story for yourself and your community.

Authors don't work in isolation, from what I've discovered. They need mirrors, others who reflect back meaningful exchanges, editors, and allies. Often the process of healing, reframing key events, and becoming an author of your life is catalyzed or supported through belonging. We need the support of people around us who align with our values because healing and becoming are also relational.

We go furthest when others hold us to account, especially when we feel like giving up. We enlist Guides and Supporters to help us overcome our Opposition, clarify our Beneficiaries, and obtain our Desire. Our StoriCompass builds our Self and identity as we make sense of our life's key events.

Key Events: The Chapters of Our Lives

Like books have chapters, our life has *key events*; some are minor landmarks, while others become turning points—events powerful enough to shift the entire narrative and trajectory of the story, which we explored in the previous chapter. Key events are notable milestones or experiences like getting married or divorced, starting or losing a job, moving to a new country, graduating from university, winning an award, receiving a diagnosis, losing a loved one, or having children. These events are often descriptive and factual, anchoring us in our life's timelines. They also are self-defining memories because key events shape the person we become.

The process of becoming can be lengthy. Each key moment connects to the next like a chain that leads us to where we desire to be.

I thought I had my life figured out as a young adult: *I'll be married by twenty-six at the latest. I'll have my first child at twenty-eight, second child by thirty, and last child by thirty-two.* A two-year gap between babies would give enough breathing space and time for my body to recover.

However, in my late twenties I was still waiting for my prince to appear. My biological clock was ticking, and he was nowhere to be found.

Life surprises us many times. My life seems to happen at the eleventh hour. I didn't marry until I was almost thirty-two, right before my carefully planned third child would have been born. I was shocked to find out later—not conceiving until my mid-thirties—my pregnancy was considered geriatric!

Many times, life does not work out as planned. Situations out of our control—love, loss, grief, opportunities—come when we least expect them. The key events in our lives can come as a surprise.

I felt like a victim in my late teens: four family members died in the space of a few months, and I was deeply burdened by grief; it was a painful time of my life. I remember these key events as a low point. I somehow managed to pull myself together from this dark period in my last year of high school and entered university.

Throughout my twenties and thirties, I was still discovering myself and my agency. I confess, I didn't know then how to take charge of my life, let alone be author of my own life. My dream of becoming an actual author felt out of reach.

I made a pact within myself: I decided that, surely, if I could successfully write a thesis—a piece of writing examined by scholars and experts in the field—it would give me the confidence that I could write. Committed to my dream, I took writing classes and completed courses outside university too.

The Journey of Becoming

The process of becoming was long. I was surprised my thesis examiner remarked my thesis was well written. *OK*, I thought, *that means I now have permission to write a real book!*

It's taken me almost six years to birth this book. I've taken several courses, written with dozens of other writers, and overcome many limiting beliefs (which I discussed in the previous chapter). Becoming an author involved a series of key events in my life; from that seed of my first box of books, to creating books as a primary school student, to completing my PhD, to completing writing courses, to joining writing groups, to writing many versions of this manuscript, and finally, to launching it to the world. Believing in my ability after I finished the PhD was the key event that became the turning point.

Writing a book is both scary and life-changing. It is not only about putting words on a page but about stepping into the identity of author, of becoming visible in the public arena. For someone who didn't want to draw any attention to myself as a child, I had many hurdles to jump to own this new identity.

That's the journey that we explore here—*becoming*—whether it's as an author, a mother, a leader, or a fully alive woman.

Navigate Your Own Becoming Journey

The journey of becoming involves reflecting on the mapping work we previously completed with the StoriCompass in part 1. It includes knowing who you are and articulating your desires, goals, and dreams, establishing your Agent-Desire relationship. Know who you are guided by and discern whether those you listen to have your best interest at heart. Know your Why and Who gets the benefit when you obtain your Desire. Be clear about your Guide and Beneficiary. Ensure you know how to reach out for instrumental support and help, as well as work through what opposes you. Understand the Supporter and Opposition in your life. With this work, know you carry a map for your process of becoming. This will also be fully explored in part 3, as an author creating your life of joy, meaning, and legacy.

When we reflect on how we became the way we are, we realize it involved a collection of memorable points in our lives: the key events. Hence, in our pursuit of who we want to become, there are key events we need to embrace to author our stories and reflect how we want to show up in this world.

Key Events and Turning Points

One of the most significant key events in my life, which was also a turning point, was becoming a mother. Motherhood stretched me in every possible way, not only skin-deep, with permanent stretch marks. It continues to stretch me as my children help me grow each day. I see being a mother as one of my greatest privileges; I wouldn't trade this valuable gift for anything in the world.

During motherhood, I went deeply within myself and decided I wanted to interrupt the old stories so my daughters didn't live them out as I had. This was what Tessa, Tina, Sarai, and others shared with me too. We all want the best for our children, and we want to stop limiting patterns that impacted our lives.

We all decided, "Hang on, I don't want this cycle of what happened to me to perpetuate. I want it to stop here and now!" Motherhood is a series of continuous key events, like intensified emotional moments in our lives. They are key because they are memorable.

Sometimes authoring our stories does not make a monumental shift in our life's directions; it comes with little things we do, like starting to respect our Self, our space, and what we need.

Clara shared her experiences of culture shock as a mother living between and within cultures. Further, how she became the author of her life rather than a victim of circumstances.

CLARA

My "mother identity" had this culture shock because I had experienced different ways of mothering in other countries that were much more aligned with how I prefer to do things. But then there was that reverse culture shock of my own.

I was already uncomfortable with certain things in the Spanish culture, but it was intensified by the fact that now I wasn't only living for me. But I think we share this commonality: that when you are in global mobility, it adds this layer of complexity and complete stress. You are in this constant multiple readjustment. You're readjusting to the place where you land in, but you're also adjusting to who you are becoming. Like this new you.

It takes time to know who you are as a mother. It's not the mere experiences, but I think place does something to identities. Because you experience a place and its culture very differently. The way you behave in a certain place may feel more attuned with your internal self. Like when I interact with people in this way from a certain culture, it's effortless, right? It flows.

But in other environments, like Spain, it has a very social culture. You're in constant social interaction. And motherhood happens in the playground most of the time. But to me, it is a space that is overstimulating. Like the children screaming, running. The constant conversation, like the constant demand from parents to bring up a conversation topic. It was very draining for me.

I realized that I had to also change the way I would mother in Spain according to my needs. I started by trying to fit in, right? Trying to be part of this group of mothers that go to the playground and then kind of prepare all these shared birthday parties. They invite the whole classroom, and the whole classroom comes to the birthday party. I was like, "Whoa, there's a lot of children. There's a lot of noise. There's a lot of..." And I started readjusting.

But this doesn't make sense to me. This is not how I would do things, and it certainly doesn't flow with how I am. It's draining. It's not fun for me at all.

So I started agreeing with my husband also, right? So, OK, if birthday parties invite the whole class, I cannot change their culture, right?

I decided, I can no longer do that. I don't go to those parties anymore, and my birthday parties for my children are not going to be inviting the entire class. And people may find that culturally difficult to understand, but I have to be genuine and align with what I can handle because otherwise, I literally...One day when I had all these people over, and they were never leaving, I brought their shoes. Because I asked the people to take off their shoes. I brought their shoes and said, "Can you just please leave now? I need you to leave. I can't take it anymore. It's too much. It's been too long. Too many people. I need you to leave."

And that's when I realized, you know, it's respecting yourself. And then you come to this overwhelming situation that makes everybody uncomfortable.

Put your boundaries down. Explain to people in advance that the party ends at seven o'clock, even if, for them, this is too early. Then they have to continue the party at the playground with the children because they're never going to go home at that time.

I am not going to take it as something that I have to adjust or accept or incorporate in my way of doing things. And I think a lot of women need to hear that because oftentimes, there's this need to please others. It comes integrated in how we were raised.

Clara's truth is powerful. She realized she could no longer live in a way that was incongruent with who she truly was.

It takes guts to go against the flow of culture's streams. Our fear of what people think is real. However, despite the awkwardness and response of others when she picked up their shoes and asked them to leave her home, she made that decision to respect herself. This was such a key event in owning her life story and becoming the protagonist.

Small Steps

Clara demonstrates the process each of us must make, the small steps we take in daily life. Drawing healthy boundaries between what's OK for us and what is not. Taking steps to establish boundaries, such as when we're tired, giving ourselves permission not to attend events out of guilt; it's OK to withdraw from others and recharge. We can communicate with others about our boundaries and what we are and aren't available to do. Stop pleasing people. Start respecting yourself and let your behaviors reflect this; it is one of the most important steps toward no longer being a character or victim but taking back authorship.

Clara shared about grieving her old self, letting go of the old patterns that didn't serve her anymore. It didn't stop with herself; Clara set up healthy boundaries with immediate family and extended family. She had to fight for what was important to her, even if that meant arguing with her husband or standing up to the other mothers. What she shares is refreshing and shows how she developed assertiveness and confidence. She's choosing to embrace self-respect and be the author of her life.

CLARA

You're just this backpack that follows along, and you just do what you're told, and you just go along and sing with the flow.

But the truth is that some adult Third Culture Kids (TCK) who are also parents come to this kind of realization that they tend to be pleasers.

Around the age that it came to me, I realized I can continue going this way and going to the playground and to attend these birthday parties and everything. But then I would be kind of stuck to this loyal system that my TCK kind of brought me into. But it wouldn't be aligned with who I really am and what makes me really happy and well and balanced.

So, I had to grieve a lot, like grieve this self that was very people-pleasing; and it takes time because you kind of feel lost at some moments. It's like, so if I'm not a people-pleaser anymore, what am I? Am I this ogre that is always going to be grumpy? Or can I find this middle ground where I can still please people to an extent that is not draining and overwhelming?

And that took time because it was a lot of trial and error.

It was like, "If I go too deep, how do I feel? If I don't go there, how do I feel?" And finally, the agreement also with my husband that he's not highly sensitive. He's 100 percent

Spanish. And he's an extrovert. So, people, people, people.

And he comes from a large family, what we call this agglomerate family system where everything happens together all the time. So, if somebody's missing, there is something wrong. So, dealing with this as well, right, which won't work for me without interfering too much with how it works with these other relationships that are also in place within my marriage.

So, for instance, Christmas has, like five, six, seven, I don't know how many days of meetings in Spain. You have the wise men, you have New Year's, you have Christmas, you have Saint Steve that also is celebrated in Catalonia.

How many days do we go? But not only how many days do we go to your family, but how long do we stay? What time do we get there? How do we do things? Like, can I just take breaks and go for a walk while we're there? Instead of being by the table the entire meal and coffee that lasts until five o'clock, can I just skip the coffee and go for a walk? You know, like finding this agreement for our individual well-being, take time out.

I'm not telling you the days where we were fighting to get to the challenges because they were there too. And you know what? That's something that many people don't talk about in couples. But I always say fighting is actually healthy because you can really be yourself when you're claiming something; you're defending something of yourself, and you're putting yourself out there. And you're fighting for something you believe in. That's why I think arguments can be very healthy. They are.

When couples come to work with me, one of the main things that they tend to say is, "We're fighting too much. Can you just help us to stop fighting?"

And I'll say, "Unfortunately, if that's what you're seeking, I can't help you with that. Especially if you're in a cross-cultural relationship, forget it. You're going to fight over many things. What I can help you with is to make those fights productive. Constructive. There's a resolution. And there is a purpose. Like the fight is not just for me to vomit over you, all my frustration, resentment, but rather to speak about my needs. What are my needs? And understand that it's going to create some tension and resistance on your end. And this is what we're going to have to work on. This resistance and tension that is going to take us some time to find how we make space for my needs without my needs invading yours. That's right. We need to find a space for yours and my needs to coexist."

This is when we become authors of our lives. We allow space for us to exist. We use our voice so that we all coexist respectfully despite our differences.

Sarai had to discover her own voice, too, after her key event of moving to Australia. She hoped the situation would be different with her husband, that their family would have a new start in a new country. However, she discovered something else. This is her story.

SARAI

We moved to Sydney, and after a while, that cycle started again. Lots of abuse. It just persisted up to the point where I couldn't take it anymore. My mental health was being affected. I couldn't keep up, especially as a mental health clinician, when sometimes I work with women that have gone through domestic violence.

I know the cycle of domestic violence. I know the cycles of the perpetrator and what they do. But I was a victim and then trying to pretend to do my job, advocating for these vulnerable women. But I couldn't do that for myself.

I think the day came when I made that decision. I remember

he just got angry, something about the kids, I can't remember what it was. And he threw the laptop at me, like one of those heavy MacBooks. It just narrowly missed my head. Like, oh my God...

I couldn't stay. And then I had to get a restraining order from the police. He got extremely angry after that.

It was so hard.

Also, I've had a work life where you went through a lot of racial discrimination because of your skin color, both in the UK and also in Australia. You're having to prove yourself, go extra above and beyond to be able either to be selected in a role in the UK and in Australia too.

It was difficult, but you grow up. There's an African proverb, which says, "If there's no enemy within, the enemy outside can do no harm."

And embracing yourself, embracing your difference, is what's going to shift things. That's what's going to make you happier and more accepting of yourself; you realize people don't have to like you. You just got to be yourself, but sometimes they'll be different, too; they'll love that difference in you.

So that's what I always teach my kids. Don't be the same, try to fit in, do what Caucasian people do. But you are who you are, so don't try to feel like every other person. Otherwise, your whole life will just be like acting and trying to be someone that you know you aren't.

So, I always teach my kids that it's good to be different and to stand out. It's all about being and doing things that bring joy to you. It's been hard for me to get to this.

For Sarai, coming out of domestic violence and abuse, owning her story, and authoring it the way she knows best has been liberating. She is working through memories of her deepest pain and suffering she endured in silence. Hers is an ongoing process of healing, as she continues to thrive in her family life, as a single mother, and in her work.

If you are reading this and you have experienced what Sarai went through—or something similar, pain of a different kind—I have only love and an embrace for you. I deeply respect you. I know what pain is, as someone who has endured and healed. You are not alone. Please, reach out to those you trust. The road of healing is available to you.

You can start from anywhere in your life—even rock bottom—to author your life and rewrite your story. In the next section, I encourage you to deal with painful memories. I have found, in my life, how journaling is a powerful tool alongside therapy.

Strength is found in the struggle and character is forged through pain.

As part of my training to become a psychotherapist, I attended individual and group therapy for two years. I highly recommend professional help for mental health practitioners. We don't realize our blind spots until others point them out to us.

Healing from Painful Key Events

Whether single, married or divorced, we have all experienced pain that has left its mark. Most problems I have helped people work through in my practice involve relationship issues, both the relationships within oneself in terms of the *I* and *Me*, and relationships with others. It's important we don't avoid these difficult issues but address them.

Expressive Journaling for Healing

One of the most helpful tools in my healing journey has been journaling about painful events. I encourage you to do likewise. As renowned social psychologist Dr. James Pennebaker found, expressive writing (the act of writing your deepest thoughts and feelings concerning a significant emotional event, stressor, or trauma without worrying about grammar, spelling, or structure), can lead to long-term improvements in both mental and physical health. I found journaling has therapeutic benefits, like: improved physical health, better mental health outcomes, increased self-insight and coherence, as well as greater emotional recovery, which Pennebaker has researched. We also know it activates our DMN and the meaning-making process. So, feel free to pick up your pen or type away.

Do not overthink it, write with love and freedom. Love is the source of healing and the fountain of all nurturance. Write and rewrite the scenes of your life that are or were painful. Even if it's not emotionally charged, write. Writing brings clarity and expresses what is innermost when we allow it to emerge. If you find it hard to write, draw or speak it out, share with a trusted ally or therapist.

If it is painful, feel the rising emotions as you write. Cry. Let the tears flow. Feel the pain but know that pain doesn't kill us; it merely shows that we are alive. We feel. We hurt. We are of worth. Know that when you write or share what transpired and how you understood it, your emotions and your story will merge. The intensity of the past can be released. Reframe the experience in such a way that you pick out the wisdom, the lessons.

All our life experiences—the pain, the heartache, the hurt—they all have something to teach us about life and our Self, our identity. They show us what happened to violate the facets of our Selves, and they show how what happened still impacts our present and future Self. They show us what was maimed, but they also unravel what needs to heal and be built up again. Like fragmented pieces in the dark, what is brought into the light, expressed in language, and articulated, can heal. Reframed and processed by our DMN, these pieces can be grafted back into the whole Self, transformed. This becomes our "Aha!" or gestalt moment.

Healing Is Relational

Healing memories in the key events of our lives is one powerful pathway to emotional healing, especially when pain is rooted in past experiences. But healing can also happen through the body, the present moment, or through new relationships and beliefs. Cultural, spiritual, or relational shifts spark emotional healing by restoring connection, belonging, or purpose. Sometimes we heal not by looking back but by living forward differently, with new meaning and purpose.

Understand that healing is relational. Our stories foster connection so we feel seen, believed, and held.

You aid your own healing when you find people who reflect the "you" you're becoming, not just who you've been. Look for values-based connections, not only shared interests. Form a support group, which could be a therapist, such as a psychologist or other mental health professional, a mentor, coach, or trusted friend. It could also involve a writing group or a group of like-minded women who have your best interest at heart.

Become the Author of Your Life Story

Becoming the author of your life doesn't mean writing your story in solitude; it means choosing collaborators wisely, building a circle of people who see you clearly and reflect your worth, not only your wounds, back to you.

You are reading this book because I healed and dared to dream big. I shared in the introduction how, as a young mom and a graduate student, I used to feel like a character lost in my story. However, after working with the StoriCompass, it helped me to understand my underlying narrative, my story loop, and I explored elements in my life story I could work on so I could move toward my dreams. I looked at the people and circumstances I needed to enlist as Guides and Supporters, my Who and my Why, my Beneficiaries, and how, as an Agent of my life, I could overcome Oppositions to obtain my Desires.

The StoriCompass helped me realize the elements associated with key events in my life, which were stepping stones to get me to my dreams, including producing the book you now read. My road to authorship had many bumps and detours, but all the twists, turns, and rocky jolts of my journey were worth it if this book helps you.

I am ever so thankful for that initial key event of receiving the box of books from my first Aussie teacher. If she is reading this, thank you for being part of my journey, for planting the seed of a dream that helped me become an author, not only of this book but of my life.

Key Takeaways

* Becoming the protagonist in your story means letting your authentic calling, desires, and values—your true self—define who you are and contribute to your story as the author and Agent.
* Key events are notable milestones or experiences, often descriptive and factual, anchoring each of us in our life's timelines.
* We become who we are from the key events in our lives which are associated with the elements in our StoriCompass life frame.

Deeper Actions

Reflect on your life and answer the following questions:

1. What are five key events, whether positive or challenging, that impacted your life path?

2. Express through writing, sharing with a trusted friend, or another artistic way like drawing how you felt about these key events. What beliefs and stories did you start weaving about these key events? What key events were associated with the elements in your StoriCompass structure? Revisit this in chapter 8 with your own StoriCompass. Note that we learn from both positive and negative key events of our lives.

3. How can you reframe these key events and see them from a learning point of view? What did these events teach you? What were the lessons?

4. What future key events need to take place as you map and navigate your path to your Desire? Do you need to enlist a Guide or Supporter, reframe an Opposition, or clarify your Beneficiary?

11

Living Aligned

Great necessities call out great virtues.

—Attributed to Abigail Adams

Be true to yourself.

— Attributed to Louisa May Alcott

Fiona couldn't take it anymore. When her parents immigrated to Australia from Zambia for a better life, she moved to a Catholic school in the south suburbs of Melbourne. All the students there were White except one Asian girl who would hide in the library because no one wanted to play with her. When the kids found out Mary, a new student, was from Africa, they asked her, "Do you have wild animals in your backyard?" and "I thought everyone in Africa was Black. Why aren't you?"

Fiona often wondered why her Scottish-born parents had moved her from a private middle-class international school in Zambia that was fully diverse to a place where differences were frowned upon. At her international school in Zambia, the children had embraced all cultures, all races, all manner of people around the world. But here, in Melbourne, Australia, Fiona felt she didn't fit in at all. School days became nothing short of a nightmare.

One day, she expressed her despair to her mother. "Mom, I can't take this anymore. I need to get out of here. I am not accepted here." Her mom didn't know what to say. She was also navigating this difficult life transition and missing Zambia terribly.

The minute Fiona finished school, she left for Europe and the UK, where she spent the next seven years living and working. She wanted to live in places that felt more aligned with her values of diversity.

In her late thirties now, Fiona told me, "I was Zambian, but I have lived the majority of my life here in Australia. So, I'm Australian, but then I'm not. When I see my Zambian friends, I'm not them anymore. I'm Australian now; but when I'm with Australians, I think, well, I'm different to Australians. I'm neither-nor. I'm in between. As I've grown older, I've learned to embrace all parts of me. My uniqueness is my superpower."

***

I wonder if you have felt—or still feel—cultural conflicts the way Fiona has? Is your life out of alignment with where you want to be? I certainly have. Even in diverse societies, many people struggle to find their place and feel a sense of belonging. We may feel we fit in some aspects, but then we may not feel in alignment in other areas, such as our workplace, neighborhood, or peer group. All of us have multiple cultures influencing us, and in some cases, putting pressure on us to act in certain ways. Many of us balance different cultures in our life.

What Is Living in Alignment?

In this chapter, we explore what it means to live in alignment. Alignment in our life story means living in a way that is consistent with our core values, authentic self, and evolving purpose, rather than being shaped by external expectations, cultural scripts, or inherited roles. In other words, alignment is when what we believe, who we are, and how we act are in harmony.

Here, we focus on understanding and bridging gaps between

your inner values, cultural expectations, and real-life choices, so you can live a more fulfilling, congruent life. An authentic life. Brené Brown suggests that being authentic means regularly letting go of who we think we should be and choosing to live as who we really are.

In chapter 2, we explored embracing who you are through exploring your CulturAlign blueprint and StoriCompass, which help you identify as the Agent of your story. If you haven't completed your blueprint where you identify your personal values in chapter 2, go right now and use the QR code there to generate your CulturAlign blueprint, because it's so important you have that information in this chapter.

Now is the time to understand how you can live aligned, based on your values.

This is important because if your personal values and cultural values aren't aligned, you will sense an invisible force working against you when you try to live your story authentically. The author Roy T. Bennett urges each of us to shape our lives by choosing paths that reflect our deepest values and purpose. Echoing this, American author Frank Sonnenberg highlights that staying grounded in our values is essential; without them, we risk being influenced by anything that comes along.

Alignment versus Misalignment

I remember when I went to live and work in Canada, I fell in love with the country and its people. I felt that Canadians were so welcoming. It was a culture I could easily adapt to because of the friendly people. Belonging and becoming both matter in the sense of the alignment we feel. They always involve relationships, even the relationship within yourself between I and Me. Remember, wherever you or *I* go, we cannot escape from the *Me* within.

Alignment happens in certain places, cultures, groups, families, or with a person. When our inner sense is in sync with our outer reality, we feel psychologically safe.

On the other end, I bet you have walked into a room where you felt vibes of tension and conflict and felt uncomfortable, as Fiona did in her school. We may sense the culture of a place and feel misplaced. This can impact our inner reality, as it did for Fiona when she felt dissonance with her new home after leaving Zambia. Sometimes the circumstances might be an adjustment time. However, if time passes and there are still signs you don't feel aligned, it's important to pay attention.

Signs of living in misalignment may be feeling uncomfortable or drained in a situation or context, or finding ourselves second-guessing, feeling obliged to do things we don't want, or feeling guilty for saying no. Or we may feel restless, with a sense of striving toward something else. This is when we may be living like a side character in our story.

Fiona felt like she had to leave Australia to regain her sense of authorship when she felt intense cultural conflict. Sometimes, like Fiona, you may have to take that step to leave a cultural misfit—whether moving to another area, leaving a workplace, or ending a relationship—if the culture doesn't align with your inner values or with your Desires.

Such a misalignment may reflect a period when you can work through that conflict, regaining yourself, and then return to the situation with a different mindset or approach. Or it may mean it's time to make major life changes and find opportunities that help you remain in alignment.

Research tells us that people who migrate to countries where cultural practices align more closely with theirs improve their psychological well-being and social integration. This implies that when our cultural and personal values are in harmony, we enjoy better health and well-being. We are more likely to operate in the world more effectively as an authentic author of our life.

Personal and Cultural Values

As I've discussed throughout the book, cultural values are shared priorities and ideals of a group, society, or culture. They define what is considered "good" or "normal" in various groups. These values are reinforced through family, education, religion, government, peer groups, and media to guide collective behavior and expectations.

We've explored how some of our personal values originated from our family's cultural values. In the CulturAlign blueprint, we may find that original values no longer align with our current values, however, if they persist and we still want to hold on to them, they can live in our present and future values. If this is the case, our current values align with our ideal self, which is also our future self.

However, as we develop, our values can change over time. Our goals change and may not be what our family or culture wants for us anymore. If your past and present values conflict with your future values of your ideal self, it's important to unpack your personal and cultural values further. For example, you may be living in a collectivist society that teaches the values of being a "good" and "obedient" girl, but now, as an adult, you value more autonomy and innovation. In this case, you may no longer be sure how you fit within your family and community.

On the other hand, there might be values you don't hold personally but that are important to others—your family, religious community, or a workplace—that you choose to uphold under certain circumstances because that helps you meet other life goals. Take the example of Cristina. Though she no longer adhered to some of her family's religious values, she still respects her earlier upbringing in an Orthodox home and communist country that emphasized hard work and family. In her words below, keeping these values alive is consistent with how she would like to navigate her path forward.

CRISTINA

I am proud of my family values. The traditions and religion. I'm not a religious person now. My grandmother was very religious. My uncle is very religious in the Orthodox Christian religion. My uncle still does a little prayer before eating and before bed, all that sort of stuff. My grandmother did the whole fasting every Wednesday and Friday. In the Orthodox religion, you're not allowed to eat any animal products. She still did that her whole life. I love the traditions that come with the religious stuff. Like the Christmases, the Easter traditions of going to the midnight mass. And I went to that when I was a child with my parents.

I think I try to keep those traditions alive but not necessarily through religion. Romanians are religious, though I know that a lot of people are like my uncle and auntie; they live in Spain and they're like, what do you mean you don't pray every night? I don't pray every night. But I love the people that I am associated with. My family and extended family. My cousins, we have a ball when we get together. So yeah, I love my family.

I also value hard work. When we grew up, like we grew up in a communist country, and we had to work hard for money. Everybody had to work. We went to school six days a week in Romania. So yes, those values of hard work and those values of family I've got, they will stay with me forever.

She has chosen to reframe her experiences in a communist country as a positive in her life. Her values of family and hard work are what guide her as she rebuilds her life after her break up. Though she is no longer religious, she still values her Christian foundations. She is not broken but has found strength in both individual values she's developed as an adult and the cultural values she grew up with, even though her priorities changed over the years. She can still value her family's beliefs, while living her values and without rejecting theirs. In this way she feels she could move forward to a healthy life that includes her family and her history.

For others like Fiona, though, the values conflict between personal and cultural is real, and resolving this is important.

Understanding Personal and Cultural Tensions or Conflicts

A common cultural script found across many cultures involves the following: Be a good child, study hard, get into university or have a solid education, find a good job and work hard, get married, have children, and then teach your children this cultural script. This is how most societies function; cultural scripts are held up in all cultures to help each member understand their roles and the culture's values. Each culture has a different way of expressing cultural scripts; there may be sacred texts, stories, rituals, and ways of living passed down through generations.

Oftentimes in the clinic, I see clients in conflict because their lives have not followed their cultural scripts and/or their personal values clash with their partner's, family's, community's or workplace's values. That's why it's so important to understand each person in their unique cultural contexts. These cultural contexts cue the frames of mind through which we interpret life's experiences, which will be covered in part 3.

Fiona moved from Zambia to Australia. In Zambia, she felt free to show up as her whole self because it was community-oriented, expressive, and connected. In Australia, she struggled to fit in with the cultural emphasis on individualism, independence, and competition. The racism and bullying she saw in Australia didn't help her feel aligned with the values of her school or classmates. It wasn't only homesickness that made her finally admit to her mom that she didn't like Australia; something deeper felt misaligned. The culture around her didn't reflect her respect for diversity. She especially saw this when she saw how other Australians treated the Asian girl and her African schoolmate, Mary.

This tension between personal values and culture has been studied by social psychologist Shalom Schwartz and his colleague Lilach Sagiv. I had the pleasure of attending one of Schwartz's talks at an international conference. His work impresses me deeply, since I have lived in cities around the world with distinct cultures, places such as Baucau, Dili, Lisbon, Melbourne, and Toronto. I understood from lived experience how cultural surroundings affect us, and how we can struggle to fit in when the cultures around us are different from our values.

From Schwartz's work, I understood that, in Zambia, Fiona felt at home because she had grown up in a culture with values that emphasized benevolence, tradition, and universalism, that is, caring for others, respecting elders, honoring community rituals, and living with purpose. These values supported who she was becoming: someone who valued connection, stability, and contributing to something greater than herself.

But after moving to Australia, she'd experienced different cultural values, and in her school, differences and diversity were frowned upon. This was unlike anything she'd experienced in Zambia. She also felt an invisible pressure to succeed on her own by Australian standards, to move fast, protect herself, be assertive, stand out, and succeed. Values like achievement, self-protection, and self-direction were more dominant in Australia. While these weren't necessarily wrong, Fiona felt these weren't her personal values.

As a mature woman, her diverse cultural experiences have given her an awareness of cultural tensions with which she is still reconciling. However, instead of running away, now she has reframed it as a "superpower." Even though she doesn't feel fully Zambian or Australian, she has gained better understanding of her values, along with the power to make good choices.

You may not need to choose between cultures like Fiona, but you need to know what you stand for. Which of your values feels supported in your current context? Which feels stifled? What might need to shift in you or around you for more alignment?

Author Rick Warren teaches that integrity means living as the same person in every area of life, so that your actions consistently reflect your deepest values.

Doing this work means you may live with integrity by being able to finally put your finger on the invisible forces of your culture's values and how they influence your life. When we name the values that shape us—both personal and cultural—they become visible. And we can work with clarity and care through what is visible. We can make better decisions.

Using CulturAlign to Assess Your Alignment

The British sociologist Anthony Giddens argued that in modern society, we no longer have a fixed identity; instead, we build a life story (a "trajectory of the self") by reflecting on who we are and making choices over time, in what he called "the reflexive project of the self." As we've discussed, we don't do this in a vacuum; social structures (like rules, family roles, work, faith, and school) shape what feels possible, and our choices and actions reshape those structures (which Giddens referred to as "duality of structure"). I call this the dance of culture and self co-construction.

Every social structure—family, school, workplace, community, peer group—influences the person we become. They cue the frames we see through and interpret our experiences, so over time, we develop the life story frames highlighted in chapter 8 with Tessa, Tina, and Tre's examples. This is covered more in part 3.

In this section, to see whether you are living aligned or not, you need to situate yourself in your story and cultural contexts that shape your life and values. This is where CulturAlign makes it easy for you, by surfacing your values and significant cultural contexts operating in your temporal self. If you still haven't completed chapter 2, I encourage you to return and use the QR code so when you go through Tina's story, it prompts your understanding of your own Cultural Identity Blueprint.

Using Tina's CulturAlign blueprint (illustrated in Figure 11.1), you can go through each step to check whether you are living in alignment. Remember, alignment means our core values, authentic self, and evolving purpose are in harmony. We might not always be able to achieve alignment perfectly or consistently due to things completely out of our control, and that's OK, as long as you reground yourself, keep coming back to your values, and are kind to yourself.

You mapped out your story landscape in chapter 8 and part 1 using the tools in this book, the StoriCompass and the CulturAlign. Now, ask yourself: "What are my Desires?"

We know Tina had dual Desires: a life worth living; to be positive, healthy, energetic, and happy; and to set a good example so her kids would have moral foundations for their lives.

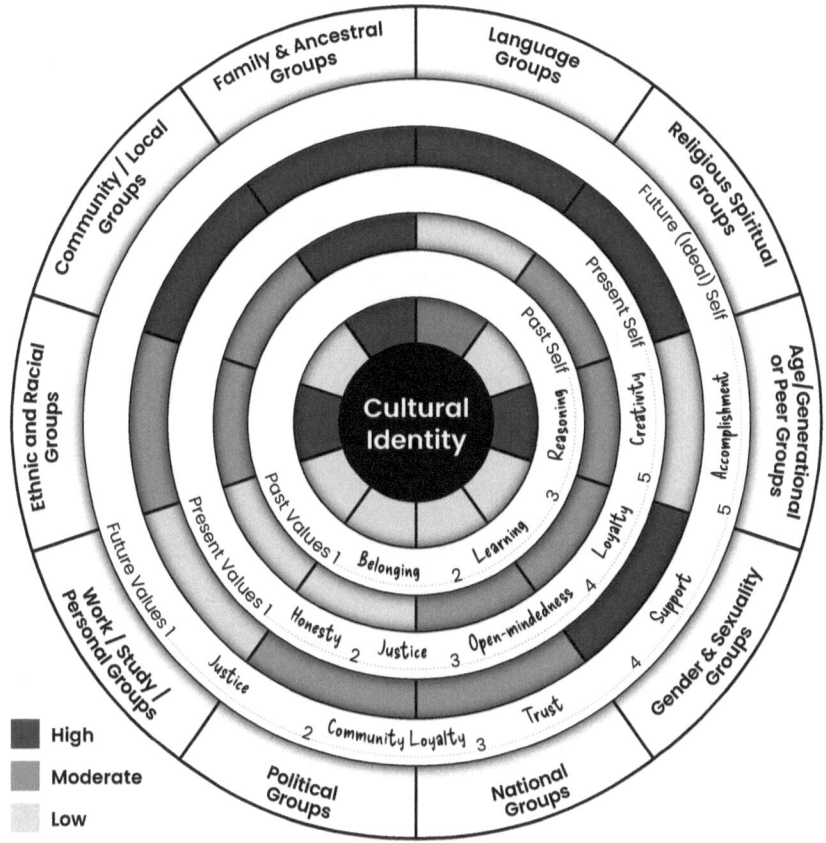

Figure 11.1 Tina's CulturAlign Blueprint to Assess for Alignment

Now, look at Tina's Cultural Identity Blueprint. She places great importance on the family and ancestral cultural context consistently, in her past, present, and future selves, highlighted in dark grey. This is also in line with her evolving purpose of wanting to set a good example to her children. Her family is indeed of utmost importance to her.

Look at your Desire and cultural context. Are they aligned? If not, ask yourself, "Why?" Become aware of your situation. Then, examine your values.

We see for Tina that justice and loyalty are consistent values in her present and future selves. She also presently values honesty, open-mindedness, and creativity. In her future Self, she values accomplishment, support, and trust. Due to her values, she took the risk of opening up to her partner to discuss their marital issues because she wants to reach her Desires.

What are your values from your CulturAlign, and how can you make your own decisions to take action toward fulfilling your Desires?

When your personal values align with your cultural contexts, you feel steadier and more energized; when they clash and are misaligned, your mood and motivation can dip because the environment blocks what matters to you, invites pushback, or creates an inner tug-of-war. Sometimes, there might be a mix of alignment and misalignment between your personal and cultural values.

Where alignment is strong, lean into where you are presently. Where it's weak, try three moves: adjust the context (negotiate hours, roles, or boundaries so you live closer to your values, such as setting boundaries for when you can be available and when you can't for nonpriority tasks), build your "valued networks" (friends, teams, mentors, or communities that share your values), or, if needed, change the setting such as your work, your peer group, or aspects of your family, like what Tina did in speaking with her husband. You don't have to solve every clash at once. Protect the spaces that matter most to your cultural identity first, and review how your well-being shifts as you experiment and make changes.

Exploring Values as a Couple

As I found out from Tina, who asked her husband to complete both StoriCompass and CulturAlign with her, both are useful tools for couples. Both helped them understand where each other was in their lives and how to build a family culture that aligned with both people's values. Tina's husband shared how he wasn't given permission to pursue his own Desires by his parents as they didn't value autonomy. She finally understood why he didn't take more initiative in their own family because he was never encouraged in his family of origin. The tools also provided them the language to name their personal and cultural values and to work through conflicts in their relationship using the pathways and elements of their life stories.

Taking Steps to Live Aligned

Living aligned doesn't always mean making one big choice and action, like Fiona did in leaving Australia. Sometimes, it's about redefining how we show up each day and taking a step-by-step approach before a turning point, like what Tina is doing. We can shift our focus from chasing outcomes to honoring the process.

For many women, the deeper question becomes "What brings me alive, regardless of where it takes me?"

That was how Pranjali navigated her journey. From taking one step to change from dentistry to psychology, then taking another step to change her mindset and align with what she valued. From pleasing her parents to following her heart to pursue her passion and do what she found meaningful. This is her account in her words.

PRANJALI

I feel in my life what I do out of passion always ends up having flow, with outcomes. So, TED Talks were very powerful in helping me through my career confusion. I have grown up on it, in a sense. They've really helped me. So, it was a full circle moment when I got to actually organize one.

When I got my psychology degree, I didn't know if I wanted to go into counseling. So, I was in that middle road. I had already taken a huge leap. From science to arts. So, I also have that sort of internalized shame. What if it doesn't work out? Like, I've taken such a big step, and I'm doing what I love, and you know, what if I'm bad at what I love?

Oh, that was really scary. So, I used to do a lot of research. And I'm a person who needs to love what I'm doing in order to do it well. Otherwise, I just cannot do things halfway, you know? Like, I really need to be the best because of all the years of academic validation.

So, while growing up, also, I was very much a straight-A student. And you know, very particular about grades. I feel my school life was only about grades. But when it comes to your bachelor's or your master's degree, you can't just do a checklist and get those grades. You need to immerse yourself in the subject. So, when I got into psychology, it was the first time I was doing something I loved. I had worked hard in science and math. But they were just not what I liked. I just did it because of the grades. Maybe subconsciously, it was kind of to please my parents, my family.

It's very sad how we are just meant to select one thing at such a young age. You don't know what you want then. Not even young people, or maybe, like people in their fifties. Even in their sixties, people may still not know what they want to do with their life.

> I think that, now, it's really powerful because I sit here in front of you. I have done science, arts, and commerce, as well. It's not like I just did arts, or I just did science. I also did commerce. I feel like I bring a very holistic sort of perspective to what I'm doing. And that has really helped me because I see people who have just done science or arts.
>
> Before I came to Melbourne and applied for my Master's course, I worked with a small business, and I worked with the ad agency to get sort of that varied perspective in marketing. The consumer side. And yeah, that's how I convinced my parents. And I think my parents saw that I was so passionate about it. That's how I got in.
>
> I feel like the most important person I needed to convince was myself.

Throughout Pranjali's journey of becoming and living aligned, she realized she needed to pursue her Desire and grow. She had to shift her focus from outcomes to the process, let go of the need to please her parents, and pursue her passions, while also showing them she was serious about changing careers.

Her last sentence, "I feel like the most important person I needed to convince was myself," is so powerful. When we are aligned with our deep core values and Desire, we oftentimes refer to our heart or intuition, then we seek cultural contexts, like a different country, field, or discipline, that fit better. Our *I* is at peace with *Me* within because our purpose is aligned with our values. We discover the power to believe we can fulfil our Desire, as Agent in our StoriCompass. We have conviction within that leads to an authentic and content life.

StoriCompass and CulturAlign: Tools for Alignment

Pranjali, Fiona, Cristina, and Tina are women at different developmental stages of life and cultural backgrounds. Yet today, they are each Agents authoring life in their own ways, in various fields of work. Using their skills to meet the world's needs and create sustainable livelihoods for themselves and their Beneficiaries: their Selves, children, families, and/or communities. They have found and are working out their place in the world, negotiating different cultural dimensions of life to embrace their cultural identities.

Despite the challenges each had in balancing personal and cultural values, they have been able to resolve conflicts showing up between personal and cultural values and between actual (past and present) and ideal (future) selves. They are living out aligned identities, pursuing Desires, and building support networks, including Guides and Supporters.

You can use both StoriCompass and CulturAlign when life changes. After a heartbreak, motherhood, career transition, or cultural dislocation, use your CulturAlign blueprint as a recalibration tool to understand where you are aligned or where you aren't.

Creating a Great Life

In fact, I believe those who can read the cultural climate and understand the interactions of personal and cultural values are well set up to thrive. They are more able to navigate individual and collective values and create innovative solutions to cultural conflicts that meet the needs of our world.

When you are on an aligned path, you create awesome things.

There is greatness within you.

You are also likely to meet other people who share your alignment and values. You start attracting the kind of people whom you can go the distance with. Knowing who you are, what you stand for, and where you are heading using the StoriCompass and CulturAlign gives you that edge because you can be strategic.

Share these with people you care about who may be struggling; it can change their life course. Hearts can be fragile; they hold sacred beliefs, emotions, and trust. Hearts are valuable, and when you give yours only to people who uphold its value, the experience is life-changing.

As Tina shared the tools with her husband, it opened up conversations with him that aligned both of them with shared purpose and values. They are now on an aligned path, creating a healthy family culture and pursuing shared goals that benefit their family.

Living aligned is not only an agreement we make with ourselves. When we feel coherent in the way we live, it also impacts people around us.

There are positive ripple effects when others in your life see you are no longer in conflict, but instead are more sure, confident, and at peace within yourself. The energy in the room changes; the vibes people pick up in your space start to feel different. Other cultural dimensions in your life can also be changed when your core feels authentic and aligned.

The Key to Traveling Light and Aligned

There is a final step to living aligned; it is to travel light. We have all been weighed down with the baggage of past hurts and conflicts in our lives. We are all in need of healing. Forgiveness is a powerful key to that door that unlocks healing. When we create safe spaces for people to share, to open up about wounds and receive appropriate interventions within a supportive environment, that is when healing takes place. It is within cultures of acceptance, safety, respect, understanding, connection, and belonging that we forgive, let go, and become whole.

I know this because I witnessed it firsthand again and again. I have also lived it. Before I became more aligned in how I live, I avoided pain and anyone who hurt me. But as I grew in my understanding of aligned living, I chose to forgive for my well-being. This didn't mean I forgot, but the choice to let go created an inner shift within me that released me to become my whole Self again rather than holding myself back to avoid pain.

What I share is not new. Probably deep down, you know you need to get to that place of letting go. Making that decision can be the hardest, but it is life-changing. It's time to let go of hurt and negatives and to choose forgiveness. No doubt, forgiving would enable you to release the positive energy to create the life you truly desire!

You may also need to forgive yourself and let go of pain and obstacles that held you back, as Tessa did in not being her worst enemy anymore. And as Fiona did by becoming aware of conflicting cultural values she lived through in Australia. We live out life's internal conflicts, keeping us imprisoned, but it is time to let go.

Live in alignment, as expressed in the wisdom of many traditions: "Keep your thoughts positive because your thoughts become your words. Keep your words positive because your words become your behavior. Keep your behavior positive because your behavior becomes your habits. Keep your habits positive because your habits become your values. Keep your values positive because your values become your destiny."

Key Takeaways

* Living in alignment is when our beliefs and values, who we are, and how we act are in harmony.
* Your personal and cultural values can be unpacked using CulturAlign and StoriCompass to help you towards alignment.
* When personal values align with cultural contexts, you feel steadier and more energized; when they clash and are misaligned, your mood and motivation dips, but sometimes, there might be a mix of alignment and misalignment between your personal and cultural values. Be kind to yourself.

Deeper Actions

Reflect on each of the questions:

1. What are the cultural values in the place or setting you live and work in right now? How aligned do you feel between your values and places you live and work?
2. Using your completed CulturAlign blueprint, answer or reflect on the following questions: What are your past, present and future values? Are your future values aligned with who you desire to become? Are your values reflected in the importance you place in your cultural contexts?
3. To live aligned, what do you need to let go from your life? Name them and take a small step to let go.

PART 3

Creating a Life of Joy, Meaning, and Legacy

Life is a sum of all your choices.

—Attributed to Albert Camus

Imagine being gifted with a box, and when you open it, you are surprised to find two wrapped rectangular parcels with a note on top. The note has instructions that read, *You can open both presents, but you can only choose one frame to keep, which will affect the rest of your life.* This comes as a shock! What kind of a gift is this?

When you open the packages, you look closer at the frames, and you realize they have different headings with inscriptions. One is labeled, *The Life You Are Living.* The other one is labeled, *The Life You Are Creating.*

Puzzled, you read each description again. You want to make the right choice.

The Life You are Living description reads: "In this frame, your future is sealed. The script has already been written. You will have the same experiences, play it safe, stay where you are, and live out the rest of your years with no change. Accept your lot in life. In this story, you know how your life is lived; it may or may not be the life you truly desire, but it's familiar, safe, and routine. This frame is the life you are living."

The Life You are Creating description reads: "In this frame, your future is blank. It is entirely up to you how to write it. You can start anywhere, at any point in time, no matter where you are in life. In this story, you don't always know where you are going next, but you are in charge of the following chapters. This is the path where you follow your heart and put your dreams and desires into action, plans that would only be ambitious goals in your current life. You might succeed in this life frame, or you might fail, but you can always reframe. There are no guarantees. But if you pick this frame, you choose to take that chance."

Whatever you decide, it will be your legacy.

There are no judgements about whichever frame you choose; your life is yours. You've made it this far. You mapped out your life story. You worked out how to move beyond your cultural script and embrace aligned personal and cultural values. This is the final passage to a life worth living and owning, where you close the gap between your present and ideal selves.

In part 3, you will learn about *Life Framing*, how to be joyful and successful, and how to create a meaningful life. Remember, our stories are what creates our cultures and Selves in the dance of co-construction. Make your choice about how to frame your life because however you choose, you are living your legacy.

12

Framing Your Future: Your Next Chapter Starts Now

We are a race of women that of old knew no fear and feared no death, and lived great lives and hoped great hopes.

—Olive Schreiner

The mind is the architect of its own frame.

— Attributed to Ralph Waldo Emerson

Susan experienced oxygen deprivation when she was born. She had to stay in an incubator, and it was a few weeks before her parents, Bridget and Patrick, took her home. The doctors were concerned about possible brain damage, so they followed her development.

She was the youngest of nine children, so home life was loud, full of commotion and music. Her parents often sang around the house. As devout Scottish Catholics, the family always attended nine o'clock Mass on Sundays; it was more than a religion for them, it was their identity. Susan enjoyed being involved in their church; her mother encouraged her faith.

But both her faith and self-confidence were tested when she started school. She struggled with learning difficulties, and other kids bullied her, leaving lingering insecurities. The shame cut deeply when they mocked her, calling her "Simple Susie." She felt isolated and misunderstood.

Coming home to her mother was the solace that held her together. Bridget encouraged Susan to sing to express herself, and this developed into a lifelong passion for music. She also spurred on Susan to sing in the church choir and participate in local competitions. As her staunchest supporter, Bridget believed in her youngest daughter's talent and urged her to pursue her dreams.

Susan stayed close to her mother and cared for her until Bridget's death at the age of ninety-one in 2007. The loss hit Susan hard. She withdrew, deeply stricken with grief. She cried a lot; she couldn't manage nor cope. However, during the darkest and lowest moment of her life, Susan knew even though her mother wasn't with her physically, she remained with her spiritually. Bridget meant for her to do something with her life, and it dawned on Susan that it was now or never. She had arrived at her turning point. She could either stay where she was, or she could listen to her mother's encouragement to move forward.

It was time to reframe her life, figure out the next chapter on her own. When she shared with her siblings what she wanted to do, they discouraged her. This led her to question and doubt herself. Had she gone mad by signing up for the audition?

In 2009, Susan showed up for an audition for the third series of *Britain's Got Talent*. She wore a lace dress with black stockings and white shoes; when she appeared onstage, her hair was dishevelled and her stress showed. The judges, Simon Cowell, Amanda Holden, and Piers Morgan, didn't seem impressed.

Simon Cowell asked Susan to introduce herself on stage. Susan appeared slightly awkward but answered with a cheery grin, "My name is Susan Boyle. I am forty-seven. And that's just one side of me!" She added that her dream was to be a professional singer and to be as good as Elaine Paige, the English singer and actress. That got the judges and audience rolling their eyes and chuckling with disbelief.

Yet, undeterred, Susan opened her mouth to sing "I Dreamed a Dream" from *Les Misérables*. Her powerful voice reverberated through the theater, stunning everyone present. The rest is history.

I saw her performance on TV. How could you not? It was everywhere! Overnight, she became a world sensation, with her performance going viral.

I was mesmerized. Her voice ignited in me the possibility that no matter where you come from, what you have been through, whatever you look like, or the age you are, you can still make it! You can dream a dream and go for that dream.

Susan's Reframe

In this chapter, we explore how you can change your story with Life Framing. *Life Framing* is the process of understanding the invisible frames that shape how you see yourself, your story, and your world—and learning how to reshape them to live more intentionally. This chapter pulls together the previous two parts, from understanding and mapping our lives with the StoriCompass to breaking our story loops, living aligned, and moving beyond our cultural scripts with CulturAlign. What we've covered so far is about embracing our cultural identity, who we are. Now, we focus on the creative process of framing our life stories so we can live more fulfilled, as Susan and others have done.

Susan Boyle didn't win the show; she was a runner-up. However, she went on to record her debut album, *I Dreamed a Dream*, which became the UK's fastest selling debut album with over 410,000 first week sales. It then sold over ten million copies worldwide. She took a risk and stepped into the next chapter of her life story, one she never could have imagined. If Susan can do it, so can you!

In 2010, her autobiography, titled *The Woman I Was Born to Be*, was released. It touched countless lives, including mine. Her story showed that fame hadn't changed her; she still lives in the same modest house she grew up in, and she has stayed true to her roots, her faith, and her belief that it's never too late to grasp your dreams. Three years after her viral performance, she was diagnosed with autism, which helped her understand her lifelong challenges.

Despite obstacles, Susan has continued to pursue her passion for music, releasing multiple albums, performing globally, and spreading the message of not giving up on your dreams. She has taught countless people that they can achieve their desires, no matter what challenges or judgements they face. It simply requires taking the risk, knowing the alternative is repeating the same day over and over again.

Susan may not have known at the time she decided to audition that this would open the door to the next chapter of her life. Neither did she know she engaged in the process of Life Framing. Despite the discouragements from her family and the nervousness she felt as she filled out her application, she knew she wanted to create a new life for herself. That seed her mother planted, the dream of becoming a professional singer, was calling out to her, catalyzed by the loss of her mother.

What Is Life Framing?

Life Framing acknowledges that we all move through life inside frames—beliefs, expectations, and cultural scripts—that structure our perceptions and inform who we should be. Some empower us; others limit us. Life Framing helps you see these hidden frames, make sense of your story, and rewrite it with purpose and joy. Like a house is built with frames to hold it up and within it are different frames like doors and windows, our stories build us up, and we have multiple frames we use to make sense of our life events and experiences.

Throughout our lives, we all walk through doors and see through windows—both types of frames—that provide us experiences through our senses. For example, we walk through a door frame into a room where we meet someone who becomes significant, or where we find an opportunity that changes our life. Or we take in the views through a window frame that shows us the vision of life or a landscape that feeds our soul. However, two people can walk into the same room and see through the same window but report different experiences. That is because frames—our mental and cultural lenses—are unique interpretative systems that make sense of what events mean to us, our sense of agency in managing events, and how they impact our future. Frames shape literally everything we see, feel, think, and decide.

Life Framing is about making a deliberate choice of what frames of experience we desire in our lives rather than going through life on autopilot.

By changing a default frame that's not serving you and replacing it with a wiser, values-aligned frame, you create clearer direction, steadier emotions, and real momentum. Small, well-timed *window* reframes refresh perspective; bigger *door* reframes move you into healthier rooms. For example, in Susan's life, at her lowest point, when she grieved her mother, she saw with fresh eyes that her mother wanted her to pursue her dreams, and she realized the time was upon her. This new perspective of how her life could be so different was a window frame, where she reframed her loss as an opportunity to go for her dream. Then she took action by using a door frame when she auditioned and stepped onto the stage. By doing this, she experienced a totally new chapter of her life. It literally opened the door for her to live out her dream of being a professional singer.

The Science Behind Life Framing

The concepts of frames and reframes were developed in parallel across multiple disciplines in the mid-twentieth century. American literary critic Kenneth Burke wrote about interpretive frames where our words can pre-frame our perception. For example, framing a relationship conflict as "my fault" (acceptance frame) creates self-blame and silence, but framing it as "our dynamic" (rejection frame) creates room for shared discussion and change in the relationship because it takes two to tango.

Anthropologist Gregory Bateson later defined a frame as the context that influences how we interpret the meaning of a message, such as interpreting whether something our partner said was meant to be taken seriously or as a joke. His work influenced Paul Watzlawick, John Weakland, and Richard Fisch, leading members of the Palo Alto Mental Research Institute, who popularized reframing in therapeutic contexts. They defined reframing as the process of reconceptualizing a problem with different meaning so the shift in meaning changes how you feel and what you can do next, despite the same problem. For example, if a son feels reactive and irritated because his mother "nags" him to get a better job, his therapist might suggest a reframe that interprets her behavior as caring for him and showing her deep commitment to his success. This reframes her pressure on him from an annoying problem ("nagging") to a sign of commitment ("encouragement"), which changes how they both feel about her behavior. The son is more likely to appreciate her support, and the mother may feel less frustrated and change her tone so he is more open to her suggestions.

In the 1960s, Aaron Beck, widely known as the father of Cognitive Behavioral Therapy (CBT), defined the internal frame, or schema, as a deeply held belief structure that colors all perception. Frames/schemas influence how we respond to what happens to or around us. Reframing or restructuring these schemas is a core component of CBT; reframing helps us examine the stories we tell ourselves about what's happening. If the stories are negatively impacting our mental state, we can reframe them so the narrative has a healthier effect.

Sociologist Erving Goffman showed how each situation carries a *scene frame*—a social context—that gives us clues as to how to behave, and psychologists Daniel Kahneman and Amos Tversky demonstrated how *wording frames* (whether a message is presented with negative or positive framing) sway our decisions. It has *framing effects*, which means you'll probably choose the chocolate bar labeled "90% Fat-Free" (a gain frame) over the exact same bar labeled "10% Fat" (a loss frame), because the way the words are presented instantly changes how you feel about the choice.

In 2000, a team of researchers—Ying-yi Hong, Michael W. Morris, Chi-yue Chiu, and Verónica Benet-Martínez—proposed the concept of cultural frames as invisible mental 'lenses' shaped by your culture and upbringing, along with cultural frame switching, which shows how people who bridge cultures can naturally shift between different 'versions' of themselves depending on the situation.

Life Framing draws from these concepts with the idea that you can craft, design, and take charge of your life through choosing your desired frames.

Framing Your Own Life Story

Life Framing is the deliberate, evidence-informed practice of noticing the frame you're using to interpret your past, present, and future, and then revising that frame so your life story becomes more aligned with your values; so your story becomes one of progress and growth rather than stuck in a frame of victimhood, resentment, or disappointment. Life Framing can take you from your present self to your ideal self in four core steps.

These four steps are:

1. **Situate** yourself in your story with CulturAlign. Know who you are, what you want, what you value, and the difference you hope to make as the Agent in the StoriCompass.

2. **Structure** your life story with the StoriCompass, so you understand the pathways and elements of your story.

3. **Shift** your framing of what's happening in ways that align with your values and support your vision, with reframe(s).

4. **Shape** the person you are becoming, knowing there may be ripple effects on the culture around you. Take small, steady actions, acknowledging that a change to your Self is a change to culture because every culture is influenced by those in it. Use your understanding of your life narrative to deepen larger cultural narratives.

The Power of Life Framing

I am moved every time I hear stories like Susan Boyle's. After the turning point of her mother's death, she was inspired by the vision her mother always held for her. She situated herself as an Agent on the borrowed belief of her mother even though she felt trepidation about taking action to move herself toward a singing career. She remembered her mother's encouraging words, which helped ground her in her mother's confidence in her, and she took action to acquire her Desire and become a singer. After grieving the loss of her mother, she restructured her life in a way that put her on the path to acquire her Desire and shifted her life frame from one of struggle to one of stardom. This, and her mother's support, gave her the strength to take a risk and apply for *Britain's Got Talent*. By applying, and by showing her true Self on stage, she not only achieved her Desire, she became a culture shaper. Her story has shaped the culture in which we all live.

Our stories may touch hearts, they can open minds, and they often become entangled in others' life story structures. We make a difference in peoples' lives. Our conflicts, and how we resolve them, can become a Supporter in another's life because shared stories have the power to inspire others to pursue their Desires, or to become the Guide and/or Supporter in another person's StoriCompass. This is how selves and cultures build, intertwined like a DNA structure. This is how cultures are sustained and changed.

One story can change many lives, the way Susan's has for others by giving hope and a reason to persevere through difficulties.

Yes, creating change in our own lives will require facing our fears, being uncomfortable, and taking risks; it may mean changing career direction from something safe to something more aligned with our values but that poses challenges, doing something we've never done before (like auditioning on TV!), or making a decision that feels scary, such as leaving (or committing to) a relationship. It may mean dropping people from our lives who aren't healthy for us anymore as we prioritize our values, how we spend time, and what kind of energy we want in our lives.

It's about gaining clarity about what you truly want, then making concrete plans to achieve your Desire; it's about examining the Agent-Desire relationship, as well as Guide-Beneficiary, and Supporter-Opposition relationships in all contexts to structure your life so you live it fully. Where StoriCompass and CulturAlign are the meaning tools, Life Framing is the process that uses both tools to get you from where you are to where you want to be.

In any endeavor of making changes in our lives, designing and crafting better lives, we need to engage this process of Life Framing.

How You Can Frame Your Life Story

What life chapter do you want to write next? What is stopping you? Let's gain self-awareness with Tina as she goes through the Life

Framing process. Wisdom is born of experience. But it doesn't have to be our experiences only. Many people have shared theirs in books, poetry, art, and many forms of expression. Let us be wise to learn from the wealth of experiences. Time is short; life is very brief. To shortcut our mistakes and failing, we embrace the wisdom of others. We learn from their lives.

Tina had begun the process of Life Framing by completing her StoriCompass and CulturAlign blueprint. Once she completed these tools for her own life, she encouraged her husband to complete them for his. As Tina and her husband found out, Life Framing can be a helpful process for couples who want to grow in their relationships.

Before their discussion, this is what she shared: She was already coming to the realization she couldn't change him, that she could only change herself. Understanding how some of her problems stemmed from the culture she grew up in, from her parents and their history, she's now in a better place to own her life story and examine her cultural frames. The following is her account before she used the Life Framing process to explore the next chapter of her life. As you read her account, think of where you are within your story. Write down your story if it helps or speak it out and record it.

TINA

My husband just makes me angry because he brings so much negativity to the house by his whinging and complaining. And I keep telling him, you know, you need to get rid of your negative energy around the house. You need to be more present.

He's always there. He does the washing. He does the laundry, the floor, but then I feel bad saying, "Oh, but he's not present at that moment."

He's there in the same room, but he's not actively playing with the kids or engaging with me. He's not, like, a bad father who doesn't do anything; he does do a lot.

He does wash them, bathe them, and look after them. But then he'll go to sleep early, and I have to be in charge. It's like, we're ticking each other off.

And at the end, it's like, there's only so much I can tell him that he doesn't change himself. Maybe I should change myself, but how much more do I have to change myself? That it's kind of like an imbalance, and I don't want to have that. I want more of an organic flow in our relationship, and that's something I'm not going to get.

And so, therefore, the helplessness and then the anger sets in. So, I need help in reframing. The other one is relationships. And setting up a foundation for my kids.

These are the struggles that most women my age are going through. Lack of energy, wanting to leave something behind for the kids, setting a good role model, having good relationships, being able to be more productive, being able to be more calm.

So, it's about breaking that cycle of where I am now. It didn't start with my journey. It started before me. I would say it started from the foundation of my journey where my parents came from, their struggles. The way I see the negativity in my husband was the way my mom saw my dad. The cycle continues, like what I thought had started with me really started with my parents, and how that set my life up. There's the deeper roots to my problems.

It's something that I've just acknowledged that it is what it is. And I'm grateful for having a history of struggle; it's better than not having anything and no understanding of it. It's like, if you can understand your roots and your foundation, it just makes it easier to know where to fill in the extra gaps so you can stand tall and go forwards.

I also want to change careers, and I think, in my mind, I am already planning to when my son starts school. I want to have a more stimulating and meaningful career that also pays what I am worth. I know I am meant for more.

The Process of Life Framing

The same way Tina went through this four-step process of Life Framing, you can also work through the steps yourself. Start by *Situating* yourself—know who you are as the Agent in StoriCompass, what you want, and the cultural context you're in through CulturAlign. Then *Structure* your life story using StoriCompass (Agent, Desire, Guide, Beneficiaries, Supporter, Opposition) in an aspect of your life in which you want to see change, for example, at work, at home, in your relationships, or in your health. This is the context. You may also choose to look at your overall life story. *Shift* the frame by choosing to understand the situation or interpret its meaning differently. Use this reframe to choose behaviors, responses, and actions that move you toward your dreams and goals. And reframe past behaviors and actions—maybe mistakes you feel you made, or choices that were not ideal—as a part of your growth path rather than proof you're a failure or you make "bad decisions." Over time, those steps *Shape* the person you are becoming, as well as the culture around you. As we know, we are not only influenced by culture, but we affect culture as well.

Here are the steps in more detail, including questions for you to answer for yourself. Feel free to write your answers in a journal or in a blank computer document along with the work you've previously done with the StoriCompass and CulturAlign tools. After a review of the basics, I'll revisit Tina's story to illustrate how she used the Life Framing process to get clearer on situations she experienced.

Step 1: Situate Yourself

This step is about clarity, context, and knowing yourself as the Agent and author of your life within your cultural contexts. The questions to answer here are:

* From part 1, with your StoriCompass, what does your current life frame look like? How are you interpreting your life? Are you a victim, a character, or an Agent in your life story currently? Do you feel like you are the Agent of your life to author your story? If not, why?
  * (Note: If you haven't completed part 1 yet, go to chapter 8 and use the QR code or go to **www.lidialae.com/readerhub** to map your StoriCompass and complete your CulturAlign blueprint.)

Know yourself as the Agent of your life story so you can become the author.

---

* What cultural contexts cue the frames you are operating in? Which are most important to you?
  * Use the information in CulturAlign about your personal values and important cultural contexts in your life. These cultural contexts cue your frames by activating the stories that drive choices.
  * Identify what truly matters to you. Reflect on moments when you felt most alive, proud, or fulfilled. What did you value about those moments?

In your CulturAlign, what are your past, present and future values?

As we saw in Tina's StoriCompass in chapter 8, Tina identified herself as the Agent. When she completed the CulturAlign blueprint in chapter 2, she noted that her values for her past self had been Belonging, Learning, and Reasoning; her present values were Honesty, Justice, Open-mindedness, Loyalty, and Creativity; and the values she hoped to embody in the future were Justice, Community, Loyalty, Trust, Support, and Accomplishment.

Reviewing her cultural frames—the way she sees her world shaped by culture and the way she prioritizes what is most important—we can see (in dark grey) that her family and ancestry had always been high importance. She was always likely to make decisions based on family values. Increasing in importance for her from her past, present to future self is her language, religious/spiritual, gender/sexuality and community/local contexts. What she used to value, which she finds is diminishing in importance in her life, is her ethnic/racial and age/generational/peer contexts. What stays in the low (light grey) to medium (moderate grey) importance is occupational and political contexts. Nationality wasn't as important to her in the past but is currently in the present, and it diminishes slightly in her future.

* Look through your CulturAlign and summarize: What is most important to you? Use what matters most to you to guide your decisions.

Knowing her values and what matters to her, Tina could use the Blueprint to structure her life story in step 2 and use her values as guiding principles for her decisions in daily life to remain aligned with those principles. This is what you can do too!

Step 2: Structure Your Life

Be clear about your Desire and your role as Agent in your life. Remember, what you pursue defines you. Use your CulturAlign blueprint to guide you in terms of your ideal future Self so your Desire is grounded in personal and cultural values.

From Tina's StoriCompass in chapter 8, we see she has two main

Desires rooted in her present and future values: 1) She desires a life worth living: to be positive, healthy, energetic, and happy; and 2) She desires to set a good example to her children so they have good morals and a strong ethical foundation.

During her explorations, she realized she had to unearth the foundations of her family of origin, not let her past and limiting cultural scripts she was given hold her back; she needed to reframe her experiences and circumstances in a way that emphasized the challenges she'd overcome to be where she is now, ready to move forward and live a life of meaning and purpose, an aligned life.

* At this point, what are your Desires? Are they grounded in your values?

Tina's pursuits are grounded in her values; as the Agent of her life, her family is the most important thing to her, and her identity as mother creates the Desire to impart strong values to her children. This is her Pathway of Pursuit; her role as a mother serves as the road to reaching her Desire. She values justice and loyalty in her present and future; with honesty, open-mindedness, and creativity in her present self, she seeks to accomplish her main Desire: a life worth living. Her ideal Self further values trust, support, and accomplishment.

From her StoriCompass, we can see she enlists Guides: her friends, family, and clinical professionals (including me). When she accomplishes her goals, her Beneficiaries are her wider family, her nuclear family of husband and kids, along with her community and friends.

* Identify your Guides and Beneficiaries. Do they overlap with other elements?

Tina reported some of her Guides (family, friends, and professionals) also acted as Supporters, along with her husband and workmates, to help her reach her Desire. However, she realizes during her exploration that she placed her husband, the needs of her children, her health, financial restraints, and time as

Oppositions. She explained that her husband and children drained her energy and time. This was her Pathway of Forces, which she frames as getting in the way of her ideal life. She realizes she feels conflicted in her relationship with her husband, seeing him as both a Supporter and Opposition to reaching her Desire. Her goal is to give her children a good foundation, but their needs seem to have overwhelmed her, so they are currently an Opposition also.

In StoriCompass, we can see how the same people (her husband and kids) can appear as different elements, as Supporter, Desire, and Opposition in Tina's case, and this helps us surface the underlying conflicts that need to be resolved for Tina to move forward in obtaining her Desire. What she listed as Oppositions are externally what stop her from reaching her Desire, which would lead to the next step, where she needs to make a shift.

* Does your StoriCompass reveal underlying conflicts or roles in different elements you were surprised by?

Step 3: Shift Your Frame and How You See, Make Meaning, or Act by Reframing

Identify what kind of a shift you need to make to develop the right mindset to support movement toward your Desire. Does it require a window frame shift of seeing the situation differently? Or a door frame shift that involves not only different perspectives, but a change in your life story structure that affects your experience? You literally have to get up, take action, and enter another door frame to a different room.

For Tina, when her StoriCompass revealed how her marital conflict played out in her Pathway of Forces, she realized she needed to make a window frame shift. She needed to shift to seeing her husband and children as Supporters, which meant she had to create new meaning about their relationship to her and their roles in her life. For example, from "I feel overwhelmed because of his and the children's neediness" to "I have a chance to set a good example by establishing steps for all of us to achieve our goals." She had to see them with a different frame, *reframe*, and tell herself a different story so she could engage all of them collaboratively as a family to support each other. She had already achieved her short-term goal of opening up to her husband and getting him to explore his life story using StoriCompass and CulturAlign. They are now working together to build a values-based foundation for their lives and their children.

Identify what you need to do, a window frame shift where you see your circumstances differently and/or a door frame shift where you have to literally act, like make a career change, make peace with someone, take an audition, etc. You can take a step by step short-, medium-, and long-term approach like Tina, illustrated in the following.

Tina's Short-term Shift

Reframe her relationship with her husband and children using a window frame, a different way of seeing them and their roles in her life, as well as her role in their lives.

A big door frame shift Tina reported was within her medium-term goal; she wanted to change her job and career entirely. She was plotting this next chapter of her life once her son completed preschool and attended elementary school. She felt her current job was unstimulating and didn't offer professional growth. However, it gave her the flexibility to attend to her young children when they needed her. She was willing to accept the trade-off in her life plan of having flexibility over professional growth as she worked toward her Desire.

Tina's Medium-term Shift

Tina's medium shift was to frame a new work chapter for her professional career using a door frame.

When we consider what kind of shifts to make, it's important to think about the life stage we are in. Sometimes we can plan our turning points, like when we choose to marry, have a child, or embark on a career, but other times unplanned life-changing events such as illness, loss, or accidents take over, and we may need to spend time reframing what's happened so our outlook supports movement toward our Desire. When life surprises us, we can continue to focus on obtaining our Desire and develop the meaning-making tools to help us get there through reframing our circumstances.

Tina's Long-term Shift

Frame a life story where she is positive, healthy, energetic, happy, and enjoying a life worth living, as well as setting a good example and foundation for her children.

What this means for her is to learn to reframe negative interpretations about events, experiences, and memories to more growth-oriented interpretations; this builds a growth mindset. If her stories keep her in a negative frame of mind, drain her energy, and keep her unhappy—for example, if she tells herself she won't ever be happy if her husband doesn't change—then she gives away her agency to him. She needs to develop new stories that give her hope and help her flip from negative to positive; for example, "Even if he doesn't change, I will keep up with my exercises to improve my health and model a good example for my children." This shift allows her to find joy by focusing on what she can do to build the life she wants, create new stories that will empower her and her children, and make choices independent of her husband's behavior. This shift will not only empower her and teach her children to be independent but affects the culture around her as others see her creating empowering narratives.

In short, for Tina, a consistent frame repeated over time builds a mindset, and a set of mindsets integrated over a lifetime creates a powerful, stable Life Frame, which helps Tina move toward her Desire. This is summarized by the sequence below.

Figure 11.2 The Four Step Process of Life Framing.

* **Frame:** How I'm seeing the situation now.
* **Reframe:** How I can see the situation to make my interpretation more empowering.
* **Mindset:** How this reframe can change how I see the world and my role in it to develop my mindset.
* **Life Frame:** How I now approach events, people, situations, and circumstances while staying connected to my new mindset. This Life Frame shows up in our StoriCompass.

Step 4: Shape

Let steady choices and actions ripple outward. Once you've shifted your Life Frame, it is time to shape the person you are becoming and the cultural contexts around you. Use CulturAlign to keep, update, or retire outdated frames and scripts so your changes gently shift your experiences with home, work, and community.

* What are your future (ideal) Self's values? Use the CulturAlign tool to identify these values, then let the values guide your choices and actions. Consistent action has compound effects. By investing in your future through focused action, you become your ideal Self.

When you've made a shift, the change you make eventually shapes not only who you are becoming—your new self and identity—but also the culture around you.

For Tina, small steps toward implementing her intentions helped her make different choices when confronted: "If X happens, then I will do Y." For example, Tina wrote in her journal, "If I feel overwhelmed, I will take ten minutes to journal, take a break to problem solve, or walk before continuing with what I'm doing and before making any decisions." She began putting her to-do lists and other noise from her head onto her phone. This cleared her mental space so she could take aligned actions. She used her CulturAlign blueprint to examine whether her past, present, and future selves were aligned, which of her personal values were aligned with the values of her cultures, and where to focus. These choices helped structure her life in a way that she could reach her Desires. Her pursuit of her goals has inspired her husband to pursue his goals of getting healthier and happier, and now both are committed to their shared values of cultivating a healthy family and building foundations for their children.

As Tina engaged with the Life Framing process, so can you, to answer the questions, "What is the story I want to live? What title will I give to this next chapter of my life?"

These exercises engage our DMN, linking our autobiographical memory and imagination. This supports our agency, cultivates hope, and helps us create meaning, which are the key ingredients of a fulfilling life.

We Can Frame a Better Future Together

We are all living architects of our culture and society. We are not only culture makers but also culture shapers and culture managers, actively participating in how culture is created, shaped, and sustained. Our time on earth is a creative contribution to a world that longs for fresh insight, new wisdom, and grounded presence.

What we dream of, conceive, and bring into the world through our ideas, stories, and action, touches other lives through the window of experiences we collectively share. I would never have gotten where I am today without the support of others who believed in me, gave their time to help me, and put their trust in me.

I believe in you! I believe that as you work through the StoriCompass, CulturAlign, and Life Framing processes, you move closer to living the life you truly desire.

Right now, you're reading the result of my journey, the culmination of my childhood and adolescent desire to write a book. To help people. To make my life count. To empower people to know that we are all creators, building up not only ourselves through daily narratives and actions but others who inhabit our shared cultures. I had to undergo Life Framing by using CulturAlign to situate myself, structure my life story with StoriCompass, shift my life frames by exploring StoriCompass pathways and elements, close my story loop, and create new meaning by reframing my story, so I could shape my new identity, which is intertwined with the cultures I am embedded in. Through this process of Life Framing, I was able to write this book, which has connected me with my readers; we're collaboratively making meaning. This is how books change lives!

When I see Susan Boyle—who practiced singing in her church choir, who sang in competitions and kept her dream alive until she entered the public arena to share her life with others—that touches my life. Witnessing Susan and Tina reach for their goals, build meaningful lives, and impact people, it impacts my life as well. Together, we are building our world with our lives, our gifts, our energy, and our passion, and we collaborate with each other in creating a better world.

Key Takeaways

* Life Framing is the deliberate, evidence-informed process of noticing the frame you're using to interpret and choosing a better frame, a reframe, to help you.

* The Life Framing process takes you from your present self to your ideal self in four core steps: Situate, Structure, Shift, Shape.

* We use window frames to see differently, and door frames to experience a significant change in our stories. These frames and reframes shape our mindset and, over time, form our life frame.

Deeper Actions

Reflect on and work through each question:

1. What is one area of your life where you desire change?
2. How are you currently situated? Refer to your StoriCompass and CulturAlign.
3. What is your structure? Draw it or write it out.
4. What is a situation you would like to reframe? Remember the process and work through it.
5. What shape would your life look like after you have shifted your life frame?

Remember, if you can visualize all the changes and take action on a daily basis, you are becoming and framing your life, owning and creating a life you want.

13

Reframing Success: What Joy Really Looks Like

I slept and dreamt that life was joy. I awoke and saw that life was service. I acted and behold, service was joy.

—Rabindranath Tagore

To leave the world a bit better, whether by a healthy child, a garden patch, or a redeemed social condition; To have played and laughed with enthusiasm and sung with exultation; To know even one life has breathed easier because you have lived—This is to have succeeded.

— Bessie Anderson Stanley

In July 2023, I was riding a wave of upward momentum, working on the completion of my debut memoir.

The year held so much promise. A piece I wrote for an anthology of creative nonfiction that featured the introduction of my memoir was set for publication in December, and I was consistently engaged and excited about writing and content creation. Then, our family embarked on an enjoyable whirlwind tour of Europe. However, as I repeatedly learn, life's high points can swiftly plummet into deep valleys.

I remember that night so clearly. Freshly arrived home from Europe. Cutting onions for a spaghetti bolognaise when Ma called. Her voice was calm as she asked me in Hakka how we were doing.

Then she told me not to worry, but a gut feeling told me something was terribly wrong.

"I've had some scans while you were in Europe," she said.

"Why didn't you tell me?" I was concerned that she had hidden this.

"I didn't want you to worry," she answered. "But I need to tell you..."

Calmly, Ma let me know that they had found a tumor that might be cancerous.

In that moment, my world changed. The sting of the onions paled in comparison to the news, which unleashed a floodgate of tears.

We can be so fragile as people. One minute we can be standing tall, but the next, collapsing in a heap on the floor.

It would be almost ten months later when I was finally able to recount this event without crying, when I wrote about the ordeal in a blog.

Multiple scans showed that Ma's tumor had grown to the size of an elongated cantaloupe. It had wrapped itself around her colon, pressed upon her bladder, and displaced her ureter. She also had fluid in the abdomen, dispersed around her gut area, and further tumor growth on her liver. She was diagnosed with stage four ovarian cancer.

It was difficult news for our whole family. She needed urgent surgery, or her chances of survival weren't good at all.

Since both my parents barely speak English, I knew that, left to their own devices, they would be lost in the public health system, trying to navigate four different hospitals. I stopped working. Almost everything in my life came to a halt as I became her advocate, researching her condition and relaying the latest medical updates to our extended family.

It was gruesome seeing her go through this ordeal, being

undressed, pricked with more needles than I could ever stand. Yet, through all the blood tests, scans, and procedures, she remained serene and composed.

Only one time did I see her upset in the colorectal surgeon's office. He explained to her there was a possibility she could come out of surgery with a permanent stoma bag. Once I translated for her, it hit Ma like a ton of bricks. She sat silently with tears streaming down her cheeks. I felt all the waves of grief and shock along with her. But I was alarmed in that moment. *What if she doesn't sign the consent to go through with the surgery?* I wondered. She desperately needed the surgery. It was her only chance of survival.

I whispered to her in Hakka, "Ma, you need to sign the form." She sighed heavily, wiped away her tears with a Kleenex, and then signed to accept her lot. Since then, she has shown a faith, resilience, and strength in quietness that I marvel. Even on the day of her complex operation.

My heart thumped on the big day as I drove to the hospital. Ma stayed overnight to be prepared for the operation. I met Ba at the entrance; he seemed nervous too. But, when we entered Ma's room, she was as calm and peaceful as the day she told me about her diagnosis.

The surgery was expected to take four to five hours. But there were complications and she ended up in the operating room for almost twelve hours. One of the surgeons tried to untangle the solid tumor mass from the colon but accidentally cut into a major artery; Ma lost so much blood that she required over eight bags of blood transfusion.

We nearly lost Ma that day. Even thinking of that trauma still tears me up. I had never seen my hardy father so shaken as I did that evening. We were told Ma wasn't going to wake up that night, and she would need to go straight to the Intensive Care Unit.

It was a miracle Ma opened her eyes the next day in the ICU.

But she woke up to see she not only had a stoma bag, but a catheter attached. Her ureter had also been accidentally injured when the tumor was removed. Seeing her all wired up, kept alive by machines, my heart sank. It was a wake-up call about the fragility and briefness of all our lives.

I've come to realize that the allure of life's achievements dims in the face of looming mortality—not my own, but one of the people I most cherish. This realization sparked deep questions in me: *What constitutes a good life? What truly matters?*

Most of us chase success in the form of achievements, climb the corporate ladder, get that promotion, make more money, earn further degrees or certifications. I have certainly been on that route before. But so often, when we accomplish something we've dreamed of, we can feel an emptiness, an anti-climax, and we look for another pursuit to divert our attention from the futility.

Pursuit of achievements without an aligned value that connects to the bigger picture of life can leave us with a sense that our effort is meaningless.

Like running on a hamster wheel, the pursuit of achievements without an aligned value connecting to life's bigger picture can leave us living what King Solomon wrote in the book of Ecclesiastes, a sense that things are "Meaningless! Meaningless!...What do people gain from all their labors at which they toil under the sun?" (Ecc. 1: 2–3, NIV).

In this chapter, we explore what *real* success is and why we need to redefine and reframe it. After all, we can't be truly successful if we're not joyful. *Real* joy requires the whole package: a life aligned with values, supportive people around us, and dreams we aspire to. What does research reveal about what a successful and joyful—a *happy*—life looks like? What frames and reframes would you need to develop to achieve success and joy? These questions are the focus of this chapter, with stories of how women create lives of joy for themselves, their families, and their communities—and how you can too.

Well-being and Happiness

Ancient Greek thinkers Aristotle, and Epicurus had very different ideas about what it means to live a good life. Epicurus believed happiness came from enjoying the small things—a holiday, a delicious meal, time with friends, the absence of stress. That's what we now call *hedonic* happiness, the kind that feels good in the moment. Aristotle, on the other hand, believed real happiness, or *eudaimonia*, came from living a life of purpose and integrity. Not the easiest path, but the most fulfilling. It's the kind of joy that comes from knowing your life means something, that you're becoming more of who you really are. We've explored this together in the previous chapters.

In the 1980s, psychologists Edward Deci and Richard Ryan brought these ideas into modern psychology in what they called Self-Determination Theory. They found that we feel most alive when three basic needs are met: autonomy (the freedom to choose our path), competence (the opportunity to grow and improve), and relatedness (deep connection with others). When these needs are met, we thrive both inside and outside. And when they're missing? Even success can feel hollow.

I've seen this play out over and over in the lives of women. All the money in the world cannot buy true joy and happiness. One friend had the career, the income, the house, and felt completely flat. "I've achieved everything I set out to do," she said quietly, "and I feel nothing." Another friend left a job she'd outgrown, not because she had a better offer, but because she couldn't keep pretending it still mattered to her. She started working part-time in the community sector, walking her kids to school, learning to slow down. "It's not glamorous," she told me, "but I finally feel like myself again."

And I've lived this too. In my culture, success was tied to sacrifice—doing the right thing, carrying the weight, honoring your family. I worked hard. I pushed through. But when my mom was diagnosed with cancer, everything inside me shifted.

I watched her face each day with courage and softness. She wasn't chasing anything anymore. She was simply present. And somehow, even in all that pain, there was quiet joy about her. Like she had stopped worrying and enjoyed being presently alive.

That season cracked something open in me. I realized I had spent years doing what was expected—being the responsible one, the achiever, the strong one—and I hadn't stopped to ask myself what I actually wanted. What mattered to me. Not what looked good on paper, but what felt honest and alive.

Since then, as I've shared, many women from different cultures and different seasons have whispered versions of the same thing: "I don't know who I am anymore." "I'm tired of proving myself." "I just want to feel like I'm living my own life." We've witnessed their journeys throughout this book.

This is where it all comes together. The ancient philosophy, the modern research, and the stories we carry. Hedonic happiness has its place. We need rest, pleasure, and soft moments. But also eudaimonic joy, the kind that runs deep, comes when our life starts to reflect our values. When we stop performing and start showing up as we are. Our whole selves. When we stop living by rules and scripts we don't choose and begin listening to what's true for us.

For me, faced with my mom's cancer diagnosis, joy didn't return until I started asking different questions. With the time I have left of my life: *What's mine to carry? What can I let go of? How can I build on my relationships? What does success look like now?*

I am teaching my daughters to ask such questions at a young age so they build a solid foundation to launch their lives. Why? Because I don't want a trauma or tragic event to be their wake-up call, like it was for me. My desire for any young person is to discover their core values, their foundations, so they cultivate eudaimonic joy from a young age. It may spare them from several dead ends as they navigate the maze of life.

One thing is for sure: Whether we're starting out in our careers or at the stage when we're ending them, there is no better time than now to focus on foundational values, personal and cultural scripts to chase after eudaimonic joy, as well as build hedonistic happiness into our lives, because life is not only work, it's also love and play.

Pivoting Your Life for Both Success and Joy

What makes for a good life? That was the question researchers Robert Waldinger and Marc Schulz asked in the Harvard Study of Adult Development, the world's longest study on happiness. Exploring eighty years of research, they concluded their findings in their book, The Good Life:

Meaningful relationships and social connections are the single most critical factor for a long and thriving life.

As I've traveled, I've asked women around the world, "What brings you joy?" Captured in mini Instagram reels, unsurprisingly, many of them echoed Harvard's research findings. Having friends and family is, according to many, the real source of happiness. We are social beings; our joy is usually contingent on having meaningful relationships.

Relationships can be the source of great joy but also sorrow.

What happens when your relationship breaks down? We learn from Sarai (chapters 4, 7, and 10) about not only her marriage breakdown but how it impacted her friendships too. How do you recover your joy after that? Her life shows the frames of strength after reframing her suffering.

SARAI

You know, we had friends, but when you separate or you divorce him, none of your friends...they would all just disappear. So, you just live by yourself.

You go through the motions and come to terms and support your children through that difficult journey. Making sure they continue to feel loved and having that understanding. And also myself, looking after myself, which was really difficult, like mentally, because you'd be kind of conflicted about your decision. But yeah, I had to pull through.

I've always been active in terms of health and wellness. I loved my exercises, which I used as a coping strategy.

Also just getting some support, someone to talk through, like a psychologist to help getting through that journey. To make sure I come out of it strong, and kind of finding myself again. Gaining strength, finding yourself again...took maybe two years or more. It was quite a process.

So, finishing high school, getting married straight away, I don't think I'd had that opportunity to really know exactly who I was as a person. And what I wanted in life. So probably, maybe, that's why I was in that life I'd gone through. Because no one talks about it in our culture. When you've been subjected to abuse from your stepmother or never had a present parent.

So, I don't think I'd have the opportunity to do that, know myself. And of course, when my marriage finished, it was like a complete failure. Coming from a broken family, I wanted my kids to grow up in an intact family. And you do worry a lot about the stigma attached to that. So, I had to get through all of that.

And the shame of being exposed in a domestic violence sort of relationship. So, it was really difficult. It took a while. I just had to remain strong as a mum, but behind closed doors, you'd be crying, getting through the motions as a parent with no support. I took up studying and finding myself.

I want the patterns to break. I told you about my dad struggling with alcohol. There's no connection with him, even to this day. The relationship is very interesting. He just sent me a text message saying, "Please, send me money." Full stop.

He doesn't even know the names of my children! He never, ever provided for me financially. Also, he never protected me from my stepmother. But culturally, even if he was in need, and even if your family was broke, you just needed to still support him. That's our culture sadly. He never paid school fees, not even one penny of my high school fees. Not even buying my uniform. He worked as a teacher. He never asked me, "My daughter, how are you doing?"

I always wanted to impress him, to impress people, and there was a time when every single thing I wanted to do, it would be about "What would this person say?" Needing the validation. And because I think it was also to do with my personality of just impressing everybody. And I think also, the first identity from an African culture, you have to be everything, to be perfect. You have to be right. You have to lead by example.

But I am moving beyond this.

I don't think back then, "I own my life," like, "I own it now." Now I'm able to talk about it. But I never used to, of course. I didn't tell everybody; being vulnerable was hard. But now I want to focus on health, wellness, and helping people who have been through similar challenges using my story.

Sarai went through the Life Framing process, situating herself after her marriage breakdown, structuring her life after enduring domestic violence, moving beyond her cultural script, and closing her story loop of needing to earn approval. She realized her lack of parenting and love caused challenges, especially from her father, that created a story loop of earned approval, but she was not going to let that frame her life. She "wanted the patterns to break." She reframed her narrative, reminding herself that she had done what she could with what she was given, and she was successful despite not having effective parenting. She could now move on by developing her new narrative, owning her life story, and focusing on her values: keeping herself healthy, supporting her children, and helping people in her community.

Sarai continues her story, which now shapes her reality.

SARAI

I am continuing to live my true and authentic life, and I think that's kind of my desire: being useful in helping others. And it's just having appreciation for the small things. Understanding that it's not the things that I do have or whatever my job is that brings joy. I just want to intrinsically become an authentic person and be fulfilled. And also, being able to move, like get exercise, that's a big thing for me. I love moving my body.

I've seen God coming through for me. My faith is strong. So, I think maybe that's one thing that takes me through. And of course, that's what got me through a lot.

I want to have joy, so whoever comes in my life, I want to be able to share that joy with them and also love. So, I went through that period, just enjoying being by myself, doing the things that I love, like enjoying my solitude, reading books, exercising, sitting down doing the things that bring me joy again.

I value integrity as well. It's important for me, so I hold

myself to quite a high standard. Friendships give me joy, having people around me. Just seeing my kids grow, be good humans and respectful.

I think I would just love to be remembered for my strength. I didn't want to be defined by my struggles nor just the things that I went through. I want to be remembered for my joy because suffering might happen through the night, but joy comes in the morning. So, I always tell myself that.

There are different seasons in each of our lives. Sarai went through many seasons of suffering but is now in a period when she has built new friendships and is living with joy. Having accomplished her professional goals, she has made peace within herself and enjoys the relationships she has with her children and friends. Confidence has arisen in her heart that her life has unfolded well.

The Frames for Confidence, Joy, and Success

Confidence comes from the types of frames we choose to adopt and how we put them into action. If we want or need anything, we must act to obtain it, otherwise we go without. Confidence is showing up no matter how you feel. Let the fear pulsate through you and use it for action. Confidence grows each time we choose to step into reaching for our Desires. When we have overcome the obstacles and the Oppositions in our lives melt away, we gain confidence in what we can be and do.

Time and effort are required for any achievement. Not all of us are in the same situation. Some have more constraints on our lives than others, in terms of access to resources. For example, I don't think if I stayed in my birth country I would have had the same education I had in Australia. Some have more constraints in terms of ability levels and opportunities. However, given we all have twenty-four hours a day, why do some with similar circumstances succeed in fulfilling dreams while others fail?

Estée Lauder, entrepreneur and founder of the famous cosmetics brand, believed in the power of a focused frame of mind. She saw her success as the result of holding on to a clear goal and not getting sidetracked. For her, dreams, whether big or small, were fulfilled by staying steady, showing up, and keeping attention on what matters most. She saw this as the key ingredient in turning dreams into reality.

As I have mentioned previously, whatever we focus on determines our life. Focus shapes outcomes. Lauder was convinced that a focused frame of mind was the key to fulfilling her dream. She started from humble beginnings and learned from her chemist uncle how to make lotions and creams. From there, she faced the challenge of selling her creams and launching her business with her husband.

Lauder believed in her dream, gaining momentum in her business with innovative methods. For example, she introduced the "Talk-Touch-Teach" method as she demonstrated and taught about her products to women, starting by selling products to women in beauty salons as they had their hair and nails worked on, and she included sample gifts after a purchase, which revolutionized beauty industry practices. The Estée Lauder brand is still one of the most recognized brands in the world, even after her passing in 2004, and continues to be run by the Lauder family.

As Estée Lauder demonstrated, success and joy demand we adopt certain frames to pivot ourselves for our best life.

Frames refer to our specific, conscious internal interpretations and beliefs. The right frames help us work with what we have to achieve our dreams. Anyone can adopt frames that foster success and joy.

How we frame events, circumstances, and stressors influences how we perceive challenges, opportunities, and our own coping capabilities.

We see life through frames. How we perceive shapes how we feel and act. With positive valence of frames, joy grows; with negative ones, it dips. Notice your frames and choose ones that help because setting the right frame means the difference between feeling confident or defeated. For example, think about a responsibility you have, such as an upcoming presentation, exam, or deadline. If you focus on how much is left to do, how overwhelming it is, and how uncertain you feel about tackling it, worry and self-doubt surge. How does that feel? Now try a different frame: "Even if I'm overwhelmed, I can handle this. I'll make a plan, take the next step, and give it my best." Notice the shift?

The G.A.M.E. Frames

When I help women reframe stressful situations—from negative frames such as "I will never finish this project!" to a constructive "Each time I work on this project, I get closer and closer to finishing it!"—they often report their stress dropping from high to low almost immediately. By choosing a better frame of focus, you change your perspective about how you're experiencing challenges. The challenge doesn't change, your attitude toward it does.

There are four main frames that help people shift their mindset to see challenges in ways that foster growth, confidence, and fulfilment. From clinical experience and studying life stories, I have witnessed how these frames help my clients. I have come to call it the *G.A.M.E. (Growth, Abundance, Momentum, Empowerment) Frames*, which enable you to reinterpret challenges and opportunities so you can move forward with clarity and strength.

Let's see how these frames played out in the lives of Estée Lauder and Sarai, two women from very different backgrounds who both learned to reframe their experiences.

Growth Frame (G): Turning Challenges into Opportunities by Learning/Expansion

When life presents obstacles, a *Growth Frame* invites you to see them as opportunities to learn, adapt, and strengthen your skills. This is where you learn how to see the Opposition as an opportunity for growth and go after your Desire using the StoriCompass tool.

Sarai reframed her failed marriage as a chance to "find [her]Self again," treating the end as a new beginning for learning and self-discovery.

When major department stores initially refused to carry her products, Estée Lauder didn't see rejection as failure. She reframed it as a chance to build exclusivity and market through high-end salons. Every "no" became fuel for innovation and resilience.

What are you going through right now in your life that is challenging? How can you adopt the Growth Frame to turn the challenge into a learning opportunity?

Abundance Frame (A): Seeing the Plenty

Abundance Frame is about seeing resources—emotional, relational, spiritual, and creative—as expandable rather than scarce. That there is enough for everyone! When we view the world through abundance, our attention widens, we become more open to opportunities, and we experience higher intrinsic motivation because we believe "There is enough: time, love, opportunity, possibility." It shifts us from fear to gratitude and generosity. It enables us to trust that new meaning and resources emerge when we align with purpose. Even in your StoriCompass, you can see Guides and Supporters and clarify your Beneficiaries, the elements that can help you obtain your Desire in your Pathway of Pursuit. You can see possibilities to overcome your Oppositions.

After her divorce, Sarai found meaning through her faith. She trusted her God and saw the abundance of joy and love that was still possible; she saw that pain could be transformed into joy. She remarked, "My faith is strong" and reframed her period of loneliness to abundance, where she explained, "So, I went through that period, just enjoying being by myself, doing the things that I love...that brings me joy again." Sarai teaches us that how we see our circumstances is paramount.

Are we seeing with abundance and positivity or lack and negativity?

Estée Lauder was born to immigrant parents and began her business in a time of economic uncertainty and strict gender roles in the 1940s. She reframed her humble beginnings not as a deficit but as an education in human connection and aspiration. Rather than wait for capital or status, she built her business through relationships, such as giving free samples, touching faces, talking directly to women. She consistently perceived abundance—ideas, relationships, confidence, and vision—even when material resources were scarce. She found joy in her work as she embedded the abundance logic of "Give first; generosity builds loyalty."

Think of your life: *Where are areas of abundance and areas of lack? Where there is lack, how can you flip into an Abundance Frame and see your situation with possibilities instead of limitations?*

Momentum Frame (M): Putting Agency into Action

At the basis of a *Momentum Frame* is the core belief that small, consistent acts compound into lasting impact. Momentum is realized through the micromovements and daily rituals we establish in our routines and the meaning we give that enables us to move forward. Each small act reinforces who we are becoming, like the fact that, every day, I try to write one thousand words in the morning; this has helped me identify as a writer. When I have setbacks, which always come, I reframe by being kind to myself when it's hard to write so I can start again the next morning.

During that painful period in Sarai's life, she focused on what she could control and the steps she could take—seeking therapy, improving her health, and studying to build a new future. Each small win created momentum for healing and growth.

For Estée Lauder, she didn't achieve success through giant leaps but through micro-behaviors repeated daily: personally demonstrating creams at department stores, writing thank you notes, remembering clients' names. Even setbacks, like early rejections by big stores that didn't want to stock her products, became *proof* of persistence, not failure. She reframed "no" as feedback, a classic Momentum Frame response: action as feedback loop. She kept refining her approach and didn't give up until she secured a placement at Saks Fifth Avenue. Her steady action turned vision into reality. Her identity thrived on forward motion, fuelled by her sense of mission: bringing luxury beauty to everyday women.

What is one area of your life you want to flourish and succeed in? What small steps do you need to take to build momentum? Commit to them now!

Empowerment Frame (E): Owning Your Progress and Potential

The *Empowerment Frame* helps you notice what is working, builds on the strengths you are developing, and helps you remember to speak to yourself like someone you trust. It turns your awareness of your gains into grounded confidence that stays with you, no matter your circumstance. When you recognize progress, even small steps, your sense of capability grows, and your next step becomes clearer. The Empowerment Frame helps you look at your StoriCompass elements and ask, "What's working? Do I have agency and clear desires? Do I have the appropriate Guides and Supporters in place to overcome Obstacles so I and others benefit from my success? What can I do to keep moving forward in an empowered way?"

Remember, your inner narration engages the Default Mode Network, which activates when you reflect on yourself and imagine the future.

When that narration is harsh or hopeless, that damaging, challenging story makes every circumstance harder. But when you consciously practice empowering self-talk and when you celebrate your progress, you give the DMN a new script. The DMN works for you, boosting your focus, helping you stick to your plan and supporting your wise choices.

Sarai shifted her narrative from "when my marriage ended, it was like, I was a complete failure" to "I don't think that, back then, I owned my life the way I own it now." Her empowering inner dialogue shifted her frame and restored her identity as a capable person with an aligned purpose. This is the kind of self-talk that ignites the Empowerment Frame to work for you.

Estée Lauder often emphasized persistence and focus as keys to success. This reinforced each small win, empowered her, and sustained her momentum as she built her business.

What is an empowering self-talk you can adopt and engage in as you go through your Life Framing process?

* Remember to focus on the Growth you seek, see the Abundance of the challenge you face as a learning opportunity, build Momentum in with change through small steps you commit to, and Empower yourself through the words you use to build yourself up.

This is how you can use better frames, reframe, and take ownership of your life. Both Sarai and Estée Lauder learned to adopt significant frames to empower themselves in their circumstances and, in doing so, changed their brain's default mode of thinking.

By practicing the G.A.M.E. Frames you learn to turn obstacles into growth by seeing obstacles as opportunities to learn and build momentum through small steps so you are empowered to reclaim and build your life the way you have always wanted. Ultimately, these frames help you see, interpret meaningfully, and speak to yourself with empowered self-talk while owning your progress toward your goals.

Living Your Dreams

To get to where she wanted to be, Estee Lauder not only had to frame her focus, she had to step into the limelight. She had to step into the "public arena" and risk failing, risk being ridiculed and judged. When we use our talents to serve the public, we take the risk of being known by the public, which may or may not respond in the way we expect. People may criticize us, leave negative reviews, or not understand what we're doing.

Maybe your dream isn't in the public arena, but in the private one. You may have the dream to run a loving and functional home for your family, which is a noble goal. In this case, you will need to step into your role as a frame builder whose job it is to shape the culture of your household; ensuring you and your partner are making, shaping, and managing a culture of belonging, connection, and safety; and instilling hope and motivation into your children. Or if you are single or living solo, your role is to create a nurturing home, a place where you'll feel safe to personally grow. These are the most important dreams and goals; it is from our homes that we not only launch our lives and pursue our dreams, but, if we have children, our family homes offer a steady, safe environment from which they go after their pursuits.

To become a patient mother, an efficient worker, a successful CEO, or a skilled singer, we must stay focused on the beliefs and actions that take us there. We need to drill down deeply into our thoughts and emotions to understand, manage, and direct them into focused action to reach our Desire.

If the mind can conceive the goal and outcome, it will push through to existence when we apply belief and action by adopting the G.A.M.E. Frames to restructure our life stories. Movement repeated over time toward what you Desire, despite the Opposition in your life, will bring you to your desired outcomes. When you change your *frame*, you change your *game*.

What We Think, We Do

The level where we can trip is the level of thoughts and feelings. If we think negatively, that we can't do it, then we feel defeated. If we stop the action and focus, then there is no movement. Unfortunately, many seeds of goodness or greatness are like that in our lives. We abort the growing belief that we can become more.

However, we can find a way to tackle the negative thoughts, to acknowledge our feelings, as they can come and go. And if we can continue to persist with action, we will move toward our Desire. That desire and action creates a feedback loop. If I have done it before, I can do it again.

Sarai and my Ma showed that, despite the pain and suffering of life, there is joy in quiet trust and confidence that better days will come. Through their endurance, they became women of strength and influence. And, of course, their life stories have impacted my own.

My debut memoir evolved into this book; I didn't take my eyes off my focus of becoming an author, and I pivoted to a new project when I saw that this book would achieve one of my most persistent goals: to empower women to own their life story.

Like Sarai, Ma, and Estée Lauder, when we embrace the joy of becoming who we are meant to be, securely anchored to our values, we can achieve what once seemed impossible. Life is like a game. How we frame a situation and play in life shapes our emotions, motivation, and performance.

We need to approach life with G.A.M.E. Frames for both success and joy and allow ourselves to have fun when engaging with the Life Framing process. These skills and tools propel us forward to the life we seek. Seeing you succeed gives others hope and deeply impacts them to live a meaningful life.

Key Takeaways

* Our lives are brief on earth. Focus on what is truly valuable: meaningful relationships as you pursue your dreams.

* Choosing the frames we interpret life with is pivotal. With positive valence of frames, joy grows, with negative ones, it dips.

* The G.A.M.E. (Growth, Abundance, Momentum, Empowerment) Frames help people shift their mindset to see challenges in ways that foster growth, confidence, and fulfilment.

Deeper Actions

Reflect and journal or draw about the following questions:

1. What do success and joy mean for you? What do they look and feel like?

2. What is your current frame of life at the moment? Think of a specific situation or circumstance you're in, like work, family, creative pursuits, etc.

3. Which G.A.M.E. Frames do you feel you have developed and regularly use in your life? Which do you think you still need to develop and use to help you achieve your goals and dreams?

4. How might you plan to nurture new frames to better reflect your skills, strengths, and resilience?

14

Living Your Meaning and Legacy

The universe is made of stories, not atoms.

— Muriel Rukeyser

The great use of life is to spend it for something that will outlast it.

—William James

Angela was born in 1925, two years after Theresa, her older sister. She was the fourth child to her Cantonese Chinese father and mixed-heritage Hakka-speaking mother in a village town called Baucau, in East Timor. She and Theresa were very close, like two peas in a pod.

Their father began as a jovial chauffeur and became a successful businessman owning his bakery and restaurant, well known in their village community. He threw many parties for his large family during the weekends. Angela recalls dancing with joy at the extended family's weekly gatherings. It was a merry yet simple life, one where they felt loved. After Angela came three more siblings. When she was twelve years old, her mother passed away. The family was heartbroken.

During that time of great loss, she clung to Theresa; her older sister was the closest she had to a mother. In a few years, her father remarried, and to their immense relief, their East Timorese stepmother was kind and loving toward them, as were her children.

Gaining new siblings from their father's new union, both Angela and Theresa felt welcomed and part of a new, blended, big family.

In the Second World War, the family dispersed for survival, and Angela moved in with her paternal uncle in East Timor's capital, Dili. She babysat her younger cousins and taught herself sewing. She was blessed with a quick-witted mind and possessed a knack for creativity. At about eighteen years old, she was married off to a rich old man, but in a little over a year, her groom passed away. She hardly spoke of this low point in her life.

Her turning point came when she fell in love with a shoemaker from Macau named Francisco. However, her father disapproved of their union and didn't communicate with her for three years after she married Francisco. Undeterred, she started an import business with her new husband and brought in shoes and fabrics from overseas. Angela was an intelligent woman with an entrepreneurial mind. When her customers bought shoes, she would offer them custom-made orders for wedding gowns. She taught herself all the knowledge and skills she needed to grow her business and create job opportunities for her family too. Her generosity knew no bounds in providing food for her extended family, and when her father saw her success, he finally accepted her husband.

People in the Dili community used to say of Angela that she was "able to turn anything into gold," for she had a knack for making money. Yet she lacked what Theresa had in surplus: children of her own.

Theresa lived in Baucau, which took a whole day's journey in a car to Dili if the dirt roads weren't flooded. The two sisters stayed close despite the distance. She had married Siu Kiat, a Hakka man from Meizhou, China. They started a family, which quickly grew. Theresa's husband tried his hand at many different business ventures like agriculture, retail, and others, but unfortunately, he did not find the same prosperity that found Angela so easily.

Angela had tried to conceive, but she grieved that her womb was barren. Theresa knew of Angela's pain of not being able to have children; she loved Angela, and she had several children, so she offered her third daughter, Mimi, for Angela to adopt. After all, they were family.

Family is what bound them together; their meaning and purpose were found in the survival of their clan.

As Theresa's children grew, they married off and started having their own families. East Timor became an unstable and unpredictable place to bring up a young family in the mid-1970s. Civil unrest spread throughout the land, with rumours that the Portuguese, who colonized East Timor, were going back to their homeland. This was an anxious time for young mothers.

When Theresa's oldest daughter, Lucia, had children, she struggled with her youngest one, the long-awaited daughter. She had already borne two sons, and so, with two young toddlers and this unsettled newborn, life was extremely difficult.

Lucia hardly slept; she often walked the dirt roads trying to calm her baby's screams. The baby girl couldn't keep down any solids. It was such a distressing time. Her husband was away for long periods, trying to build up his transport business to support not only his own family, but help out with Lucia's family too.

No matter how much they tried to comfort the baby girl, she was in agony. She could only keep down rice congee liquid, but that didn't provide the nutrition her body needed to grow. Whenever Lucia tried to feed her breastmilk, she kept screaming and crying as if in deep pain. Lucia felt helpless and distraught.

When Angela heard of her niece's struggles, she reached out to her. Learning that Lucia's baby was undernourished, and had severe diarrhea, she had to find a way to help. She was that kind of a woman: heart in her hand, with sleeves rolled up, always willing to give support.

"If that baby doesn't get any medical attention," Angela said to her husband, "she might die."

There were few doctors in the whole country. In fact, they knew of only one pediatrician in East Timor, located in Dili. The flight from Baucau was exorbitant, a fee out of reach for most people. And the bus trip could be a journey of several days on treacherous dirt roads if it flooded; it was a dangerous ride for mother and child. The baby might not survive such a road trip.

Without hesitation, Angela reached into her pocket and handed over a bundle of cash to George, Lucia's older brother. She asked George to organize the flights and take the baby and Lucia to see the pediatrician.

In Dili, the pediatrician diagnosed the baby as suffering from a severe dairy allergy and prescribed medication for an accompanying infection. The medication worked, and the baby soon after outgrew the dairy allergy. Without Angela's kindness and help, the baby would never have thrived and possibly not even survived long term.

That baby was me.

How Are We Framed?

As we come to the end, let's reflect on our journey from the beginning. From the cradle to the grave, we all live out our life stories. Mine began dramatically with civil unrest and then war. I came from humble beginnings. Born fragile and unable to thrive; then along with my family, I became an asylum seeker and refugee in Portugal. But that beginning didn't have to define me. I used the support of my family to pursue goals that no woman in the family had ever pursued before. Within the constraints of each of our lives, we have choice. In that consistent choice, the frames of our lives form.

Legacy is how our life is framed.

In my family, Great-aunt Angela is framed as a generous, intelligent, and thoughtful woman who is remembered fondly. I will never forget Great-aunt Angela's kindness toward my family and what she did for me. Great-aunt Angela was approaching her last days in the world when I learned this early part of my story from Ma. It was only a few days before my Aunt Mimi rang to tell me Great-aunt Angela was in the hospital. When I heard the news, I could not contain my tears. I knew the end for her was approaching, and I wasn't ready to let go yet. We had lost Poh Poh, our beloved Theresa, several years beforehand, and to lose another elder was like losing the pillars of our culture.

I made it to the hospital in time to see Great-aunt Angela. She had turned ninety-eight two months earlier.

At the hospital room, I took her soft, fragile hand. She looked at me with a faint smile. Her twinkling eyes welcomed me with warmth, but I could see the great pain she experienced. Through tears of gratitude, I thanked her for loving me and giving me a chance at life when I was a baby. I shared with her that Ma had only recently told me what she had done for me as a baby girl. I was sobbing. She nodded, her eyes moist as well. More tears rolled down my face seeing her so frail. When visiting hours were over that evening, I felt an ache in my chest that weighed heavily as I walked out of the room, knowing it might be the last time I see her.

The next day, Aunt Mimi called to let me know Great-aunt Angela had passed away peacefully. It was hard to accept the passing of another great woman in my life. However, her legacy lives on because Great-aunt Angela, along with Poh Poh, is woven into the fabric of my being. The lessons they taught have become the elements of Guide and Supporter in my life story.

Great-aunt Angela and my Poh Poh instilled in Ma and her siblings strength found in meekness. A love and harmony that sustains our large extended family, which keeps our bonds alive. It is the kind of love that Leo Tolstoy wrote about in *War and Peace*, which underscores their own lives: "Love is life. All, everything I understand, I understand only because I love. Everything is, everything exists, only because I love. Everything is united by it alone."

That kind of love lives on in my mother, father, and my family. Love is the value that my family embedded into my life and from which all of my life makes sense. It is the same value I will pass onto my children. For such a life of love is worth living. It is their legacy for my family. The very one I want my life to be framed by.

Rethinking Legacy

We will leave this life once we've breathed our last breath. We don't have a choice about that. But we can decide what kind of legacy we will leave behind.

I used to think legacy was something you leave behind when you depart, after your time on earth. Now I am realizing that legacy is a living, breathing thing, something we live every day of our lives. It is what we're doing as we build long-lasting meaning and purpose, when we impact the here and now. What we do *now* matters! Our legacy is the impact others feel, what the people around us see, hear, feel, believe, and experience of us.

We're always creating legacy, intentionally or not.

Legacy is not only what we are remembered for, it is the life story we live now, how we contribute to our cultures. Our story gives context to our legacy. It connects the past, present, and future into a coherent life narrative.

Legacy is identity in action. It reflects how you live your values and tell your story—loud or quiet, public or personal. Legacy is cultural identity, the story of who we are, what we value, what we have become, and whose lives we touch and impact. You shape your legacy by living in alignment with your values. I love what Oprah shared at the 2025 *Oprah in Conversation* event in Melbourne, because it reinforced my own views. Our legacy is shaped by the lives we touch and the people we lift, and the best way to live is to become our truest and highest self.

The wonderful news is that you can revise your legacy at any point in your life. It's never too late to live in a way that reflects what matters most to you. You can make intentional choices today and take action.

You can revise your legacy at any point in your life.

Clara recognized this. Despite her struggles, she's intentional about creating experiences for her children, to leave a legacy of an international upbringing, which she hopes will foster empathy, sensitivity, and curiosity in them, along with the ability to adapt and grow in a multicultural, multinational world.

CLARA

Am I seeking to leave a legacy to my children? I probably am, maybe from a very unconscious level. So, one of the things that I'm definitely conscious about, and this is what brought me to kind of create this international environment, is that I really embrace my international upbringing. And I see that as a gift that I can honor and I can embrace.

I really like how it's made me "me," right? All this international experiences. And I don't deny the grief, the opportunity losses, the difficulties that came with it. But I definitely made it through the healing process of seeing how much beauty comes out of it.

And I really want to transfer that to my children. And this is why we speak to my children in different languages, we expose them to as many culturally different experiences as possible. Because I strongly believe that not only because the world is becoming this globalized environment where everybody is growing and working and living in, but also because my experience as a global citizen is that I have much more empathy.

I have much more sensitivity that I think goes beyond my neurological sensitivity.

It's very difficult to deny the existence of others or other needs or other realities because you grew up in it. It's almost like, you fell in this water, right? And there's nothing you can really do about it. It becomes part of who you are and how you see things and how you interact with people.

So, I'm hoping to leave, probably, this legacy to them, like this opportunity to see the world from these 360 degrees with a little bit, at least, of empathy, a little bit of cultural sensitivity, and a lot of curiosity. The best blessing that you can leave a child is that curious mind so that they are hungry to be learners themselves.

Clara's intention is to take the reins of authorship and instill her values into her children. She is showing up each day, learning, and quietly building the architecture of a life that will outlast herself in her children. She is imbuing her children's life with meaning, which I believe is admirable and makes me reflect on my childhood.

A Meaningful Life Is Legacy

My mind was as awake as my eyes. Even when I shut them, sleep did not come. I looked through the window at the twinkling stars, gleaming with brilliance in the night sky. I felt insignificant observing the vastness of space in my eight-year-old body. Overcome with the wonder of life, my thoughts turned to questions: *What is the meaning of my life? What is my purpose? Why am I here?*

Ma tells me I was an inquisitive child. She was often surprised by the many big questions I asked. I laid in bed many nights, churning over the questions of existence.

Ma and Ba stayed up late most nights, sewing clothes to make ends meet. Once, in exasperation because Ma was tired and didn't have the answer to my question of "What happens after we die?", she replied, "I will one day die and come back to tell you." She was stunned by my thinking about death at such a young age. Her answer shut me up because the thought of her dying terrified me.

Looking back, I was already trying to make sense of my young life. *You live, you die. What was the point of it all?* From the time I could think, I grappled with meaning.

So, in my thirties, imagine my delight when I turned up to my PhD supervisor's office to discuss my thesis topic, and he suggested that I focus on semiotics—the study of signs and symbols, and how they create meaning—to understand cross-cultural differences. I didn't tell him during our meeting that he literally handed me my dream topic on a silver platter! After all, I had been thinking about meaning-making since I was a child.

My research not only took me around the world—I presented my findings on the continents of Africa, Europe, North America, and Australia—but more importantly, it was an internal journey of self-discovery and personal integration. It took me to the edges of what I was capable of, brought me up against my limitations. And it led me to understanding how I make sense of my life to gain coherence, and how others can too.

Pursuing this degree made me realize that, for my whole life, I was in a pursuit of truth and love, understanding and connection. And this pursuit became a major part of my life story. Through my research and clinical practice, I've found that we all try to make sense of our lives using our life stories. We seek coherence, significance, and purpose. We all want our lives to mean something.

My pursuit of truth and love, understanding and connection—ultimately, meaning—has led me to write this book for you. We are collaboratively building meaning through the exchange of words, me sharing my life story so you can reflect on yours and see what is possible for your life. A meaningful life is not something we find; it's something we build, and that meaning becomes our legacy that touches other lives.

When Stories Touch Others

When I lived in Toronto, I felt very lonely in the first few weeks because I didn't know anyone except my then-boyfriend, now-husband. I'd roam Eaton Centre and the streets of Toronto aimlessly, then return home to call family or friends in Melbourne to share my stories of life in Canada. I realized the truth of narrative psychologist Theodore Sarbin's insight, that loneliness can arise when we stop sharing our stories with others. In my case, in a new city, I didn't have many people around me to share stories with.

In my attempts to integrate into Torontonian life, I was thrilled to meet Elizabeth Vervey, who spoke at the lunchtime business meeting I attended. Elizabeth is the type of woman who is beautiful inside out, oozing with joy and life. She invited me to my very first writing group in her home.

Elizabeth has become a friend who always inspires me. I felt sad when I learned her marriage fell apart. However, she shared with me that it was in those difficult times some friends came to console her, and each woman took a chance to "bare their souls" to each other, creating an inclusive community. Before she knew it, more women joined, and they grew out of her apartment to venues. From her pain, she founded Spoken Lives, a platform in which women share their stories to encourage and uplift others.

As I write this last chapter, Elizabeth has already moved through many new chapters of her life, now remarried to a loving husband, she has continued her creative contribution to society. She launched her book, *Brave New Endings*, about her experiences of caring for her ex-husband and many true stories of others who have shown the same care and compassion.

Elizabeth simply told the truth and shared her life story. When we express our authenticity, we give others permission to do the same. That's the real power of storytelling. It doesn't only heal us; it humanizes our spaces. Meaning is contagious. Elizabeth took her pain and shifted it to weave a collective story of human connection that touches other lives.

Impact is meaning made visible. It flows from a meaningful life.

Meaningful living isn't about perfection, having it all together or constant positivity. We've got to be real, life is often painful and messy, but there is growth and healing too. A meaningful life is about coherence, purpose, and significance, about integrating who you are, what you value, and how you contribute. When you live from that integration, your life begins to tell a story of its own. A legacy in the making.

Meaning Multiplies When Shared

A meaningful life is one that makes a difference. It's a life that recognizes the power of story as both mirror and bridge: a mirror that helps us see ourselves more clearly, and a bridge that connects us to others with empathy and hope.

I got to witness this firsthand on stage, listening to Verity Price, the 2021 World Champion Public Speaker from South Africa. I was deeply moved by how much her story spoke to me and connected with mine. She shared how, as a thirteen-year-old, she dreamed of being an actress but was so bullied by her peers when she got the leading part in their school play, that it crippled not only that dream but her confidence. From that moment, she feared getting on stage to be visible. However, at the age of twenty-four, when her beloved father died unexpectedly, she came to a turning point. She realized how fragile and brief life is. She could stay hidden, in fear, or she could pursue singing, which she wanted to do. Eventually, through her process of Life Framing, she found herself back on stage speaking and sharing her story that words build our reality. We are all made up of stories in the end, even our cultures.

The Call to Create Your Legacy

Our lives on earth are fleeting, like a vapor that disappears, but what remains are words and deeds long after we are gone. Both in life and death, we are reduced to narratives that formed our Selves, our identity, and our meaningful acts. Therefore, our life stories, backed by actions, are really our legacies, the only remnants of our walk through this world in time and space.

Why did I write this book? Because I wanted to awaken you to see that you are valuable, you bring your uniqueness into this world. That we all live our legacies through our life stories daily.

When each of us owns our life stories, we create lives we want to live, ones full of joy, meaning, and legacy. At the end of the day, we all contribute to this world through our shared responsibility of creating and maintaining collective cultures. It is up to us to make this world a better place for all, by living lives that create strong connections and communities, and in which we contribute to the well-being of one another. Thus, we cement our legacy.

We do not wait to leave a legacy; we are living it, moment by moment. Every word we speak, boundary we set, time we stand for what matters, we write the story others will remember through the life we've built.

Throughout this book, we learned that StoriCompass is both a compass and a framework. It helps us navigate what matters most and provides the elementary structure of our life narrative. It's the architecture within which our experiences find coherence, the scaffolding that holds the unfolding story of who we are becoming. We don't merely navigate life with it, we build life through it. It becomes our life frame. Each element represents a pillar, and every moment of clarity about our pathways is a beam that holds up our life frames and represents our identity.

Through the StoriCompass, we build our life frame, pillar by pillar, beam by beam, chapter by chapter. It helps our Default Mode Network edit and weave together our life story, identity, and sense of meaning and purpose.

Our CulturAlign blueprint reminds us that this construction doesn't exist in isolation. We exist within a landscape of shared values and meaning—our cultures, histories, lineages—that reflect in the narrative of our lives. To align our story with cultural contexts is to contribute to something larger; a collective narrative that exists beyond us. When we reshape what we inherit and offer authenticity in return, we transform culture itself, and that transformation is our legacy.

CulturAlign invites us to align our personal story with the wider narratives that shape our world. It reminds us legacy is both personal and collective. The stories we live are woven into the stories that hold us.

Legacy is about our life story's structural integrity. A life with a clear direction holds together; it resonates with purpose and meaning. We are integrated into others' lives, and vice versa, depending on the decisions we make about how we interact with and respond to others. The others we encounter may play roles in our narrative, as co-Agent, Desire, Guide, Beneficiary, Opposition and/or Supporter, as we play roles in their stories.

I was taken aback and honored when Tina named me as a Guide in her life while I interviewed her. Witnessing her using StoriCompass and CulturAlign to make progress through reframing not only her narrative, but exploring her family members' values, Desires, and legacies, confirmed for me, along with the breakthroughs for many other clients, the need to get this book out into the world.

What I have come to understand is that both StoriCompass and CulturAlign are actually meaning-making tools. They help us make sense of our lives and live the legacies we want.

I seek to live a legacy of alignment, as I realize alignment is really a dialogue between authenticity and belonging. It means asking: How does my life contribute to the greater story I am part of? How can I honor what I inherit, while daring to reshape my story to live a more wholesome life? When we act from awareness, our journey expands beyond individuality and into legacy. We are all part of something bigger. We become bridge-builders—carrying *what was* into *what can be*. Legacy becomes the meeting point between the Self we author and the culture we influence.

With This One Life

Why, when we realize we are dying, do we live more fully? It's as if, when we realize a product is close to its expiration date, we consume it. Much of life is like that. We often don't grasp the urgency of things, of life itself, until we get close to the end. When it is touched by the idea of death. When it's approaching termination.

I shared about my last turning point after finding out Ma's cancer diagnosis. Ma continues to surprise me; she recently returned from a trip to Meizhou, China, where she and my aunties discovered their father's birthplace and saw his and his forebears photos displayed in their village hall. My Aunt Mimi told me that Ma was so moved her eyes were moist with grateful tears. She survived cancer and is living her life with a great sense of urgency and meaning. That's why Life Framing is so powerful. If we can frame our lives as finite and live each day as if it may be our last, many more people would go after their Desires rather than wait until a faraway future.

If there's a dream waiting within you, enlist Guides and Supporters so you can overcome the Oppositions that arise. Understand the reason for your being and doing. Know your Beneficiaries, your Why and Who; they will give you the motivation to move forward when the going gets tough. Use the G.A.M.E. (Growth, Abundance, Momentum, and Empowerment) Frames to overcome the obstacles that emerge. Keep going for your dreams.

We need to frame our lives today with vision through StoriCompass and CulturAlign, with the conviction that each of us are apportioned a finite time on earth. We must ask ourselves the question: What is it I love to be and do? What will I be remembered for?

In doing so, we Situate, Structure, Shift, and Shape our lives for more joy and meaning. Because to pursue what we love aligns with authenticity. Love is what gives life joy and meaning; it is what touches others.

We never truly know how another human life touches us. But we sense it when they share their stories. I felt Tessa and Sanhydra's pain under the weight of their husbands' Oppositions. I felt the heartbreak Sarai, Aylin, and Cristina endured through their relationship breakdowns, yet also the strength they found in forging a life despite these setbacks. I was lifted up, seeing how Clara, Tre, and Pranjali's parents shared timeless wisdom and lessons with them, and how their parents' belief in them supported them to live their lives. I could relate to Fiona, Tina, and Colleen's cultural tensions and the societal expectations they experienced. Each of these incredible women touched my life with their stories. And I would never have known their life stories if I had not pursued writing this book.

With this one life, we have the opportunity to fulfil our dreams, encourage each other to live our best lives by embracing ourselves and each other. We can create cultures of belonging, connection, and flourishing by sharing our stories with acceptance and dignity.

Live Your Legacy

Our stories are the threads that weave our history, experiences, memories, and Self to propel us into the future. Without these stories, we may be lost.

Stories become bridges between lives. Stories keep this web of culture alive. They allow the connections that provide us with collaborative meaning-making. Our lives are so interconnected, past, present, and future. We must find the courage to share our lives and cross that bridge.

The courage to be who you really are is your greatest gift to the world. To share your unique life story, one that you have fully owned, is to have lived your legacy.

What about you? What is the story you need to share? Who inspires you? And what future do you hope for? What do you want your life to look like? How can your life story touch and move the hearts and minds of generations to come? How would you like to be framed?

This is the power of our life stories, of living our legacy, of living beyond ourselves. Immortalized by the words with which we build our realities.

Through mapping my story landscape and embracing my cultural identity, I now know who I am. I know where I am going. I know why I am doing what I do, as I create a life and a being that are all I ever dreamed. I am not perfect, but I have given up closing the 1 percent gap. I am deeply flawed, like every other human, but I embrace my imperfections and weaknesses along with my strengths. My life is not my own; it is intertwined with many others, like my family, my communities, and the world in which we all live. The difference is that now I own my life story and choose how I show up in the world.

My Desire and intention are to awaken you to see how unique, beautiful, and special you already are. The seed of greatness is already there within you. Whether you realize it or not, living it or not, I thank you for opening that gift box and choosing the life frame of contributing to making this world a better place for all. I embrace you and cheer you on as you own your life story. Your story is part of the bigger story of our world.

No matter where you've been, what scars are on your heart, what bruises you have acquired through life's difficult path, you are still here. You are here to make your life count, to arise and claim your voice. Make your distinctive contribution to society and shape a world where everyone thrives. Embrace who you are, your cultural identity. All of life is creation. Create the life you've always desired as you pursue joy, meaning, and love. Thus, you frame your legacy as you live your own life story!

Helping Children Build Healthy Life Stories

Many parents have asked me how they can help their children build healthy life stories. Over my years as a psychologist and trained teacher, I have had the privilege of working with children and young people in many settings. Drawing on training across developmental psychology, child and adolescent mental health, family systems, cross-cultural psychology, and narrative identity, this combination has given me an in-depth understanding of children.

I have seen how children grow, struggle, and flourish in real classrooms and real families. Having my own children as well, I was eager to learn how to shape their stories, help them make sense of their world, and grow into confident young people. I have walked alongside many parents, enabling them to understand their children's needs, build their confidence, and support their well-being.

From this work, I created a special bonus guide for you. These ten evidence-based guidelines bring together the most important things I have learned about how children develop their sense of self and their life stories. The guide gives you clear, practical steps you can use at home to support your child as they grow into a healthy, grounded young person who can make good choices, take ownership of their life, and pursue the goals that matter to them.

If you would like to feel more equipped and confident as a parent, I invite you to download this guide as a companion to the book and use it as a gentle roadmap for your child's journey.

Download it at www.lidialae.com/readerhub to get started.

Acknowledgements

First and foremost, I would like to thank all the women who trusted me with their stories and shared their lives so generously. You know who you are. Thank you for your vulnerability and honesty. Your life stories have enriched my own.

Writing this book has been a transformative process of becoming, moving me from writer to author. Like any meaningful journey, it's richer with companions. This book would not have come alive without the support of so many wonderful people.

I am especially grateful to Dr. Wendy Cahill for taking the time to write such a thoughtful and insightful Foreword. Also, thank you to Dr. Daniel Wong, Talisha Bassett, Graeme Farmer, Gina Mu, Dr. Lisa Miller, Katerina Roukakis, Julie Postance, Dr. Sarah Craze, and Andee Tham for reading the manuscript and providing perceptive and invaluable feedback.

To my wonderful editors, Cortni Merritt and Melissa Kirk, I truly appreciate your craft, and it was such a joy to work with you both. Thank you to literary agent Amy Collins for expanding my reach to get this book to the diverse world in foreign languages.

My sincere thanks to Julie Postance for walking alongside me in this writing and publishing process. Also, to the amazing women I met through Julie who were instrumental in helping me gain momentum to complete this book.

Thank you to the amazing Sophie White, who turned the look I envisioned for this book into reality. And to Ashish Joshi for the awesome book cover. I would not have come this far without Daniel Mu's contribution. I am thankful for all his hard work and building the digital platform of StoriCompass and CulturAlign, along with Ethan Lae's IT skills. Both worked tirelessly.

Thank you to the various writing groups and the generosity of members who have helped me develop as a writer and evolve my ideas. To fellow writers, Vicki Milliken and Anastasia Panayiotidis, for both of your encouragement along the writing process. I stay indebted to my creative friends, Caroline DePalatis, Colleen Higgs, Laura Cox, Rhoda Bangerter, and Steve Brock during this process of becoming.

I am so grateful to all my amazing friends who have filled my life with joy, love, and support. My life has been enriched with all the special moments we shared. A special thanks to Elizabeth Verwey who has encouraged me throughout my writing journey! To all the women who supported this book, I am deeply thankful!

I also extend my thanks to my friends and colleagues at the Centre for Theology and Psychology, Dr. Michael Bräutigam, Dr. Lisa Miller, Dr. Judy Willkie, Dr. Rosemary Wong, Judy Lillis, Dr. Kuruvilla George, Benjy Soosai, Dr. Brian Edgar, and Aaryan De Bruyn. To all my clients and work colleagues in the different organizations I have the privilege of working with, thank you for enriching my life with meaning and purpose.

To my extraordinary Ma and Ba, you have framed my life with a solid foundation of love, peace, and harmony, for which I am deeply indebted. To my brothers Sien and Kian, and my big family, thank you for shaping my Self with great joy and meaning. A special thanks to my aunts Ana, Mimi, Lydia, and Donna for their unwavering support, as well as my mother-in-law, Margaret.

To my husband, Daniel, and my precious daughters, Gemma and Ella, you are the love of my life. Thank you for your patience and loving me as I am. To my Creator who sees me and who makes all things possible, thank you.

Finally, thank you, my reader. This book comes alive as your own story unfolds. Meaning is something we create together, and it is a privilege to share this space with you.

Bibliography

Al-Sharif, Manal, with Carolyn Jess-Cooke. *Daring to Drive: A Saudi Woman's Awakening*. Simon & Schuster, 2017.

Angelou, Maya. *Letter to My Daughter*. Random House, 2008.

Anusasananan, Linda Lau. *The Hakka Cookbook: Chinese Soul Food from Around the World*. Illustrated by Alan Chong Lau. University of California Press, 2012.

Aristotle. *Nicomachean Ethics*. Translated by W. D. Ross, revised by J. O. Urmson. Princeton University Press, 1984.

Assaf, Michal, Kristin Jagannathan, Vince D. Calhoun, Michael Kraut, John Hart Jr., and Godfrey D. Pearlson. "Abnormal functional connectivity of default mode sub-networks in autism spectrum disorder patients." *NeuroImage* 53, no. 4 (2010): 1036–44.

Austen, Jane. *Pride and Prejudice*. Penguin Books, 2003.

Bateson, Gregory. "A theory of play and fantasy." In *Steps to an Ecology of Mind*, 177–93. Ballantine Books, 1972.

Beck, Aaron T. *Cognitive Therapy and the Emotional Disorders*. International Universities Press, 1979.

Beck, Aaron T. *Depression: Clinical, Experimental, and Theoretical Aspects*. Harper & Row, 1967.

Bennett, Roy T. *The Light in the Heart*. Roy T. Bennett, 2016.

Berman, Marc G., Scott Peltier, Derek Evan Nee, Ethan Kross, Patricia J. Deldin, and John Jonides. "Depression, rumination and the default network." *Social cognitive and affective neuroscience* 6, no. 5 (2011): 548-555.

Boyle, Susan, with Simon Heptinstall and Lorraine Kelly. *The Woman I Was Born to Be*. Bantam Press, 2010.

Brontë, Charlotte. *Jane Eyre*. Smith, Elder, 1847.

Brown, Brené. *Daring Greatly*. Gotham Books, 2012.

Brown, Brené. *The Gifts of Imperfection*. Hazelden, 2010.

Bruner, Jerome. *Acts of Meaning*. 7th ed. Cambridge, MA: Harvard University Press, 1990.

Bruner, Jerome. "Life as Narrative." *Social Research* 54, no. 1 (1987): 11–32. https://www.jstor.org/stable/41411426.

Bruner, Jerome. "Life as Narrative." *Social Research* 71, no. 3 (2004): 691–710.

Bruner, Jerome. "The Narrative Construct of Reality." *Critical Inquiry* 18, no. 1 (1991): 1–21. https://doi.org/10.1086/448619.

Bruner, Jerome. "The Narrative Creation of Self." In *The Handbook of Narrative and Psychotherapy*, edited by Lynne Angus and John McLeod, 2–14. California: Sage Publications, 2004.

Bruner, Jerome. "The 'Remembered' Self." In *The Remembering Self: Construction and Accuracy in the Self-Narrative*, edited by Ulric Neisser and Robyn Fivush, 41–54. Cambridge: Cambridge University Press, 1994.

Bruner, Jerome. "Self-Making and World-Making." *Journal of Aesthetic Education* 25, no. 1 (1991): 67–78. https://doi.org/10.2307/3333092.

Bruner, Jerome. "Self-Making Narratives." In *Autobiographical Memory and the Construction of a Narrative Self*, edited by Robyn Fivush and Catherine A. Haden, 209–25. New York: Psychology Press, 2003.

Buchanan, Tony W. "Retrieval of Emotional Memories." *Psychological Bulletin* 133, no. 5 (2007): 761–79. https://doi.org/10.1037/0033-2909.133.5.761

Buitelaar, Marjo, and Hetty Zock, eds. *Religious voices in self-narratives: Making sense of life in times of transition*. Vol. 54. Walter de Gruyter, 2013.

Burke, Kenneth. "Terministic screens." In *Language as Symbolic Action*, 44–62. University of California Press, 1966.

Cameron, Julia. *The Artist's Way*. TarcherPerigee, 1992.

Chandler, M. J., M. Boyes, L. Ball, and S. Hala. "The Conservation of Selfhood: A Developmental Analysis of Children's Changing Conceptions of Self-Continuity." In *Self and Identity: Perspectives across the Life-Span*, edited by T. Honess and K. Yardley. Routledge & Kegan Paul, 1987.

Charon, Rita. *Narrative Medicine: Honoring the Stories of Illness*. Oxford University Press, 2008.

Chiao, Joan Y., Tokiko Harada, Hideto Komeda, Zhang Li, Yoko Mano, Daisuke Saito, Todd Parrish, Norihiro Sadato, and Tetsuya Iidaka. "Neural Basis of Individualistic and Collectivistic Views of Self." *Human Brain Mapping* 30, no. 9 (2009): 2813–20. https://doi.org/10.1002/hbm.20707.

Chiao, Joan Y., Tokiko Harada, Hideto Komeda, Zhang Li, Yoko Mano, Daisuke Saito, Todd Parrish, Norihiro Sadato, and Tetsuya Iidaka. "Dynamic Cultural Influences on Neural Representations of the Self." *Journal of Cognitive Neuroscience* 22, no. 1 (2010): 1–11. https://doi.org/10.1162/jocn.2009.21192.

Chirkov, Valery I., Kennon M. Sheldon, and Richard M. Ryan. "Introduction: The Struggle for Happiness and Autonomy in Cultural and Personal Contexts: An Overview." In *Human Autonomy in Cross-Cultural Context: Perspectives on Autonomy, Social Integration, and Development and Well-Being*, edited by Valery I. Chirkov, Richard M. Ryan, and Kennon M. Sheldon, 1–30. Vol. 1. Springer Netherlands, 2011.

Choy, Bennett, K. Arunachalam, M. Taylor, and A. Lee. "Systematic review: Acculturation strategies and their impact on the mental health of migrant populations." *Public Health in Practice* 2 (2021): 100069.

Cohen, Adam B. "Many Forms of Culture." *American Psychologist* 64, no. 3 (2009): 194–204. https://doi.org/10.1037/a0015308.

Cohen, Adam B. "Religion's Profound Influences on Psychology: Morality, Intergroup Relations, Self-Construal, and Enculturation." *Current Directions in Psychological Science* 24, no. 1 (2015): 77–82. https://doi.org/10.1177/0963721414553265.

Cohen, Adam B., and Michael E. Varnum. "Beyond East vs. West: Social Class, Region, and Religion as Forms of Culture." Current Opinion in Psychology 8 (2016): 5–9. https://doi.org/10.1016/j.copsyc.2015.09.006

Cohen, Myron L. "The Hakka or 'guest families': Dialect as a sociocultural variable." In *Guest People: Hakka Identity in China and Abroad*. Edited by Nicole Constable. University of Washington Press, 1996.

Constable, Nicole, ed. *Guest people: Hakka identity in China and abroad*. University of Washington Press, 2014.

Coolidge, Susan. "New Every Morning." In *Verses*. Roberts Brothers, 1880.

David, Susan. *Emotional Agility*. Avery, 2016.

Deci, Edward L. "Effects of Externally Mediated Rewards on Intrinsic Motivation." Journal of Personality and Social Psychology 18, no. 1 (1971): 105–15.

Deci, Edward L., and Richard M. Ryan. "The 'What' and 'Why' of Goal Pursuits: Human Needs and the Self-Determination of Behavior." *Psychological Inquiry* 11, no. 4 (2000): 227–68.

Deci, Edward L., Richard M. Ryan, and Patrick P. Baard. "Facilitating Optimal Motivation and Psychological Well-Being Across Life's Domains." *Canadian Psychology* 49, no. 1 (2008): 14–23.

Dickinson, Emily. *The Poems of Emily Dickinson: Variorum Edition*. Belknap Press, 1998.

Diener, Ed. "Subjective Well-Being: The Science of Happiness and a Proposal for a National Index." *American Psychologist* 55, no. 1 (2000): 34–43. https://doi.org/10.1037/0003-066X.55.1.34.

Doidge, Norman. *The Brain That Changes Itself: Stories of Personal Triumph from the Frontiers of Brain Science*. Penguin, 2007.

Dweck, Carol S. *Mindset*. Random House, 2006.

Eliot, George. *George Eliot's Life as Related in Her Letters and Journals*. William Blackwood, 1885.

Epicurus. *The Extant Remains*. Clarendon Press, 1926.

Epicurus. *Letters, Principal Doctrines, and Vatican Sayings*. Harvard University Press, 2010.

Erikson, Erik H. *Childhood and Society*. Norton, 1951.

Erikson, Erik H. *Identity: Youth and Crisis*. Norton, 1968.

Fivush, Robyn. "Constructing narrative, emotion, and self." In *The Remembering Self*, 136–57, 1994.

Fivush, Robyn. "Speaking Silence: The Social Construction of Silence in Autobiographical and Cultural Narratives." *Memory* 18, no. 2 (2010): 88–98. https://doi.org/10.1080/09658210903029404

Fivush, Robyn, and Katherine Nelson. "Culture and Language in the Emergence of Autobiographical Memory." In *The Development of the Mediated Mind: Sociocultural Context and Cognitive Development*, edited by Joan M. Lucariello, Judith A. Hudson, Robyn Fivush, and Patricia J. Bauer, 53–70. Mahwah, NJ: Lawrence Erlbaum Associates, 2004.

Frankl, Viktor E. *Man's Search for Meaning*. Simon & Schuster, 1985.

Frankl, Viktor E. *The Will to Meaning*. Plume, 1988.

Giddens, Anthony. *Modernity and Self-Identity*. Stanford University Press, 1991.

Goffman, Erving. *Frame Analysis*. Harvard University Press, 1974.

Grandin, Temple. *Thinking in Pictures*. Doubleday, 1995.

Greimas, Algirdas Julien. *On Meaning*. University of Minnesota Press, 1987.

Greimas, Algirdas Julien. *Structural Semantics*. University of Nebraska Press, 1983.

Hamilton, J. Paul, Madison Farmer, Patricia Fogelman, and Ian H. Gotlib. "Depressive rumination and the default-mode network." *Biological Psychiatry* 78, no. 4 (2015): 224–30.

Han, Jo-An J., Michelle D. Leichtman, and Qi Wang. "Autobiographical Memory in Korean, Chinese, and American Children." *Developmental Psychology* 34, no. 4 (1998): 701–13. https://doi.org/10.1037/0012-1649.34.4.701.

Han, Shihui, Georg Northoff, Kai Vogeley, Bruce E. Wexler, Shinobu Kitayama, and Michael E. W. Varnum. "A Cultural Neuroscience Approach to the Biosocial Nature of the Human Brain." *Annual Review of Psychology* 64 (2013): 335–59. https://doi.org/10.1146/annurev-psych-071112-054629.

Hiatt, Brian. "Billie Eilish Opens Up About Her Mental Health." *Rolling Stone*, April 24, 2024.

Hofstede, Geert. *Culture's Consequences*. Sage, 1980.

Hong, Ying-yi, Michael W. Morris, Chi-yue Chiu, and Verónica Benet-Martínez. "Multicultural minds." *American Psychologist* 55, no. 7 (2000): 709–20.

Huffington, Arianna. *Thrive*. Harmony Books, 2014.

Ingle, Sean. "Wada cyber attack: Williams sisters and Simone Biles targeted by Russian group." *The Guardian* (2016).

James, William. *The Principles of Psychology*. Henry Holt, 1890.

Jeffers, Susan. *Feel the Fear… and Do It Anyway*. Ballantine Books, 2007.

Kahneman, Daniel, and Amos Tversky. "The framing of decisions and the psychology of choice." *Econometrica* 49, no. 1 (1981): 453–58.

Kashima, Emiko S., and Yoshihisa Kashima. "Culture and Language: The Case of Cultural Dimensions and Personal Pronoun Use." *Journal of Cross-Cultural Psychology* 29, no. 3 (1998): 461–86. https://doi.org/10.1177/0022022198293005.

Kashima, Yoshihisa. "A Social Psychology of Cultural Dynamics: Examining How Cultures Are Formed, Maintained, and Transformed." *Social and Personality Psychology Compass* 2, no. 1 (2008): 107–20. https://doi.org/10.1111/j.1751-9004.2007.00063.x.

Keller, Helen. *The Story of My Life*. Doubleday, Page, 1903.

Kierkegaard, Søren. *Fear and Trembling / Repetition*. Princeton University Press, 1983.

Kitayama, Shinobu, and Ayse K. Uskul. "Culture, mind, and the brain." *Annual Review of Psychology* 62 (2011): 419–49.

Kitayama, Shinobu, and Jiyoung Park. "Cultural neuroscience of the self: Understanding the social grounding of the brain." *Social cognitive and affective neuroscience* 5, no. 2-3 (2010): 111–129.

Lae, L. L. *Culture, Self-Narratives and Autobiographical Memory*. PhD diss., University of Melbourne, 2019.

Lauder, Estée. *Estée: A Success Story*. Random House, 1985.

Lee, Harper. *To Kill a Mockingbird*. Grand Central Publishing, 1988.

Lewis, M. Paul, Gary F. Simons, and Charles D. Fennig, eds. *Ethnologue: Languages of the World*. 23rd ed. SIL International, 2023.

Liddle, Elizabeth B., Gaëlle Douaud, Barbara J. Sahakian, et al. "Task-related default mode network modulation in ADHD." *Journal of Child Psychology and Psychiatry* 52, no. 9 (2011): 946–55.

Luo Xianglin 羅香林. *Kejia Yanjiu Daolun*. Shanghai Wenyi Chubanshe, 1992.

Maehler, Débora B., and Jessica Daikeler. "The cultural identity of first-generation adult immigrants: A meta-analysis." *Self and Identity* 23, no. 5-6 (2024): 450-483.

Margolis, Michael. Story 10x: *Turn the Impossible Into the Inevitable*. Page Two, 2019.

Markus, Hazel Rose, and Shinobu Kitayama. "Culture and the self." *Psychological Review* 98, no. 2 (1991): 224–53.

McAdams, Dan P. *The Art and Science of Personality Development*. New York: Guilford Press, 2015.

McAdams, Dan P. "The Psychological Self as Actor, Agent, and Author." *Perspectives on Psychological Science* 8, no. 3 (2013): 272–95. https://doi.org/10.1177/1745691612470282.

McAdams, Dan P. *The Redemptive Self: Stories Americans Live By*. New York: Oxford University Press, 2006.

McAdams, Dan P. *The Stories We Live By: Personal Myths and the Making of the Self*. New York: Guilford Press, 1993.

McAdams, Dan P., and Erika Manczak. "Personality Development: Self as Actor, Agent, and Author." In *Handbook of Personality: Theory and Research*, edited by Oliver P. John and Richard W. Robins, 4th ed., 447–65. New York: Guilford Press, 2021.

Obama, Michelle. *Becoming*. Crown, 2018.

Padmanabhan, A., C. J. Lynch, R. Schaerer, and Vinod Menon. "The default mode network in autism." *Biological Psychiatry: Cognitive Neuroscience and Neuroimaging* 2, no. 5 (2017): 476–86.

Pennebaker, James W. *Opening Up*. Guilford Press, 1997.

Plato. *Complete Works*. Hackett, 1997.

Potok, Chaim. *The Chosen*. Simon & Schuster, 1967.

Raichle, Marcus E., Ann M. MacLeod, Abraham Z. Snyder, William J. Powers, Debra A. Gusnard, and Randall L. Shulman. "A default mode of brain function." *Proceedings of the National Academy of Sciences* 98, no. 2 (2001): 676–82.

Rain Man. Directed by Barry Levinson. United Artists, 1988.

Ryan, Richard M., and Edward L. Deci. *Self-Determination Theory: Basic Psychological Needs in Motivation, Development, and Wellness*. Guilford Press, 2017.

Sagiv, Lilach, and Shalom H. Schwartz. "Personal Values Across Cultures." *Annual Review of Psychology* 73 (2022): 517–46. https://doi.org/10.1146/annurev-psych-020821-103609.

Sagiv, Lilach, and Shalom H. Schwartz. "Value Priorities and Behavior: The Moderating Role of Social Context." *Journal of Personality and Social Psychology* 69, no. 5 (1995): 950–61. https://doi.org/10.1037/0022-3514.69.5.950.

Sarbin, Theodore R., ed. *Narrative Psychology: The Storied Nature of Human Conduct.* New York: Praeger, 1986.

Sandberg, Sheryl, with Nell Scovell. *Lean In.* Knopf, 2013.

Schwartz, Shalom H. "An overview of the Schwartz theory of basic values." *Online readings in Psychology and Culture* 2, no. 1 (2012).

Schwartz, Shalom H. "Values and culture." In *Motivation and culture*, pp. 69-84. Routledge, 2014.

Sinek, Simon. *Start with Why.* Portfolio, 2009.

Tolkien, J. R. R. *The Lord of the Rings.* Houghton Mifflin Harcourt, 2004.

Tolstoy, Leo. *War and Peace.* Dutton, 1904.

Tomasello, Michael. *Constructing a Language.* Harvard University Press, 2003.

Tsereteli, Nino, and Aglaya Tsereteli. "Sociocultural Predictors of Immigrant Adjustment and Well-Being." *Frontiers in Sociology* 9 (2024): 1251871. https://doi.org/10.3389/fsoc.2024.1251871

Turner, Tina, with Kurt Loder. *I, Tina.* William Morrow, 1986.

Verwey, Elizabeth M. *Brave New Endings: True Stories of Caring for an Ex.* Friesen Press, 2025.

Waldinger, Robert, and Marc Schulz. *The Good Life.* Simon & Schuster, 2023.

Warren, Rick. *The Purpose Driven Life.* Zondervan, 2002.

Watzlawick, Paul, John H. Weakland, and Richard Fisch. *Change: Principles of Problem Formation and Problem Resolution.* W. W. Norton & Company, 1974.

White, Michael, and David Epston. *Narrative Means to Therapeutic Ends.* Norton, 1990.

Zeigarnik, Bluma. "On finished and unfinished tasks." In *A Source Book of Gestalt Psychology*, edited by Willis D. Ellis, 300–314. Kegan Paul, 1938.

Zhu, Ying, and Shihui Han. "Cultural Differences in the Self: From Philosophy to Psychology and Neuroscience." *Social and Personality Psychology Compass* 2, no. 5 (2008): 1799–1811. https://doi.org/10.1111/j.1751-9004.2008.00133.x.

Zhu, Ying, Li Zhang, Jin Fan, and Shihui Han. "Neural basis of cultural influence on self-representation." *Neuroimage* 34, no. 3 (2007): 1310-1316.

Beyond These Pages

Some stories stay with us long after we leave the places where they began.

As a child, I spent part of my early life in Timor-Leste, a country marked by resilience, strength, and the enduring power of women to hold families and communities together through extraordinary challenges. That connection has remained part of my own life story, shaping how I think about identity, culture, and what it means to live with purpose.

In 2024, I returned to Timor-Leste for the first time since leaving as a refugee. I felt called to put into action a long-held intention to empower women in a larger way, because when women are supported, strong families and communities grow.

For this reason, I support the work of the *Alola Foundation*, a Timor-Leste–based organisation dedicated to improving the lives of women and children.

Founded in 2001 by former First Lady Kirsty Sword Gusmão, Alola focuses on four vital areas: maternal and child health, girls' education, women's economic empowerment, and advocacy for women's rights and leadership. Through this work, Alola has helped strengthen opportunities for girls, improve family well-being, and support Timorese women in building more independent and secure futures.

Readers around the world can learn more about Alola's work and how to engage at: **www.alolafoundation.org**

Thank you for being part of a story that reaches beyond these pages.

–Lidia Lae

About the Author

Lidia Lae PhD is a psychologist, author, and sought-after consultant and speaker whose work sits at the intersection of identity, culture, and meaning. She helps individuals and leaders—especially women—move beyond inherited narratives that keep them stuck, so they can become conscious authors of their life stories and create lives shaped by clarity, joy, and purposeful impact.

Trained in psychology and drawing on self-narratives, semiotics, and cross-cultural research, Lidia explores how personal histories, cultural values, and social environments shape who we are and who we become. She developed **StoriCompass**™, a narrative framework for understanding how individuals and organizations inherit, interpret, and reshape their stories. She also created **CulturAlign**™, the Cultural Identity Blueprint, and **Life Framing**, a practical process for turning insight into meaningful action and long-term direction.

Through her writing, speaking, and consulting work, Lidia works with individuals and organizations globally to foster clarity, resilience, and inclusive cultures where people and purpose can thrive.

She lives in Melbourne, Australia, with her family.

Learn more at **lidialae.com**.

www.ingramcontent.com/pod-product-compliance
Lightning Source LLC
LaVergne TN
LVHW091531060526
838200LV00036B/558